UNMASKING

A Page-Turning Espionage Thriller

RAYNE DOWELL

ISBNs: 978-0-9959167-0-8 (pbk.), 978-0-9959167-2-2 (hard cover), 978-0-9959167-3-9 (ebook), 978-0-9959167-1-5 (audiobook)

Printed in the United States of America

CONTENTS

FOREWORD

It's necessary for me to warn you: This will be the oddest memoir you've ever read. And I don't mean it to be. However, it's based on my life and my life experiences.

I follow what I consider to be "orders," and I've received many throughout my life, disguised as intuitive feelings as well as outward "signs" from the real world.

I was ordered to write this book about my journey—my life—so far.

So I began writing... unsure, unsteady, scared silly, but nevertheless determined to carry out my orders. Then, when I was ninety percent done writing the book, my intuition softly said, "... stop writing, it's not over, you have something else to learn, you're not done, be patient...". So I stopped writing. Three months later I learned why. So you see, it's been a journey and continues to be a journey.

You may find some of what I'm going to share with you unbelievable. I understand. I found it unbelievable at the time too. This autobiography is how I've perceived the unseen and how that's worked, or not, for me. As you'll see, the unseen is closely intertwined with what I consider to be "reality."

I could only have learned what I've learned (and I'm not done by any means) by using my life as an experimental lab. I've conducted thousands and thousands of experiments with intuition, energy, consciousness, intention, emotions, and dreams and learning how these things relate to, and interact with, this "reality"— too many to note here, but you'll get the gist of it, I think.

And because I don't wish to divulge private information about people, or get sued, the names and descriptions of the people I do describe are inaccurate, on purpose.

So I apologize for not providing you with people's real names and descriptions. The point of this book is to show by example how life is a wonderful, unbelievable, inspirational journey and we are so much more than we think. Sure, sometimes it gets bumpy. Sometimes it's ugly. But it's always, *always* worth it.

What I also learned, although I didn't set out to learn this, is that we ***are*** all connected to everything: each other and the natural world. I also learned much, much more that I'd like to share with you.

I'll have to ask you to keep an open mind, though, because I end up learning this, and many, many more things, in a roundabout way. If Life has shown me anything so far, it's that life can be unpredictable, but nothing trumps unconditional love, faith, hope, forgiveness, self-acceptance, patience, persistence, transformation, positivity, and believing in yourself.

And finally, I'd like to thank The Light for providing me with this life, the gifts I've received disguised as challenges, the many people who've helped me along my journey, the chance to make mistakes — lots and lots of mistakes, the people who've challenged me, the beauty and inspiration of the natural world, the knowledge that each and every one of us is unique and vital, and most of all, hope and unconditional love.

It's because of The Light I'm writing this book for you, in the hopes you find the courage to begin unmasking. ***We are all*** incredibly amazing.

DEDICATION

Young people are our future and in my view, it's important that we invest in them. The Doorway (www.TheDoorway.ca) is a not-for-profit organization that works with youth familiar with street culture, showing them a gentler, kinder way of life, full of promise and hope.

The Doorway doesn't believe in labels or boxes and encourages self-determination, inclusivity and creative problem-solving. Ten percent of this book's profits are invested in this not-for-profit, because these young people are incredibly courageous, creative, and persistent. They're taking positive steps forward, setting goals, problem-solving, thinking differently, and doing what's unfamiliar to them, with open minds and hearts.

"What lies behind you and what lies in front of you pales in comparison to what lies inside of you."

— Ralph Waldo Emerson

ACKNOWLEDGEMENTS

For my co-creators, who helped me with the editing process; without their support this book wouldn't have seen the light of day: Pat, Burt, Anna, Tyler, Christina, and The Light.

For the support of my Grandfather, "Papa Hep": may we all see beautiful sights that reflect our soul.

For Marilyn at The Doorway, whose committed, inspirational foresight continues to be a beacon for many.

For the many, many beautiful souls I've met on this life journey who've shared their lives, lessons, dreams, pain, thoughts, feelings and hopes—thank you.

Chapter 1:
Ordinary World

I just left my husband and the reason sounds crazy. It's 2001 and I'm driving my 1999 green Chevy two-door Cavalier from Vancouver, British Columbia, Canada back to Calgary, Alberta. I'm thirty-four years old. I was married for one year. Exactly. To the day. Apparently, that was long enough. I was in an on-off relationship for about fifteen years. Mostly off. He thought I had an issue with commitment, so marriage was supposed to be the cure. Turns out I don't have a problem committing. I have a problem committing to something that doesn't work for me.

My car is packed up and my two cats are nervously looking at me as we weave our way through the city streets toward the main highway leading out of the city.

Something always felt off but I couldn't put my finger on it. One thing, perhaps the only thing, I'm grateful to him for was introducing me to nature—camping and fishing. I grew up in the city and no one in my family had a love for nature. At the age of 20, when I met him, my love affair with nature and the wild began. A whole new world.

If I'm being honest with myself, the main reason I left him was because of my dreams. I was constantly dreaming he was cheating on me. When I'd tell him about my dreams he'd tell me I was crazy. Which was too bad. We'd probably still be friends if he could've been honest. I'd been interpreting my dreams since I was fourteen years old. Usually they were more symbolic—numbers, items, an animal, a place, a feeling–that kind of thing. Where it's like a puzzle you can figure out with some time and effort. But these dreams of him cheating? Well, not so much to figure out. Which made me question these dreams. Maybe this had more to do with me than him? Which it did, but for the time being I decided to call it a day, even though it seemed crazy to leave your husband because of your dreams.

I'd been told since I was a child that dreams don't mean anything. That they're just random, meaningless messages your subconscious churns out during sleep. Maybe that's how it is for other people, but for me, deep down I didn't believe that's what my dreams meant. I mean, it sounded like a logical, rational explanation. But lots of things aren't logical.

Like when I was nineteen years old, working in an office for a small company in downtown Calgary. I was working away at a computer when a strong feeling came over me, a knowing… a download of instant information. It told me that when I wanted to have children I would either experience problems or I wouldn't be able to. Concerned, and never doubting this random blast of information, I called the doctor's office that day to book an appointment to find out if it was true. I was told that unless I was trying to get pregnant they wouldn't test me. This type of "feeling," download of information, hadn't happened to me before, so I let it go.

But when I was thirty and thirty-two years old I would experience two tubal pregnancies, and while these experiences were life-threatening and difficult emotionally, physically, psychologically, and spiritually, they also gave me valuable information about my feelings and my intuition, which I found interesting, confusing, unbalancing, strange and somehow reassuring.

But not at all logical.

Another odd experience I couldn't explain was when I was twenty-four years old. I'd been living with my now-ex for a few years. That was when the dreams of him cheating first started. I didn't say anything to anyone about these dreams, but I'd started regularly going to the clinic to get tested for STDs for the past year and a half, every six months. I figured it couldn't hurt.

One day I was walking home after being tested and was thinking... wondering... what was wrong with me? Was I paranoid and going to have to experience this awful feeling of distrust for the rest of my life? Was it him? Was he not worthy of my trust? Or was it me? Did I choose, and would I be forever doomed to choose, untrustworthy partners? I felt desolate. Isolated. And sad. Very sad. My spirits sank with each step I took.

Suddenly I felt something. An energy... two energies. I stopped and looked behind and above me and couldn't see anything. But I sensed something; I ***knew*** something was there—***two somethings*** were there. Two formless, odorless, colorless energies.

Now they were hovering very close to me, one on each shoulder, about two inches above each shoulder. Next I experienced a feeling of such incredibly strong positivity, hope and playfulness. They were lifting me up, these energies... lifting my spirits. Showing me I wasn't alone and I wouldn't be alone, and that everything would be all right, telling me to take heart, have faith, be patient and keep going.

Somewhat confused but uplifted and smiling, I continued walking.

***

Which reminds me of when I drowned. People call these things "near- death" experiences, and I get it: you didn't die and stay dead. But somehow it seems inaccurate. When I drowned, I did die, and was dead for a time. I don't know how long, because time and space have a different meaning over there than here, in this reality. This dimension. This physical world.

I was three and a half years old. We were visiting my dad's parents' cabin in Pigeon Lake, Alberta, Canada. Back then it was beautiful. Clean. Relatively unpopulated. I'd just learned how to tie my shoelaces. It took me about twenty minutes to complete this task, but I could do it. I'd been looking out the living room windows overlooking the lake. It was early morning, maybe seven or eight o'clock. A cloudless day in late July. Sunlight streamed across the lake invitingly.

A new item had been added to the toy box the day before. A small, red, hollow plastic boat. At the front of the boat the plastic stuck out a little, and there was a small hole through the plastic. Which got me thinking, as I stood alone looking out the window over the lake the next morning...

If I tied a piece of string through that hole, and then made a knot to hold it there, I could put the boat on the lake and see if it floated! If it floated, then I could imagine it heading off to faraway lands, discovering and exploring new things, new places, new animals, new people. Imagine what the boat would discover! Good plan!

So I quietly set about carrying out my plan. Mom and Grandmother were in the kitchen drinking coffee and talking about whatever boring things old people talk about. I was on a mission and had to accomplish my task. I searched around, eventually finding a piece of twine about three feet long, and spent half an hour tying a knot through the front part of the boat. Then I spent another half an hour tying my shoelaces.

Inwardly victorious, I closed the front door while grasping the piece of twine and started down the dirt path to the lake, the little red boat trailing on the ground behind me, bumping and bobbing along. The sun winked at me using the tree leaves, a co-conspirator. A fat bee buzzed lazily by in front of me. I could smell and taste in the air the earth teeming with life, worms and ants and other creatures busily working away. The wind was resting.

At the bottom of the path, the wooden pier sat patiently waiting for me. I walked to the end of the pier, hunkered over the little red boat and, leaning over, reverently placed it on the water, making sure to keep one hand tightly closed around the end of the line. This boat wasn't getting away from me.

No way.

I sat patiently, watching it for a time. It seemed the little boat was happy in the water, staying adrift and bobbing gently on the current. It didn't sink! Experimentally, I gently pulled the line back and forth, watching as the gentle waves of the lake made my little boat rise and fall rhythmically. The string was holding good, the knot staying tight.

Finally satisfied my little red boat was ready, I decided - systems go! It was ready to explore more distant seas and lands! I changed positions, from hunkering to sitting with my knees under me, leaning forward and stretching my arm as far out from the pier as it could go. Slowly the gentle waves began pulling the string taut and away from me. Go little boat, go!

I kept stretching until... I fell in.

Where I discovered an amazing new world... Underwater everything was incredibly quiet. Muted.

Slow.

Ethereal.

My long auburn hair is floating around me, dancing to a soundless orchestra.

An orchestra playing a slow, beautiful, timeless song.

Looking up, I see the sun shining through the water, revealing blue-green ripples within ripples. Then, taking a breath, I notice water rushing into my nostrils and mouth.

Huh.

Strange.

No matter.

Looking down, I see the sun reflecting off the sand at the bottom of the lake, in waves.

So many waves, in the water, in the sand. The waves go on and on, forever it seems.

The color of the water is different from when I looked down into it from the pier.

In the water, looking up, the water is light green in places where the sun is shining through, and then it slowly, gradually goes to darker and darker shades as it moves away from the sun.

Taking another breath, I notice water again rushing down my throat and through my nostrils.

Then my vision begins doing something funny.

It's going black from the outsides in a perfect circle, closing in, until there's only a very small circle of white in the middle.

A pinpoint of light.

Then the pinpoint of light starts getting bigger and bigger, growing... pushing the dark away.

At the same time, I'm moving forward, toward and through the light, travelling really fast!

Until I feel like I'm light too, but I'm also with the source of The Light. It feels amazing!

It's joyful, playful, wise, powerful... and it's everywhere! I notice I have no body, no form.

I'm spirit.

And I spend time with The Light.

Where I experience and receive what I now know is called unconditional love.

At the time, I sense this is a rare thing in that other place. So I'm fully immersing myself in it. It feels so wonderful!

After some time—and like I said, time is a different concept over there—I hear a voice both in my head but also throughout every molecule of my spirit body.

It gently but firmly says, "It's time to go back now, child."

"I don't want to go back," I quickly say with my mind. "I want to stay! "I experience a warm chuckle that tickles through me. The Light. Then suddenly I'm whooshing back through that white tunnel! Back to where I was.

Except when I get back there I find I'm hovering above myself.

I look at my hands and they're see through-ish, so I'm not like when I was with The Light, where I had no form and was just energy, but I'm not like how I was when I was here... solid.

And I'm looking down over the physical, solid me, which is lying motionless on the pier.

Physical, solid me looks like I'm sleeping.

My hair looks like big, fat, wet noodles are growing out of my head, which makes me laugh.

Then I notice Grandmother is leaning over me, pushing on my chest with both of her hands and then covering my mouth with hers.

My cheeks are puffing out. She looks serious and concerned. It looks like she's blowing air into me.

Huh. I wonder what's going on?

The next thing I know, I experience feeling a violent slamming of my spirit self into my physical body.

Pain explodes behind my eyes and, turning my head to the side I begin throwing up, my stomach seizing strongly.

I keep throwing up water for awhile. My stomach feels like it's on fire.

***

And from that point on I'll experience the majority of my dreams differently than most other people.

I won't know that for many years, though. For most of my life I just assume everyone dreams like I do. But they don't. For me, I'll usually be in my dreams, as my physical self, but I'll also be watching myself in spirit form just above and to the side.

The spirit me is compassionate yet unattached to the outcome. I'm somehow both at the same time. I can see what each sees, understands, feels, perceives and experiences.

I'm so thankful I drowned, because it gives me an objective

viewpoint toward my dreams, because "spirit" me is detached... so it's a way to distance myself, look for, and appreciate the deeper, more meaningful messages, less connected to the physical realm.

The way I experience my dreams... well, I've learned it isn't rational or logical.

But life isn't always rational and logical. Rational and logical feels safe though. But in some ways, logical is an illusion, depriving us of a richer, more meaningful experience of life. That doesn't mean I'm embracing it. It just means at this point, I'm willing to dip my toes in, where others run away shrieking.

I like logical, love logical, but I'm also curious about the unknown. The unexplainable. How does it work? What effect or impact does the unseen have on the physical realm? And even though I'm curious, I'm also going through the process of being raised in a family and society that aren't open to the unseen, that are loud, insistent, violent, and arrogant in their views. And over time I notice I'm being encouraged by the outside world to ignore my inner world and the unseen and am being guided away. Far, far away from the unseen.

Regardless, as time moves on I appear to subconsciously agree to dip my toes in a little more.

***

When I was twenty-nine years old my great-aunt, whom I was close to, was admitted to the hospital. She'd been standing at a bus stop when both of her hips broke. Just broke. She didn't fall; no one touched her. She was eighty years old.

Being in the hospital was extremely hard for her, and for the staff at the hospital. She was a functioning alcoholic and also took a lot of prescription pills. So she was going through withdrawals in the hospital. I'd visited her at the hospital a few days prior and she was doing okay, not great, but she was making progress. Healing.

That night I have a dream.

I'm standing in a room looking down at my great-aunt lying on her back, her eyes closed, sleeping on the ground. I'm also in spirit form looking down at myself looking down at my great-aunt. Somewhere above there's a single light bulb shining down on us. Darkness surrounds us.

As I'm looking down at her body, I watch as her spirit wakes up and at the same time steps out of her body. Silently, her spirit self starts walking away, into the darkness. I look from her sleeping physical body to her departing spirit, wondering, Why did her spirit leave her body? And where did her spirit go?

Eventually I hear a voice calling my name. My great-aunt's spirit self. "Where am I?! I can't see anything?!" she's crying.

Panicking.

Then she's calling my name.

"You're okay, it's okay. You can hear me, right?" I call out to her.

I sense her confusion, then her relief at the recognition of my voice. "Yes… I can hear you," she replies falteringly.

"Just start walking toward my voice then. I'm right here, you're okay," I say into the darkness. Then I start singing 'You Are My Sunshine'.

She taught me that song when I was a child.

Soon I see her spirit self walking toward me. She's smiling. Relieved. I stop singing and smile back at her. As her spirit self gets close, she sees her physical body. She moves beside her physical body then changes from standing to floating horizontally and above her sleeping physical self, then lowers her spirit self down until she's merged with her physical self.

The dream ends.

After waking I'm not quite sure what to think of this. I haven't had a dream like this before. I don't know if we shared the same dream somehow or not. It sort of feels like it, but I'm not sure. Afterwards, I don't talk with her about this dream, ask her if she experienced the same thing, if she remembers this.

I don't ask her because I've been trained, or brainwashed, to disregard, ignore, things like this, and because most people feel uncomfortable talking about these things. I don't know why. But it leaves me feeling like I have to be quiet about it, like I've somehow done something wrong or bad, or there's something wrong with me.

It doesn't feel like I've done something bad or wrong. But it makes me feel alone... isolated. Because I have no one to talk with about these things, to help me understand what they mean, why I'm experiencing it, and how I can understand it better.

Which leads me to the last one of these experiences before I need to make a decision: to either take the "red" pill or the "blue" pill.

***

I am thirty years old and on a retreat in the countryside just outside of Calgary, Alberta, Canada. It's autumn and orange, yellow, red and green leaves and pine needles are crunching under my feet as I'm hiking in a forest. The air smells fresh with earth and pine. I'd finished climbing a ridge overlooking a river and had stopped to enjoy the view. When another one of those strong feelings came over me. The same type of feeling I'd had when I was twenty and later on learned I'd have problems having children.

Except this feeling is telling me something different. It's telling me that in the future something is going to be asked of me. Something very difficult, that would challenge everything I'd been taught and had learned so far.

That this something was very important to The Light.

This makes me feel very, very uneasy. Because being prepared is something I fully subscribe to, and I don't know how to do this, to prepare for what The Light wants me to do. I don't like making mistakes and I make fewer mistakes when I'm prepared. It just doesn't feel like I have a way to prepare for this, though. I'm just supposed to have faith.

But also, it scares me and I just want to be "normal" like everyone else.

But this feeling that I'd need to do something difficult for The Light would return from time to time as my life continued.

Each time, the feeling is stronger than before.

***

I look in my rearview and side mirrors. Driving gives you a lot of time to think. I'm on the number one highway now, passing out of the city limits of Vancouver. The highway stretches out in front of me. A new life. I don't want to think about those illogical things now.

I just want a new, normal life.

I open my cigarette pack and pluck out one of the four pre-rolled joints I prepared for the ten-hour drive. I've smoked pot almost daily since I was eighteen years old, mainly because it dulls my senses. I experienced a lot of violence, drama, negativity and chaos throughout my childhood and teen years and am pretty sure I have PTSD.

Which isn't special, but I think it's what's causing me to be acutely aware of energies. I can't think of any other reason for this. People, places, things. I pick up on a lot. And I don't want to. But I don't know any other way to block or dull how much I pick up on. I don't like pills or needles, and my body doesn't handle alcohol very well, so I smoke pot. A lot. Sometimes three joints a day in the evenings on the weekdays, and whenever I need to on the weekends.

This is the best way I know to cope.

The only problem is that pot is different now. It's a lot stronger than when I first started smoking it. While everyone acts like this is a great thing,

I don't like it. I try different kinds, but all the strains seem to be getting a lot stronger. I've noticed that over the past ten years or so there aren't any seeds in the bags I buy, either. I'm not sure what this means; all I know is it's stronger and the side effects are worse.

For me, short term memory loss is one of the side effects, and the other is loss of balance. Everyone I know just thinks I'm "creative and absentminded" so the short-term memory loss isn't noticeable and doesn't really bother me or anyone else very much, but the loss of balance thing is annoying me.

Sometimes I'll just be standing there and it feels as if the earth just got suddenly tilted and then set right again, but I lose my balance and have to take a few steps to regain it. I know this is a side effect of the pot and I also know I have to look into other ways to deal with the "picking up on energies" thing. I'm not sure where to start with this, though, but it is on my "to do" list.

I light the joint and inhale while rolling down the window. I can see the mountains in the distance.

A feeling comes over me. A gnawing sense that energy has been lowering in nature.

That if it continues it's going to affect our ability, as a species, to survive.

I exhale, slowly blowing smoke out the window, thinking, *That's crazy*, to myself.

But I've had this feeling before. It's coming more often and stronger.

I dismiss it. Because, well, what am I supposed to do about that?

And besides, I just want a normal life.

Like everyone else.

I play a Chris Rock standup comedy CD and continue on my way, listening, laughing, smoking and driving my way back to Calgary.

***

After I get back to Calgary I settle in. I start slowly furnishing a basement suite, get an office job downtown and begin filing the divorce papers myself. I begin waiting for the year-long separation process to be over so I can officially be divorced.

After a few months, my family and friends want me to start dating, even though technically I'm separated and not divorced yet. It makes them feel uneasy that I'm single. I don't know why. Why do they think being single is a bad thing? But I decide to give them the benefit of the doubt. They have my best interest at heart, know me well and it can't hurt, right?

So… I give it a try.

The problem is I haven't dated since high school. When my ex and I would split up, sometimes for years at a time, I'd just do my own thing—work, read, exercise, go hiking, visit distant countries, take night courses, visit with family and friends. I liked the freedom. Besides, most married people I knew didn't seem that happy to me.

Ok. Dating. It's supposed to be fun, right? So I start dating two guys. Both are friends of friends. After about four months I decide one is definitely an alcoholic, so I stop dating him. He was funny, though, and open to trying new things. I'd taken a course and learned how to kayak the year before and he was game to try it. My ex wasn't interested in trying anything new. I always tried new things on my own, whether we were together or not.

I date the other guy, Leslie, a few months longer but something feels off. I can't put my finger on it, but something's not right. It feels to me like he's seeing someone else, which is no big deal; we're just dating, but there's just something else not quite right going on. I just don't know what it is. Also, I don't really have fun with him. He seems a bit too controlling. He insists on talking with me at a certain time every night, no matter what. This feels kind of weird. Like a job or something.

I conclude I must be feeling this way because I'm just not ready to date yet, and I'm choosing people to date that aren't right for me because I'm not in the best place to be making good decisions. After all, I'm not divorced yet.

The divorce course I've started going to at a nearby church advises to not date for quite a long time, even after your divorce papers have been processed. In fact, they advise you to be on your own for a third of the time you were with your ex, and that's after the divorce papers go through.

I'm not sure how to calculate mine, though, because my relationship with my ex was an on-off thing. But it does feel to me like I'm not ready for dating. So I stop dating Leslie too. The only thing I had in common with both of the guys I was dating was pot.

A few weeks later strange things start happening. Hang-up phone calls at my home and work, daily. A cat dies mysteriously on the sidewalk in front of where I live. And I'm getting a feeling that I'm being watched. Watched and followed.

I've never had that feeling before.

My friend calls and tells me she saw Leslie slowly driving by my apartment. Which is odd. I didn't get the feeling he particularly cared one way or the other about me. He seemed like he was happy "playing the field." He'd been single a long time when I met him, or so he told me. Maybe he's the one calling and hanging up?

I look up stalking on the local police website. It says the best way to deal with it is to just ignore it. If you file a restraining order it tends to escalate the situation.

Hmmmm.

Well, I don't want to escalate the situation, and besides he'll bore quickly following me around. I'm not a very exciting person.

Nevertheless, the hang-up calls and the feeling like someone is watching me continue. And I'm beginning to feel an ongoing, elevating rise in my feelings of anxiety[1] as time moves on.

***

A few months later I get laid off my job. I'm working for an oil and gas company downtown and this is normal. The oil industry is cyclical, and jobs in that industry commonly increase and decrease in cycles over the years, depending on how the industry is doing.

The hang-up calls and the feeling I'm being watched are continuing, though, and I decide the best way to handle it is to move. So, I find an apartment in a complex and move into it.

In the meantime, I've had a few dreams about Leslie, which in itself is a little disquieting. I only started having dreams about my ex after we were together for about three years. These dreams I'm having about Leslie are showing me he wasn't the person I thought he was, the person he was showing himself to be. Pretending to be.

That he's some kind of drug dealer. Which doesn't alarm me; pot hasn't been legal in Canada up until this point and I've bought pot from a lot of drug dealers. Mostly people that grow some plants and then sell it, or know someone who grows plants.

This is different though. Leslie, from what my dreams are telling me, has something to do with a more formal type of organized crime. A bigger type of business thing, which means harder drugs.

Which is about all I want to know about that, even if that's true. Because that doesn't make any sense. Why would someone like that have anything to do with me? I'm boring and pot is as illegal as I get.

Which isn't to say I haven't experimented. As a teenager, I experimented with drugs, sex and stealing.

Sex, because—what was the big deal about? I couldn't understand why everyone seemed to spend so much time and energy talking about it? As I learned more about it, I learned some people have an addiction to it, they use it as an escape, and a lot of people aren't very good at it. I'm a heterosexual female so I can only speak to that.

But I also wanted to know - what's the difference between having sex with someone you don't care for or love, having sex for money or having sex with someone you love or care for who also loves or cares for you?

Because so far,

I'd met women and men who were married, who didn't seem to love their husbands or wives, but who wanted financial security, so they stayed with and obviously slept with their spouses. So what was the difference between someone who does that and someone who sleeps with people for money? And if this was normal, which it seems to be, would this work for me?

Stealing—because other people that I knew did it and they weren't "bad" people. And, confusingly, I'd been raised for some years by an adult who made a living doing this, skirting the grey lines basically, but in the end—stealing from people.

And drugs—because they aren't all bad for you. In a lot of cultures psychedelics are commonly used in spiritual practices. Plus, if drugs were that bad, doctors wouldn't prescribe them, right?

In the end, I decided, after experimenting, I have to go with what works for me.

I felt guilty when I stole.

Sex was only good for me if I cared about or loved the other person and they cared or loved me.

I don't like the various drugs on the street or prescribed by my doctors. At least, my body doesn't like them and it shows me this using side effects (vomiting, sweating, feeling "on edge," feeling not quite myself, loss of appetite, nervousness, etc.). So for now, I don't like drugs and don't use them, except for pot, which, for now, I need to "not feel so many energies."

***

After I move into my new apartment I decide to apply for jobs where I can use my skills in a different environment, one I haven't worked in before. So far I've worked in corporate environments. I'm not sure why, but after some time I automatically start seeing patterns in the ways people work, the work flows, what isn't working and what can be improved.

Personally, I've found only a small number of corporate environments to be open and supportive of innovative ideas and ways of doing things, though. So I end up deciding on a school atmosphere. I haven't worked at a school before. I apply online for a position at an elementary school and am hired.

Strangely, the school happens to be in the same neighborhood where Leslie, the guy I think is stalking me, lives. Which is quite a coincidence in a city of a million people. But I dismiss this as a coincidence, because that might be a paranoid thought brought about by the stalking stuff.

I love the change in work environment. The kids are great. I love learning how a public school works, what the challenges are, what the patterns are, and I'm learning new skills. I'm also noticing I'm getting a few hang-up calls at work every day.

But that could be anybody. Right?

The school I'm working at is in a low-income area, and I can tell some of the kids attending this school, whom I talk with almost daily, are growing up in homes similar to the one I did, with a lot of violence and confusion. They're full of hope and are doing their very best to learn, and they're doing this without drugs.

This fact makes me feel like a fraud. I don't like that feeling. I decide to cut back on smoking pot. It just doesn't feel right, having it in my system and interacting with the kids every day. I decide now is the time to seriously start looking at other ways I can control "the energies" I pick up on, without drugs. After some research, I decide to enroll in a yoga/meditation class.

I also enroll in a weekend Wilderness First Air Training course. The new apartment seems to be working out.

Until it stops working out.

After a few months, I start hearing screaming from the apartment above me at night. It sounds to me like a couple, a man and a woman, live upstairs. The walls, laminate flooring and ceiling seem to be thin. Sometimes a child is running above me on the weekends, so one of them must have a child and have weekend visits.

But during the week I'm hearing a lot of screaming. It doesn't sound like domestic abuse. I know what that sounds like; I grew up with it.

This sounds like young people, in their late teens or early twenties. Each night one or two young people are forcibly brought to the apartment above me, held against their will, tortured for hours and then eventually killed. It feels like it has something to do with hard drugs, drug dealing.

The torturing and screaming goes on all night most weeknights, and I'm having a hard time sleeping. I'm trying cotton batting in my ears, special earpieces to cut out noise, and nothing's working. It's disturbing. Hearing young people screaming, pleading, crying. Many times I pray for the Archangels to be with them. This is what I consider those two positive energies I felt lift me up when I was younger.

I'm also noticing the tenants living in the apartments to the sides and opposite of me are moving out and the apartments are remaining empty. Which is strange.

Functioning well at work is getting difficult. This isn't… can't be happening, could it? I mean, I know things like this happen in real life, but they've never happened around me. Who would do this in a regular apartment building filled with people? I've also been told, throughout my childhood, I have an active imagination. So I'm wondering, is this my imagination?

It also isn't helping my "cut back on smoking pot" thing. Pot calms my nerves. My nerves are getting raw. But I stick with it, because feeling like a fraud when I'm around the kids at school feels worse.

I give it more time, a few more weeks, because I need time to determine if this is actually happening or if it's my imagination. I mean, the tenants in the apartment above me, a couple, could just watch a lot of violent movies on television with the volume really loud or something, right?

Eventually, I conclude this is actually happening. In real life. The couple in the apartment above me torture and kill people. This is their job. A job they apparently enjoy. Which is really odd. If someone were going to do something like this, wouldn't they arrange to have a more private place to do it?

At any rate, I'm getting irritable due to the lack of sleep so I make a decision. I complain to the Building Manager.

But still, the torturing noises continue, all night.

***

A month later, after listening to the screaming for four hours one night, at three o'clock in the morning I decide to call the police. As soon as I call the police I hear a lot of movement in the apartment above me. I hear someone being ordered to get into a trunk. It's as if they know I've just called the police because of them. I can hear them "tidying up," waiting for the police to arrive.

The police arrive at my door, four of them, with guns drawn, and ask me to confirm I heard the noise from the apartment above. I do. One gives me a business card. They leave.

Then I hear the police knock on the door of the apartment above me. The couple let them in and the police walk through their place. I can hear the couple mildly complaining to the officers, and the officers' heavy footsteps echoing through the laminate flooring above me as they walk through the apartment. The police don't open trunks or closets or anything. They walk around for five minutes then leave. They don't come back to my door to let me know how things went, or what I'm supposed to do.

After I hear the police leave, I hear the trunk being opened and the torturing and screaming begins anew. I call the number on the card the officer left for me, letting them know the screaming and torturing started again after they left. The officer who left the card doesn't return my call.

***

I mull this over for a bit and eventually conclude that the torturers don't care if they're bothering other people, or if the police visit them or not. They aren't going to stop torturing and killing people. And the police aren't going to do anything about it.

So the torturing continues.

After another month of this I talk with the Manager of the building, a young woman, and ask to get let out of my lease due to the noise. She agrees.

Then she moves out of the complex herself.

This hasn't happened to me before. I've rented apartments my whole adult life, aside from a three-year stint where I bought a condo, renovated and sold it.

I decide to move out of the city. I haven't lived outside of the city before and commuted. I browse the Internet and find a guy in his mid-thirties looking to share the expenses of a house. We meet, he seems okay, and he says he's not home much.

It's an older house but the property is fairly well-kept and he seems tidy. I move in and all seems to be going well.

My roommate isn't home much and I enjoy watching the deer grazing on the grass in the backyard, the squirrels chasing each other up and down the trees. The air is much cleaner. Clearer, crisper. The nights are quiet.

I'm not fond of the commuting, though. It takes me an hour to get to the school I work at and an hour to drive home again. Plus, the cost of gas. But it is quieter and I enjoy hiking in the nearby forests and reading on the porch outside in my off time.

The feeling that I'm being watched and followed isn't going away, though. When I drive, I get the distinct impression I'm being followed. But again, I've been told I have an active imagination, so I'm not giving this too much weight. I am noticing how this is affecting my hormone levels in my body though. It feels like they're getting out of balance. I don't like it.

I do like my yoga/meditation classes, but I'm finding that doing yoga at home works better for me. When I'm in a class setting, I get distracted by other people, by their energies. But I'm finding it easier to cut back a lot on smoking pot and am substituting yoga/meditation for pot.

So far, so good.

After about three months my roommate starts behaving differently. He seems to be spending a lot more time at home. He's inviting people over constantly, partying. I'm not sure what this is about... maybe he's going through a phase? I decide to give it a month or so and if it doesn't calm down I'll move.

Shortly after I decide this, my roommate tells me I have to move out at the end of the month. There are five days left until the end of the month. He doesn't want to give me back my damage deposit even though I haven't damaged anything. I'm not sure what's going on, but I find another apartment to rent and talk him into giving me my damage deposit back.

I'm grateful I found somewhere to live on such short notice and to leave what seemed to be the start of a rapidly degrading situation.

Somehow it feels like Leslie had something to do with the dead cat, the hang-up calls I'm getting at home and at work, the stalking, the apartment with the torturing going on, and my now ex-roommate's strange change in behavior.

I don't usually experience long strings of negative situations/ people like this, so I'm wondering if, in fact, a lot of this does have something to do with Leslie, and it isn't just my imagination.

I decide to call Leslie. His voicemail answers. I leave a message asking if we can meet and talk. I'm hoping to dispel this feeling that he's behind this negative stuff going on.

He doesn't return my call.

Which somehow adds to the feeling that yes, it could be possible Leslie has been behind the negativity that's been occurring.

For a lot of people moving three times in a one-year timeframe would be hard. Monetarily it is difficult for me; the cost of renting moving vans to move furniture and the time and effort it takes to move is mostly what I don't enjoy.

But I do like living in different areas.

I don't seem to get particularly attached to areas or homes.

***

The new apartment I find is on the third floor of a three-story apartment building in the city. Awesome. No need to worry about loud noises going on above me. I like the Building Manager, an elderly lady. I offer to paint the apartment on the agreement the paint is provided. The painting takes about four days. In the past, I've found painting walls to be calming.

As I'm painting though, I'm noticing an ongoing tightness in my chest. I'm feeling anxious most of the time and I'm feeling angry[2] about being stalked, so I'm breathing shallow a lot of the time.

On the fourth day, as I'm cleaning the paint brushes and roller in the kitchen sink I decide to sit down afterwards and do more research on yoga and meditation.

Why did I do this? Well, because it feels to me like somehow this stuff has been happening for a reason. I'm not sure how else to explain it; it's almost like destiny in a way. And that I'll need to fortify myself somehow, spiritually. That this is the beginning of a journey, some type of journey. This is how it feels, which sounds crazy even to me. But that's how it feels.

And I know somehow there are aspects of the human condition that are incredibly under-rated. It feels to me like yoga/meditation is a gateway somehow — a gateway to better understanding myself and how to manage my own energy. Even though in the West yoga/meditation is considered a form of exercise, that just doesn't feel right to me. Spiritual doesn't seem to describe it very well either, and I'm not talking about religion here; I'm not affiliated with any religion. But it feels to me as if investing in myself energetically is going to be super helpful for me on this...journey. One thing I'm concerned about, though, is that the long term negative aspects of stress, which I'm feeling a lot of currently, are a decreased life span and a decreased enjoyment of life.

After some time, I locate a specific type of yoga/meditation audio online. I decide to start practicing it on my own three times a week and monitor the tightness in my chest, my breathing and level of anxiety.

Now, because at the moment, I have a lot of stress going on, I figure the best thing I can do is to focus on transforming any fear-based energy I have into positive energy.

Any amount whatsoever will be helpful, because I don't want to make any decisions based on fear or make rash decisions, and I want to be as calm and mindful as I possibly can under the circumstances.

After practicing a certain type of yoga meditation about three times a week, I'm finding it's really helping me. It's calming, relaxing, and restorative. It's helping me focus. A lot.

And I wonder, if I concentrate on this will I be able to cut down on pot so much that I'll be able to stop smoking pot - for good? I'm hoping so.

As an aside, over the years, I've learned some ancient techniques that complement this style of yoga/ meditation and have incorporated them into my routine.

Meanwhile, I'm starting to hear voices and footsteps above me in my new apartment. The one on the third floor of a three-storey building.

Which means someone is on the roof. I don't know why, but to me it feels like it's Leslie. Which is crazy. That would be crazy.

I must be imagining it. I try dismissing these thoughts every time I hear footsteps on the roof above me. Because... things like this don't happen in real life. Right?

***

One day I decide to Google my name and find over two thousand people quite dislike me, which seems odd. I don't think I've met two thousand people over my lifetime, and most them I've gotten along with. So why would that be? I conclude there must be someone else with my name. Or something. Unless Leslie **is** some kind of organized crime leader, and these people work for him or something?

But that would be crazy. No way. That's just a way out there thought. But it could be a possibility and it would explain what's been going on. But it seems so weird. I mean, seriously?

Regardless, I decide I need to make more of an effort to calm myself and decide to practice my yoga/meditation daily. I start practicing for forty minutes every morning before going to work. I've cut back on smoking pot to once every few weeks now, over the weekend. The yoga/meditation is really helping. It feels like it's helping me balance my hormones… somewhat.

Then I start noticing something else. Friends I visit regularly, usually about once a week, have two children. The youngest is about two years old and is exhibiting behavior out of the ordinary, as if he's experiencing trauma. I keep watching him as the weeks go by and determine he's definitely experiencing trauma. I do a lot of online research on the signs and symptoms of trauma in children and how to talk to parents about it.

At this point I'm strongly feeling that all this negativity, stalking, hang-up phone calls, strange neighbors and roommates, and the trauma the child is experiencing are somehow linked to Leslie.

To me it's feeling more and more like Leslie has a lot of power somehow, and for whatever reason he's decided to spend a lot of time and effort trying to negatively impact my life and now, those I care about. Which is strange because, at this point, I don't even know who Leslie is, or why he'd do this.

I'm feeling a lot of confusion and am overwhelmed,[3] and I'm not quite sure what to do about it.

So I decide I need guidance.

I decide to start asking The Light for guidance and strength.

And I thank The Light and the Archangels (this is the closest thing in books I can find that describes the energies and feeling I had when I was twenty and the two positive, loving energies were by my shoulders - I believe they were Archangels) for helping and protecting me.

And I start practicing lucid dreaming, although at the time I didn't know this was the name for it. To me, I'm just using my imagination. Basically, after I finish my meditation/yoga exercise and I'm already in a calm meditative state, I use my imagination to express gratitude to The Light.

It goes something like this:

Sitting on the ground cross-legged, I close my eyes, keeping my tongue curled behind my front teeth and concentrating on my third eye, while breathing deeply. My hands are open, palms facing up. In my mind's eye, I see me, in physical form, standing, but I'm also hovering above and to the side of me in spirit form, just like in my dreams.

I'm standing on a large, white circular stone slab about fifty feet in diameter. There are no walls and no ceiling. The sky is clear. With love, I repeat, "Archangel Michael" slowly, over and over in my mind, calling. After a short time, I feel my fingertips begin to tingle, and the sensation begins to spread throughout my hands. This is a sign he's heard me and is on his way.

Soon, I can hear in the distance a rhythmic whoosh-whoosh sound. There're three seconds between each whoosh. In my imagination, physical me opens my eyes, smiling, and watches him land gracefully on taloned feet.

His wings fold back gracefully against his broad back. He's ten feet tall; the length of each powerfully formed white wing is nine feet, when fully expanded. His talons give way to muscular calves and thighs.

He, like all Archangels, is not equipped with sexual organs. They don't reproduce or have need to.

While he doesn't have male reproductive organs his dominant energy is male, yet is balanced with his female energy. His hairless chest rises and falls gently. His neck is feathered and, this time, his head is that of an eagle. Austere, majestic, wild, loving eyes peer through me, reading my soul.

I drop to one knee, closing my eyes, and bowing my head, lifting my hands, thanking him for being with me. He reaches down with one large hand and places it in mine. I bring his hand to my lips and place a soft kiss on the back side. Then I place his hand on my heart. Finally, I place his hand across my forehead. All the while I'm concentrating on the energy of gratitude to him and for him, for The Light. For their unconditional Love.

I release his hand and slowly open my eyes, looking up at him. His eyes look back at me with patience, understanding and kindness. His hand drops to caress my cheek. Then he places his hand on top of my head. After a few moments, his wings unfold gracefully, powerfully. I smile at him. His chin/beak moves upward slightly. He slowly takes five taloned steps back.

*Next, I call Archangel Gabriel. For me, Gabriel is female. Just as powerful as Michael and, again, no reproductive organs, but the shape of Gabriel's body and energy reminds me more of the female form. Sometimes the Archangels have an eagle head, sometimes a human head; sometimes they have talons instead of feet; sometimes their legs are covered in feathers. Sometimes their necks are skin, sometimes feathered. The constant is their energy, their wings, and their uncon-*ditional love.

I repeat the same ritual with Archangel Gabriel, then Raphael and finally Ariel. After I've thanked all four, I sit on my calves and stretch my arms out in front of me, my head touching the floor. I concentrate on The Light, the loving energy of the unconditional love I experienced when I drowned. I sense a powerful and luminous brightness and warmth growing in front of me. The Archangels drop to one knee and bow their heads.

Unmoving, I sense an energy of purity that spirals into eternity, then reverberates back, filling the spaces of seeming nothingness and connecting them like a web, connecting the unknowable, the unseen of one dimension of time and space to another.

I feel better after this. I'm calm.

I'm also getting the feeling that things — energies, circumstances, events — are colliding together to form this… journey. This journey that'll have many levels.

Because this current situation with Leslie has something to do with the feeling I had when I was on that spiritual retreat years ago. It's getting closer, the feeling of having to do something for The Light that will be extraordinarily difficult.

And it also feels like this difficult task has something to do with the other feeling I keep getting, the one where the energy of the environment is decreasing and is having or will have a large impact on our ability to be able to survive, as a species, in the future.

At the same time, it feels like it has something to do with the collective subconscious, as if it's an infected, putrefying wound and getting worse. Like in some way I'm being asked to lance it, release the pressure, open the wound.

And it feels like it has something to do with me, with how I perceive things, with how I've been taught to focus on the logical, the physical world, what's in front of my nose, and to disregard my intuition, my dreams and how they relate to the physical realm.

All of this makes me feel extremely uncomfortable, fearful. I have no idea what this is all about or how I'm supposed to do this. I'm only one person. Why would The Light ask me to do something like this?

But I'm also incredibly thankful I've discovered the tool of yoga/meditation.

***

As time goes on the unpleasant occurrences from Leslie seem to be gaining in intensity. Every morning there's something on my car window now. Some form of human liquid—sometimes spit, other times, well... you can use your imagination here.

One day, while working at my desk at the school, I smell hard drugs.

Later the Janitor finds a bag with drug paraphernalia on the roof, close to a vent that feeds into the office where I work.

Regardless, I continue practicing yoga/meditation daily, first thing in the morning before getting ready for work.

***

Finally, I decide to try to find out for sure what's going on. If I'm connecting dots that aren't connected. If I'm somehow being paranoid or something. If I'm overthinking things. Somehow...

What's been happening is too out of the ordinary to talk to anyone I know about. Because... well, this stuff just doesn't happen in real life, right? The thing is, I don't think I'm being paranoid. I just can't wrap my head around the fact that my dreams told me something about Leslie that is accurate and that would explain why this stuff has been happening. But still, I need verification. Somehow. Some way.

So, I send a postcard to an acquaintance I know. The postcard isn't really for the acquaintance. The postcard itself is a message for a mutual friend we have in common.

Kyler.

I guess you could say I "officially" met Kyler through an acquaintance when I was about twenty-five years old. This acquaintance was helping me set up for a garage sale. It was a Saturday morning on a summer day. Kyler was friends with my acquaintance and had stopped by to say hi to them.

I knew Kyler from the neighborhood. We grew up in the same neighborhood. I didn't know him well enough to say hi, but enough to recognize him. He was a couple of years younger than me. But I did know enough about him to steer clear of him.

Not that he was a bad guy or anything. He wasn't. He was just involved in things I didn't want to know about. Hard drugs mainly. I knew he had a habit called heroin. On this particular day when he dropped by he looked normal enough, fairly healthy.

The three of us were sitting in the cool shade of the garage when our conversation turned to a more spiritual nature. We started talking about God. Kyler asked me if I believed in God. I said I believed in The Light. Then he asked me if I believed God judged us when we died and decided whether we go to heaven or to hell. I thought about that for a minute. Then I replied I thought The Light was everywhere, including in us. That when we died ***we*** decided what happened to us and where we **deserved** to go. After all, who knows us better than us, right?

As I said this I looked him in the eye. And in that moment, I had the strangest feeling. Like I knew him, but from a different time and place. But I couldn't remember where or when. But that somehow it wasn't from this lifetime, which seemed really strange to me. I haven't had that feeling before, nor since, with anyone else.

He must've had the same feeling too. Because I saw my recognition reflected in his eyes.

After that he would stop by for tea sometimes, once, or twice a month. He'd call first and ask if it was okay. He never talked much during our visits. I'd talk about whatever course I was taking at night, or book I was reading, what I was learning, or just things I thought were interesting. He'd listen intently, nodding his head here and there, while sipping his tea. I understood without being told that he couldn't and wouldn't share anything about his world with me.

But he just enjoyed quietly hanging out together. It was normal and he liked it. His reality was a lot different... harsher. He wanted it to be different but he hadn't been able to change it. Without saying it, I knew he grew up in violence too. It felt to me like his mom had physically beat him as a child but also like his way of life was handed down to him, like it was a family thing or something, like he was expected to carry on the "family business". He was smart, funny, creative, talented, and caring. But in his world, only smart and violent are worth anything.

It felt to me like he resented the fact that he felt forced to live in his world.

We continued with our visits every few weeks for about six months. Then I didn't hear from him for about six months. Then one day he just showed up at my door.

He'd lost about twenty pounds, and he was lean to begin with. When he was healthy, he had a trim, athletic build.

Now he looked skeletal and had sores on his face and arms. His eyes were sunken into his head and dark half circles indented the areas under his eyes. He looked deathly. I knew he had a problem with heroin but I didn't realize it was this bad.

It took me by surprise.

Speechless, I looked at him for about two minutes without saying anything. He just stood there looking back at me. Waiting.

"You look like shit," I finally said to him.

He looked me in the eyes for some moments, nodded his head and wordlessly left.

I heard he went to jail shortly after that.

About a year later he showed up at my door again. He'd just gotten out of jail. He looked healthy. He'd had a few drinks, I think to get his courage up to visit me. I got the feeling that he'd been thinking about me in jail and had feelings for me, as I did for him, but we both had no understanding of what those feelings were, or what the initial recognition was.

We slept together that night, but both of us realized whatever we had, it wasn't sexual or romantic. It was a friendship. He knew I understood his situation and accepted him, and hoped he would find a way to live a happy, healthy life, but that I couldn't and wouldn't have anything to do with his way of life. We visited over tea a few times after that, and then I moved. Now, ten years later, I'm sending him a message on a postcard via our acquaintance.

So why did I send him the message, via our acquaintance? Because what little I did know about Kyler was that he understood organized crime. It was his way of life. I hoped he'd let me know the truth: whether I was being targeted by someone who has something to do with organized crime, or if I'm just losing my mind.

I'd rather not be losing my mind, but if I'm right, and I'm not losing my mind, I'm hoping he'll know the best way to deal with this situation. Because I'm at a loss.

So, I send the postcard and wait. The daily harassment I can deal with, but harming my friend's child, that's really bothering me.

***

In the meantime, it feels to me like my energy is blocked. I'm feeling stuck,[4] restricted, like energy can't flow. Like negative energy is trapped somehow. I'm not sure how to fix this so I start researching it online.

Next, I start experimenting with clearing energy in my apartment. I also get rid of things I've had for a while but never use by either donating them or giving items I think friends or family would want. I rearrange furniture and organize papers and items I use often.

Afterwards, the energy in my apartment feels better, as if the energy can move about more freely now. I feel lighter, clearer.

I've also started to eat less and less meat, white or red. Somehow it feels like I need to be careful about this. I don't know why. So, I check into it.

After doing some research I learn that the red meat I've been buying at the grocery store is loaded with hormones, steroids, and antibiotics. For some reason, I'm being guided to be careful about making sure the *hormones* in my body are balanced and functioning as best they can. Hormones regulate and affect the body and mind **a lot**. One of the things hormones do is affect how stressed we feel. Based what's happening in my world presently, stress is an issue.

Right now, it feels like my stress hormone is quite elevated. I'm still feeling stressed, even though I'm meditating daily, but I don't want anything else making it go any higher. I know my meditation practice is helping a lot to keep my hormones balanced, so I decide to only eat red meat once a month. White meat not at all. For now.

This change in diet is extremely out of the norm for me and anyone I know. Alberta is known as beef country and it's been a staple in my diet for as long as I can remember. My family and friends are having a hard time accepting this change. I don't know why; I'm not asking them to change what they eat, but they seem to feel threatened by my making changes. Odd.

Nevertheless, I continue making these changes. And over time, I notice this change is having a positive effect on me. I'm thinking more clearly, and my feelings of stress, anxiety and being overwhelmed are lessening as well. Not gone altogether… at all, but making things… somehow… manageable.

So, I continue with it.

***

I've been living in this apartment for about eight months now. And for about six months, every morning when I wake up, I feel like I've been

through some kind of psychic battle. I wake up psychically and emotionally exhausted.

Is that even a thing? Psychic battle? Because it feels like I've been battling something or someone in my dreams all night, but I don't remember any of these dreams. Which is odd, I always remember my dreams and have fitful, refreshing sleeps. I'm just waking up exhausted, though.

This is **seriously** out of the ordinary for me.

I decide to double up on my yoga/meditation practice, practicing not only first thing in the morning, but also before I go to sleep.

I also start doing shadow self-work. I don't know why, but it feels like I need to. I draw pictures of my shadow self. I've been taught by my family and society—no, there's a better word, "brainwashed" — to "be nice" and essentially push back, push down, any negative feelings I have. As if pushing them away negates them actually being there. It doesn't.

I want to acknowledge any negative feelings I have. Feelings, no matter what they are, are there to help me grow.

Figuring out how is the hard part.

***

My friend's child is still showing signs of trauma, and it feels to me like he's still experiencing trauma. It's now been a year and a half of suspecting that Leslie is behind what's happening to my friend's child, but I haven't heard anything back from Kyler. I decide I have to broach the subject quietly and gently with my friends, the child's parents.

I've been researching how to discuss this with my friends. Delicately.

Very delicately. To me the most important thing is that the child receives help and support. So, one evening after eating dinner with my friends, I cautiously and gently broach the subject, focusing on what I've been noticing about the child's behavior and the information I researched.

It doesn't go well.

The mother somehow makes it about her, which I don't understand. But then again, I don't understand why either parent hasn't noticed their own child's out-of-the-ordinary behavior, and why they haven't sought support already.

I'm essentially berated for bringing a problem to light.

Which doesn't help the child.

I'm hovering above myself in spirit form, watching my physical self standing in a meadow. Behind the meadow is a forest of birch trees. It's summer. In front of me is a field of wheat.

I notice a large red tractor sitting silently ten feet away from me. The mother of the child who is being assaulted, my friend, is sitting on the tractor facing the field. She's turned in the seat looking at me, smiling. Standing beside the tractor is Leslie. He's smiling at me too, extending a hand, as if he wants me to get on the tractor with my friend.

I sense someone behind me. I turn, look, and Kyler is standing with his hands in his pockets a few feet behind me. He isn't smiling, and he isn't extending his hand. But he is there.

I don't trust any of them. But if I have to choose one to trust somewhat, it's Kyler. I say nothing to Leslie and my friend, and instead turn around and walk to Kyler. He looks up at me. I'm not smiling. I hold my hand out to him and send him with my mind, "Do you want to walk in the forest?"

He looks at me. He understands I don't trust him much more than the other two, but if I have to choose someone it will be him. He takes my hand and we walk into the forest.

I wake from this dream and review it, because I'm going to have to pay serious attention to my dreams now, that much I can tell.

As I review this dream I conclude that Leslie and my friend, the mother of the child being assaulted, are somehow connected. And it occurs to me, I think my friend experienced an unhealthy, unbalanced childhood too. That she was assaulted when she was a child. And she hasn't done the work to heal, or hasn't figured out how to transform her pain into something healthy, something that'll benefit her.

Somehow this feels like it's something she has in common with Leslie.

And none of this makes any sense. I'm not sure what to make of this dream or how much validity it has to base my decisions in real life on.

Three months after I send the postcard, Kyler lets me know.

My .22 rifle I use for target shooting that I've been storing in the trunk of my car, goes missing. It's been stolen.

I report it stolen to the police the same day.

The next day at school I hear people talking about how shots were fired at a guy leaving his home in the neighborhood. The neighborhood Leslie lives in. The man wasn't shot, but he was shot at. Then I hear a young man, a teenager at a nearby high school, was shot in the groin.

This is bad. Not good at all, because I think Kyler just let me know that Leslie is behind the child's trauma and that he has been behind all these strange, negative things going on.

Kyler is telling me, without words, that I'm not crazy, which is incredibly reassuring. Life-saving. But in a way, I wish I was, because knowing this information makes things seem worse. And while I wish Kyler hadn't done what he did, I now understand in his world this is how things are done. In his world, they "do" things. They don't talk or discuss or negotiate.

The thing is I only wanted to know I wasn't imagining this stuff and what the best non-violent way forward was.

I didn't want any violence.

That he stuck his neck out in this way to let me know worries me too. I didn't realize in his world, the only way he could let me know I wasn't losing my mind was to do something like this.

And I don't know if because of me, he put his own neck on the line.

I was hoping for a note or something.

What's more, it feels like other people have gotten involved, like some sort of battle is going on, and people are getting hurt. Like chaos is happening. Some people are looking for retribution, some for redemption and some are just plain confused. And I'm helpless to stop it. It feels like I'm in the eye of some kind of storm.

For the next three months, I try to think of some way to reasonably, peacefully resolve this. So far ignoring it, like the police website advised, isn't working. I can deal with the following, stalking, hang-up phone calls, crap on my car windows, scratches on my car, hanging around on the roof above my head and other miscellaneous distasteful behavior. What I'm having a difficult time dealing with is feeling helpless to help the child. What is the purpose behind what Leslie's doing!? It doesn't make sense to me! And it continues. Until...

Three months later, I reach a decision. I'm going to have to kill Leslie.

The fact that he's doing all these things "under the radar" means he has no intention of stopping this behavior or talking with me about why he's doing it.

So, I just can't see any other way. I'll have to buy another rifle.

I started target shooting about four years previously. What I enjoyed about it was the focusing; the moment before taking the shot everything becomes so still and quiet. Moments hang suspended, almost frozen, and the slow, rhythmic beating of my heart is the only sound I hear.

I also learned that women are naturally better sharpshooters than men.

In Canada, when sharpshooting was created as a sport, both men and women competed at the same time. After women kept winning, year after year, it was decided to split the competition into separate competitions, men's, and women's. Apparently, women have better hand-eye coordination and fine motor movements. What women don't like is loud sounds.

What sucks about this recent decision is I'll be going to jail. I know myself well enough to know my conscience won't allow for anything else. I'm not sure if I'll turn myself in, but no matter what, I'll give myself away somehow, because I won't want to get away with it.

Which is fine. I guess you have to do what you have to do. Maybe that's part of The Light's plan for me. Maybe there's something I'm supposed to learn or do in jail.

So, sitting at my kitchen table after supper, I'm making a mental list of what I'll need for gear, where I'll position myself, what time of day, what to wear, where to park the car...

I pull out a piece of paper and a pen and start writing items down.

Chapter 2:

Call to Adventure

Then I sense something. Movement in the periphery of my mind, a sense of something, an energy...? Approaching me.

I stop, close my eyes, and listen.

Whoosh-whoosh... whoosh-whoosh... whoosh-whoosh.

It's strong. The energy is very strong. And somehow, it feels to me like it's Archangel Michael.

Then a loud, angry voice, Archangel Michael's voice, thunders in my head.

"YOU WILL NOT!

YOU WILL BE AN EXAMPLE!

YOU HAVE BEEN CHOSEN!"

My yes op en. I'm stunned.

Then, as the words sink in, I'm slowly becoming furious.

"NO! CHOOSE SOMEONE ELSE!" I scream back with my mind.

A moment of silence.

I sense reproach.

"YOU HAVE BEEN CHOSEN AND YOU WILL!" Archangel Michael's voice thunders back.

Then the sound of wings, leaving.

Whoosh-whoosh... whoosh-whoosh... whoosh-whoosh.

I'm swirling in anger and confusion and it doesn't occur to me to be astounded that Archangel Michael spoke to me, first, and second, that I received an outright order.

I'm too upset with what I've been ordered.

And for the next three hours I'm storming back and forth in my living room, fists clenched, as angry, hot tears form creeks, running down my cheeks.

How ***dare*** he order me to do nothing?! To stand by while some power-crazy nut job assaults a child I love! How can he ask that I *do nothing*?!

I'm unable to wrap my head around it. But I try. Try to understand why. Why I'm to do nothing.

And at the time, it also doesn't occur to me to be thankful.

But eventually I do decide to try to follow this order. And I practice my yoga/meditation, as usual, before going to sleep that night and early the next morning when I wake up.

After my morning yoga/meditation, where I spend the end of my meditation asking "why?" of The Light, and in return I receive a feeling, a soft, quiet message from The Light.

I'm being asked to have compassion for Leslie, to try to understand him, and to help him understand, warn him about the lowering energy in the environment.

Seriously? What am I? Mother Theresa? Is this a joke?

Because the thing is, at this point in time, the best I can do is not carry out my plan to kill him, let alone try to understand, communicate with, and help him.

I'm also noticing that I'm going through some type of transition into a different state of being. Maybe because of how long I've been feeling stressed, I don't know, but I'm literally sensing everything in every moment of my waking life. All my senses are sharpened. Hypervigilance.

And it takes me back to when I was a child, when I felt hyper-alert because I didn't know when the violence would erupt or for how long, but how I'd know it was coming, how moments beforehand everything seemed… enhanced.

And how the adults in my life made it clear to me I was to "act normal" to the outside world. How it was imperative to "act normal."

***

I decide to let what Archangel Michael ordered sink in. Give it time. Because this is difficult. I'll have to think about this.

It feels like I'm being asked to do the impossible. But it also feels like it's important that I listen. So, I do. As difficult as it is, I do. Contrary to what I've been led to believe in the society I grew up in, at times it's the hardest thing to simply "be," to "not take action." We're taught to react rather than act mindfully. So, while this isn't easy, at all, I know it's the right thing for me to do in this circumstance.

I continue visiting my friends and trying to help in whatever way I can. The kids and I play in parks, go tobogganing and skating. We laugh and have a lot of fun together. At the very least, they have what I didn't, someone who loves them, who knows what's going on isn't healthy, who loves having fun with them and is there for them.

***

A few other things are quietly settling into my mind too. It feels like a few different things are occurring on different levels. One, it feels like Leslie represents the "collective subconscious," what people as a whole repress and don't want to look at or heal. Which is why it feels like a massive infected wound.

Two, on another level, it feels like I'm being asked to try because I have the ability to detach myself from situations, any situation really, and look at it objectively, like an observer, even when I'm in the situation.

Three, it's as if I asked for this test before I was born, as if my soul wanted to learn something that I, in the here and now, can't remember.

Four, I'm starting to wonder if I didn't "find" Leslie, even though it looks like he's playing with me like a cat does a mouse. It feels like the way it looks isn't really the way it is.

A friend has given me a steel guitar as a birthday present and I hire a teacher for a few sessions to learn more about it. At the music store, where I go to pick up a few items, I meet a friendly guy around my age who works at the store. In his off time, he plays in a band too. He seems like a good guy.

We hang out a few times, go for a drive in the mountains. He seems romantically interested in me, but I let him know I'm only interested in being friends. He seems good with this.

I also take a few creative writing courses in the evenings. Afterwards, I wonder if I can actually write. I mean, when I was between six and twelve years old I used to love writing and would often gift my stories to family members and friends. But just because you're drawn to something doesn't necessarily mean you're good at it, right? Or maybe that's not true?

I decide to check into it some more and find an online writing contest and work on a story. It can only be one page long. Once I have it written I decide to get a second opinion on it. I invite my guitarist friend over for dinner one night and ask him if he can read it and let me know what he thinks.

My guitarist friend reads it and offers some helpful suggestions. The next day he calls me and tells me when he left my place the night before, one of the tires on his vehicle was slashed.

I'm not sure what to think about that. Would Leslie do that? The regular harassment is still occurring, and it feels to me like Leslie is still hanging out on the roof above my apartment, but I haven't decided if I'm going to do what The Light's asked. If I'm going to try to help and warn Leslie.

That would mean taking the "red pill" and I'm not quite sure about that yet.

I make the changes to my story that my friend suggested and submit it.

It's posted anonymously online, and people vote online. I don't tell anyone I know about the contest—well, my guitarist friend knows, but he doesn't know what contest.

A few months later I receive a phone call at the school where I'm working, telling me my writing piece was chosen as one of the winners. I'm asked to frame it and send it to them so they can display it and send it on a tour, and I'm given an invitation to attend a type of social event to recognize the winners.

Then I have a dream.

In spirit form, I'm watching myself sleeping naked on my side, on the floor, in the fetal position. The room is made of four by three feet pitted and chipped, worn, smooth, light gray stones. The walls, the ceiling, the floor. The ceiling is forty feet high. The room is bare of furnishings or any color. Monastic. There's one window, four feet wide and five feet tall, rounded at the top. On the same wall as the window is a massive fireplace. Three large men could sit on chairs next to one another in this fireplace. There's no fire or wood in the fireplace.

Kyler is kneeling beside me, gently prodding my shoulder, trying to wake me up. He's wearing clothes. Slowly, I begin opening my eyes. I'm now both me in my dream and watching me from above in spirit. I sit up and then slowly get to my feet, looking around at my surroundings. I doesn't seem that I feel concerned I'm not wearing any clothes. And I don't feel cold. I feel something against my back though. I look over my shoulder and find it's a very large white wing. It's part of me. It feels like an extra appendage. Startled and fearful I look back at Kyler questioningly.

Using his mind, he sends me, "It's fine, it's okay."

I look over my other shoulder and see a second white wing.

I look back at Kyler again, wide-eyed, not sure what to think or do. "Stretch them out, get a feel for them," Kyler sends me, encouragingly. Smiling.

It seems like he has some experience with this, although I notice he doesn't have wings.

Tentatively, I will it. I can feel the pulse of each individual feather as I slowly make them open. I can feel how each are separate, yet how they're all connected, a part of me. I feel the strength and curvature of the framework of bones in each of my wings. When I open them fully, they're five feet, four inches long. I stand five foot, five inches. I look at them, incredulous. Awestruck.

"See?" Kyler sends. "It's okay. Try flying... just around the room a

little." I look back at him doubtfully.

I'm willing to try, though. I concentrate and imagine what the timing of the beats will need to be if I want to lift into the air.

Whoosh... whoosh... whoosh.

My feet lose contact with the ground and I'm hovering in front of Kyler. "Wow!" I send him, excited. My eyebrows are raised and a smile is growing on my face.

Smiling, he sends, "Fly around the room a bit now." I nod and begin turning, giving energy to my wings.

Turning is a lot easier than I thought it would be. I simply turn my head in the direction I want to go and my body follows. Soon I'm flying faster and faster, swooping and swerving through the air, using the inner and outer perimeter of the room as well as the height.

It feels amazing!

After some time, I land... mostly gracefully in front of Kyler.

My wings fold automatically against my back. A little too hard, I notice. So, I'll have to work on that and my landing.

"You need to go out there," he sends as he nods toward the window.

I look out the window. It's a bright, sunny day and the odd marshmallow-like cloud hangs suspended in the light blue sky.

"But you have to break the window first."

How cool would that be to fly out there?! But break the window? With what? I scan the room again. There's nothing to break it with.

I raise an eyebrow at him.

"It's easy," he sends. "Just go to the far end..." nodding his head in the direction which is the opposite side of the room from the window, "hover and build your momentum, then in one strong move

bring your wings down hard, and at the same time flip your body horizontally so your feet are pointing at the window. Use one wing to cover your front and the other to cover your back, so when the glass breaks you'll be protected."

I think about this for a few moments.

It could work. It's worth a try.

I follow his directions exactly.

Next thing I know I'm hovering outside the broken window looking in at him. I can feel the expanse of the sky calling to me, pulling me, away. Looking at Kyler, I notice he's staring at my wings, and I can sense his longing.

Not for me. For wings.

In that moment, I remember.

We've flown together before. I also know he'll fly again one day.

I nod at him and turn, falling a little at first, and then my wings take me higher.

Flying through the open air feels amazing, the air currents and pockets different and varying. I'm noticing how my wings react to slight movements I make, and then I see a large stone turret with one side open.

It's a type of castle. The room we were in was part of a castle. I fly toward the turret and see a washing machine sitting in the turret. It has my clothes

in it. Two middle-aged, rough-looking men with sallow complexions and bad teeth are opening the washing machine. They're trying to steal my clothes.

I'm surprised and exhilarated at how fast I can fly as moments later I land between them, in front of the washing machine. I look at their surprised faces and forcefully close my wings, then position my wings across the front of my body, folded one over the other, and then push them out forcefully. The backs of my wings knock them both off the turret.

Which I meant to do. But it's a long way down…

It was cool to have wings and learn to fly… but clearly, I have some things to learn about sharing and being gentler.

***

A week later I'm woken in the night to a child's loud pleas. Below my bedroom window, which is open, I can hear my friend's child, the one who's been assaulted, calling for his daddy. And I know he's being sexually assaulted. I know I'm not hearing things and this is actually happening. And I know it won't make a difference if I call the police, and it won't make a difference if I run out of my apartment and try to reach him. The person who has him will be gone by the time I get down the stairs and out the door.

I begin praying for Archangel Michael to be with him, to protect his soul. Because what isn't well understood is that hurting someone's physical being isn't that important. It's their spirit and their soul that determine how they move forward. Still… I don't know how The Light thinks I can do this.

***

As the days turn into weeks and two months' pass, I think about what The Light wants me to do: to try to understand Leslie.

Maybe Leslie is trying to show me that what's happening to the child, what he's either doing to the child, or having someone else do to him, happened to him. That's why he's acting the way he's acting and doing the things he's doing. This is what happened to him, what his "normal" is. It's okay. To him this is okay.

On some level, I can understand this. I've had similar feelings myself. I couldn't explain what it was like to someone who hadn't grown up with chaos and violence. No one can truly understand it unless they've been through it. While I haven't been through what Leslie's been through, I do understand the feeling of isolation. I'm understanding more why The Light is asking me to have compassion for Leslie, try to understand him and to help him understand about the lowering of energy in nature, because Leslie doesn't understand this. For some reason his senses don't pick up on things like this.

Which is good that I've come this far in my willingness to try to understand Leslie. Except I have no way to communicate with him. How am I supposed to warn him about the lowering of energy in nature?

He's obviously some type of leader, meaning he has a stake in protecting and ensuring others' survival, to some extent. So logically it would make sense that he'd appreciate information that would protect not only his well-being but that of those who follow him and support him. I just don't know how to communicate with him. He's made it clear he doesn't want me to see him and he doesn't want to talk to me in person or on the phone.

So, I try to think of how to communicate with him as time goes on.

And I continue working, meditating, eating healthy and living as normal a life as I can under the circumstances. I keep visiting my friends.

***

Then I'm invited to the child's kindergarten graduation ceremony. The child is supposed to be moving forward to the next level in kindergarten. He's five now. But they're holding him back.

It's because of the trauma he's experiencing.

Driving home from the ceremony I feel the anger growing inside me. This has been going on for almost two years now. Leslie doesn't need to do this. It's helping nothing.

After I get home I silently let loose with my thoughts, directing them, looking at the ceiling.

Knowing, but not knowing, if Leslie's on the roof, if he hears me. I call him names like coward and shithead.

The next morning, I wake up and notice three things...

One, I've been drugged... I can tell because my system is pretty clean and I can feel the drugs in my system. It was some type of sedative. I feel slightly groggy.

Two, I've been sexually assaulted.

Three, there is no apparent forcible entry to my apartment. The door is still locked and deadbolted.

So. This tells me a lot.

First, Leslie **is** hanging out on the roof; second, I have a way to communicate with him and third, he's playing games—trying to make me think I'm crazy or if I tell someone what happened, they'll think I'm crazy.

That he assaulted me shows me a lot about him. First, it shows me he thinks that doing something like this toward me will make me feel badly about myself. It doesn't. I don't feel any particular way about it at all, other than it showed me this is something Leslie has experienced, and he felt badly, maybe still does, about it. Because this body I've been given to inhabit while I'm here on this earth is just that—a body. It doesn't represent my spirit, my essence, my soul. No one can take that away from you unless you allow it.

It appears he's also not that confident about his bedroom skills. But that's irrelevant.

The main thing that surprises me is I could communicate to him using my thoughts.

I also might be going crazy. Because this seems crazy to me. It isn't possible for someone to understand and receive thoughts, right?

But it must be possible.

And I'm not sure what to think about this. I've never experienced anything like this before.

I also can't report this to the police. What am I supposed to say? I woke up this morning and noticed I was drugged and assaulted when I was sleeping? I doubt a rape kit would produce any DNA. If he was smart enough to gain entry to my apartment without damaging the lock, then I'd assume he would've taken precautions so his DNA wouldn't be found in any way, shape, or form. So, it would basically make me look crazy. Funny how someone who's crazy tries to make other people look like they're crazy.

But it doesn't surprise me. I grew up around this type of mentality, and to someone like this, this is their normal.

Still, I'm doubting I can do what The Light wants. This is quite difficult.

Plus, I don't understand how this stuff works. Like sending thoughts. Can he only hear me if I concentrate on sending him a message with my mind, or can he hear all my thoughts? Do I have to guard my thoughts? How do I do that?

I don't know.

I decide to remain calm. Remain calm.

Keep practicing my meditation. And remain calm.

I get ready for work and after I arrive at the school a few police officers show up, wanting to talk with the Principal. I lead them into the Principal's office and leave, closing the door behind me.

A few nights later, after work, I'm sitting in my living room reading. I can sense Leslie on the roof above me.

Again.

Suddenly I hear him whistle loudly and I sense he's excited/agitated. This isn't the norm. He's usually very quiet and controlled. Then I hear a police siren for about ten seconds, coming from behind my apartment block, in the alley behind my building. I hear officers stop a vehicle and order people out of it. They're looking for drugs. I hear someone yell, "F**k!" through an open window from an apartment next to my building. Then I hear a lot of doors opening and closing throughout my apartment building, which houses about thirty-two units.

Huh. So. What does this mean? Did this happen by coincidence? Or do the police know what's going on? If they do, why aren't they stopping it? Do they know about the child being assaulted? If they do, why aren't they doing anything to stop it? Or is this ***their*** way of letting Leslie know they know what's going on?

Unless... unless this is a setup by Leslie. I'm not naive enough to think there isn't corruption within the police department. Maybe this is a setup, part of Leslie's ongoing need for drama. I'm not sure I want to give this anymore thought now. Because really, Kyler let me know all I need to know. It appears the police aren't helping anything. If anything, it's just making things more exciting for Leslie. Anyway, they could just be players playing in Leslie's game. Some of them anyway.

Because nothing is ever what it seems, and this realization is slowly sinking in.

Mostly, though, at this point, I want to figure out if I'm crazy or if I'm going crazy. Because all of this just seems completely bizarre.

"Perception is not reality."
— Plato

Chapter 3:

Refusal of the Call

A month later, while on summer break from the elementary school where I work, I decide to check myself into a psych ward at a local hospital because I'm not sure if I really am crazy or not. What's been happening is so far is so unlike anything I've experienced that I figure, well, I just might be crazy or going crazy.

I tell the psychiatrist I hear someone hanging out on the roof above my apartment; I can hear him walking around; I think it's a guy I dated a few years ago, who seems to be stalking me, harassing me; and that I think this same person has been and is assaulting a child I know. This doesn't sound that crazy to me.

Apparently, it does to the psychiatrist. The psychiatrist wants to know if I hear voices. Which, other than the once, with Archangel Michael, I haven't. I decide not to share that with the psychiatrist.

The thing about crazy is it's a tough thing to figure out. Most people who actually are crazy don't think they're crazy. That's what I'm wondering about. How's a crazy person supposed to know they need help if they don't think they're crazy? The doctor diagnoses me with psychosis and at my insistent request allows me to only take half of a mild sedative, the lowest. I look up what psychosis means and good grief, seriously?

After a week goes by and I watch and visit with other people in the ward, I come to the realization that no, I'm not crazy.

Maybe on the verge of some type of nervous breakdown, but not crazy.

I also decide a lot of crazy people aren't locked up in psych wards. The people who are? While they are unbalanced, they aren't fed healthy food, aren't encouraged to breathe deeply, and meditate, aren't encouraged to go for walks in nature, aren't given a homey, relaxing atmosphere, aren't encouraged and taught how to unconditionally love and accept themselves and live a healthy, balanced lifestyle.

Basically, they're medicated.

After three weeks, I leave and stop taking the mild sedative I was prescribed.

***

Maybe that's why The Light chose me to do this? As a child, I managed to deal with crazy somehow, without actually going crazy myself. Somehow a part of me knows what's right, what's healthy, and I cling to it.

The thing is, I feel like I barely survived my childhood with my soul and my sanity, never mind revisiting it again with this situation. What's more, I don't think I want to try.

Yet it feels like no one else can sense the lowering, the diminishing energy in nature. No one can feel the collective subconscious and how it's been getting worse over the years. It's as if people have forgotten who they are, where they come from and what's important. Not that I'm in any better position now, but it feels like I'm supposed to find the answers, figure it out.

Because if anyone can feel it, sense it, or understand it on any level, it feels like they either won't or can't do anything about it. No one is up for the job. No wonder. It's dangerous. On many levels. And I have to think about this some more.

***

Aside from my recent learning experience with the mental health system, which wasn't particularly helpful for me, although interesting, it feels like the changes I've made to my diet are helping. Meditating and eating less meat and more vegetables are helping me balance my hormones, keeping me on a more even keel. Helping me keep my emotions on an even keel. I decide to investigate what else can affect my hormone levels negatively and impact my system negatively.

Because I'm feeling stressed,[5] like my hormone levels need to be continually monitored.

I do some research to find out what man-made chemicals can mess with the natural production of human hormones, and find out ingredients called "parfum" and "fragrance" are particularly harmful to the natural body.

Apparently, manufacturers currently don't have to list chemicals they're using to create "parfum" or "fragrance." I check through my medicine cabinet, my makeup, my perfumes, and my cleaning products. Turns out there's a ton of parfum and/or fragrance in these products. I've been using most of these products for a long time. I had no idea they've been messing with my mind and body. Crap. So now I need to get these chemicals out of my body, which will take time.

I spend a few days getting rid of these products. Bubble baths, bath bombs, lotions, cleaning products, perfume, and anything I find with the ingredients parfum or fragrance—I throw away.

I learn that instead of using the typical cleaning products I've been using I can use baking soda and vinegar. Well, that simplifies things. I check into makeup; there are organic manufacturers of makeup. I find a lotion that's organic and doesn't contain parfum at a local store.

After a few weeks, I can feel a difference. My body feels as if it's highly tuned into what it needs to be tuned into. My mind is clearer.

I'm hovering above myself in spirit form, watching myself standing in a meadow in front of a light, forest-green colored lake. Shocking pink, yellow, blue, and white faces surrounded by a dark velvet green coat litter the meadow riotously, their faces peeking up at the sun. I'm picking small wildflowers one by one, gathering a small bouquet. Bees are humming tunelessly around me.

The hem of my plain, faded light blue sundress tickles my calves. A gentle wind cools my thighs. The sun is kissing my arms.

Then I hear something above me, like a loud, low, mechanical whining. I look up and see a large silver plane. It looks like it seats about a hundred people. I watch it and notice its flying strangely. It's swooping and swerving in the air, as if it's trying to be a much smaller, lighter, more agile plane—the type that can navigate tricks in the air with ease. But this plane is too large, too heavy.

Not built to fly like that. Odd.

Holding my bouquet of wildflowers, I watch as it attempts a difficult maneuver. It's trying to fly upside down and then flip itself right side up. Except in the upside-down position it's flying extremely close to the ground. That isn't going to work, I think to myself.

The pilot is attempting to bring the nose of the plane up quickly, while at the same time turning it, but the plane is too big, too heavy. Foot by foot it lowers until the upside-down nose of the plane begins plowing through the ground. The rest of the plane is pretty much at the same level as the nose, so the plane just keeps plowing through the soil until it reaches a full stop.

Well, what did they expect? *I think to myself. Shaking my head, I turn and walk to the small wooden cottage behind me. I turn the handle of the door and a cat greets me, purring against my ankles. His cold nose causes me to reach down and playfully ruffle his furry head.*

I fill a Mason jar with water, place the wildflowers in the jar and set the jar on a well-worn, scarred wooden table in front of the window overlooking the meadow and lake. I pick up the cat and start petting him while looking out the window. What a beautiful place.

It seems as if my dream is telling me Leslie's actions aren't doing him or the people who're with him any good, and that overall, if I stay focused on my purpose, and remain calm, things will work out.

Huh.

Well.

Okay.

I'm not totally sold.

But.

Okay…

***

Work is going well. The Principal at the school where I work, and some of the teachers, are encouraging me to go to school to become a teacher. They think I have a way with children. I'm not sure about this, but I appreciate the compliment. I decide to enroll in an online TESL course at night and earn a certificate to teach, just in case I'd like to try it sometime. I'm also feeling a strangeness, a connection, and a disconnection at the same time. I feel disconnected to humanity in a way, because I'm living two separate lives, one in "reality" and another "dream" one. No one knows me in "reality" because I have a separate life, my "dream" life, and somehow, they're connected. But it feels like I'm supposed to "act normal" and not outwardly react to all the new information I'm receiving.

It's a solitary feeling.

Chapter 4:

Meeting the Mentor

I'm in spirit form watching myself. I'm sitting with my knees against my chest, my arms wrapped around my knees with my head resting in my arms. And I'm naked.

Lifting my head up, I begin opening my eyes. I'm now both me and watching me in spirit form.

In front of me is a deep, warm, velvety black that extends forever.

Thousands of bright, shining, small beams of light randomly pierce through the black. I'm in space? I look to my left, right and behind me and notice in some places, circular pockets of black seem to quiver... to waver. As if they contain something more.

It's so silent.

So... peaceful.

I feel neither warm nor cold. What am I sitting on?

I look under me.

Nothing. I'm sitting on and in space. Interesting...

Crossing my legs and sitting straight, I look forward again.

My hands resting on my thighs.

The smell and taste of eternity is blissful. All encompassing.

Eternal.

There are sounds in this soundless place. Vibrations under vibrations.

Energy and vortexes within the blacks.

Smiling, I wink and blink back at the stars.

There's no sense of time.

No need for it here.

That felt like a good sign, as if The Light is telling me I'm just one small part of the universe, that I'm insignificant, but at the same time significant. To access the sense of peace I felt in this dream whenever I want or need to.

Okay. I'll try.

> *"Do not feel lonely, the entire universe is inside you."*
>
> *— Rumi*

I've completely stopped smoking pot now. I've decided that yoga/meditation and the other changes I've implemented are helping a lot.

A lot.

And so far, my dreams are telling me that what I'm doing is helping. Plus, I feel better, more prepared psychically, emotionally, physically, and spiritually. I decide to concentrate on asking The Light to give me more signs using my dreams. It seems as if The Light is letting me know I'll be okay, which is reassuring.

Not enough to get me to fully accept the task of trying to help/

warn Leslie about the lowering energy in nature-thing yet, but little by little I'm feeling somewhat better about it, more confident. Yet still… hesitant.

I'm watching myself in spirit form above myself and physical me is swimming underwater.

The water is a murky, light green color. In places algae and weeds dance and float deceptively. My arms are slowly and cautiously reaching forward and pushing the water away, as I bring my arms down to my sides and then back in front of me again. I'm not kicking my feet. Instinctively I know there's something else in the water I need to be aware and wary of. And to not make unnecessary movement. Making my way through the water I notice a large patch of tall weeds nearby, their tips waving about an inch above the surface.

Sensing I need to camouflage myself, I swim to the weeds. Once there I move close to the bottom, where the weeds are thickest, and crouch, all

the while looking above and around me. I notice then that air bubbles aren't escaping from my nose. I'm not holding my breath. Nor am I breathing water. Somehow, I'm simply able to exist in water.

My eyes widen as I watch a massive reptile, a crocodile, swimming into full view. It's about twelve feet long, its thick girth illustrating its hunting prowess. I'm very still, like a frozen statue. Its dry scales thrash silently against its cold-blooded skin. Its slit-eyes methodically, mechanically, move back and forth, searching, always searching to quench its unquenchable appetite, a bottomless black abyss. It moves quickly, yet somehow slowly, through the water. I know it can move much more quickly if it wants to. Terrifyingly quickly.

I watch its serpentine tail sway back and forth as it swims by me, mesmerizing in its departure, its tail swinging hypnotically—even this is a trap. Because if I move too soon it will sense my movement. So, I wait, focusing on my heartbeat. On a calm... even... heartbeat.

When it feels right, I swim out of the weeds but stay low, my chest skimming the muddy bottom, until I reach the concrete steps. I climb out of the water and I'm standing on a stoop. The front door of the house is closed. The child, the one I love who is being assaulted, is standing in front of me, his gaze searching mine. I place my forefinger up against my lips while looking him in the eyes. Turning around, I scan the still water, searching for movement.

Suddenly, ten feet in front of me, I see ripples as the top of its scaly head and eyes surface. It's heading right for us. I turn around and in the corner, behind the child, is a four-foot long wooden spear about three inches thick. The wood looks solid. I grab it and push the child into the corner.

As I turn around the crocodile is gliding up the stairs while its jaws are opening wider and wider, revealing a maw full of sharp, pointy, crooked teeth. Its intent is clear.

I take a deep breath and bring the spear up vertically in front of me, holding it tightly with both hands. As soon as the crocodile's jaw is fully open and less than a foot from me, I plunge the spear down as hard as I can into its mouth, pinning it to a step.

The spear plunges completely through the bottom of its mouth. Blood spurts from its wound, clouding the water around it and creating a sort of

mini-fountain inside its mouth. It uselessly thrashes its tail, pinned to the step. I lock eyes with it and wait a few minutes.

Then I jerk the spear up, releasing it, but holding it high again, just in case it comes at us again.

The crocodile's mouth closes slowly as it silently slides backward into the water until its snout disappears.

A door opens behind me and arms reach out and grab the child by the arm, pulling him into the house. The door shuts quickly and firmly. I turn back to look at the water.

It's been replaced by a desert.

Sand dunes gently roll in front of me, all around me. Waves of light, warm, brown.

I walk down the steps into the desert. It's as if a massive hourglass has been broken open and the sand weaves its own time.

The grains of sand massage the bottoms of my feet as I walk.

I climb to the top of a dune in time to see a spaceship landing and materializing at the same time. There's a crowd of about fifty people around it. I walk quickly toward it. A material resembling metal yet somehow organic, living... flows from the ship, creating a walkway to its entrance.

Walking briskly, purposefully, I climb the walkway toward the entrance. An intricate snowflake-like pattern creates and opens the door. A being walks out.

The being looks somewhat like us, but somehow not. It has a head, body, legs, and arms, yet it's somehow alien and seems to float as it moves. It's surrounded by a white aura. A kind, patient, contemplative look greets me. I hold out my hand in greeting. The being takes my hand.

What happens next is the most intelligent, gentle sharing of information I've yet to have with a human. We share mind to mind. I slowly begin to realize this being is from a higher plane, a plane of consciousness devoid of fear, of limitations. This being is beauty.

After some time, I realize I've been so engrossed in our sharing that I need to look around at my surroundings. I look at the crowd. They're staring at us; their eyes are fearful and an uneasy murmuring sways through them.

Disappointed, I turn to the being and with my mind, recommend it leave now. These people are getting more and more fearful, and fear, with humans, usually turns to violence.

The being slowly blinks and nods its head. Smiling at one another, we release hands. As the being nears its door I send thank you and love.

The next morning, I review this dream and the few before it.

My dreams seem to be telling me that if I remain calm, have faith, and do the best I can, signs will be shown to me, and I'll receive assistance. If my intention is pure, and stays pure, it'll all work out.

Which is fine, but I'm finding all of this pretty stressful. Because I need to "act" normal in real life, communicate with Leslie in the meantime, and at the same time depend on my dreams, and real life, to give me signs. So, it feels as if I need to be alert 24-7.

I decide to start trying, in waking life, to talk with Leslie using thoughts, while looking at my ceiling. I can sense when he's up there, on the roof, above my apartment. Which is most of the time.

I'm trying to let him know that what's happening in the environment is important. Very important.

I don't know much about his world, but I do know that organized crime is sort of like a large business; it has a lot of departments and a lot of people in charge of these departments.

Frankly, I don't know how he has the time to hang out on my roof.

So far, Leslie hasn't acknowledged he's hearing or understanding me. The regular harassment is still going on.

I know that whoever I thought Leslie was, was someone he was pretending to be. So essentially, I don't know him and know nothing about him. Which makes it difficult to communicate with him in a way he'll understand. He obviously doesn't want to talk with me in real life.

I decide I'll need to try to find out more about him. If I know more about him then it'll help me figure out a way to communicate better with him. I don't know how I'm going to do this, though.

Chapter 5:
Crossing the Threshold

I'm hovering above myself, watching myself. Except "me" doesn't look like me. Physical me opens my eyes and looks around. I'm in a very deep, dimly lit, rocky, dark pit. I'm hearing high-pitched, long, ear-splitting, shrieks of pain and anger assaulting my ears. I slap my hands over my ears quickly, wincing. It barely muffles the sound. I look down at my body. This isn't my body. But it is in this dream. My hairless skin is black and rubbery, and long, sharp, pointed claws curl out from the ends of my feet and hands. I have small pointed ears on top of my head. I have a tubby little potbelly.

I'm standing on a ledge. Behind me is a large pockmark in the wall of this pit. Below me stands the source of the screaming and shrieking. It looks like a big demon. It's about fifteen feet tall, same black rubbery skin, but it has scales too. And a long tail that ends in an arrowhead. Its tail whips and flashes through the air behind it. At times the arrowhead slams against a wall in the pit and pieces of rock explode into and through the air.

Its calves, thighs, belly, and arms are pure muscle. Long, sharp claws jab at the air, stabbing it. It's standing on bent knees, feet spread, one slightly more forward than the other. Every time it screams it juts its chest out, closes its eyes and its claws clench and then unclench to stab the air.

The pit is roughly circular. No entry or exit passages from the ground. Interspersed around this screaming banshee are groups of three and four other, smaller demons, huddled together. They look like me, but each one is slightly different. Some are a little taller, some are thinner, some stockier. All of them are cowering away from the big demon-like thing. The shrieking is painful. It feels like my brain is going to split open. Agonizing pain. I slap my hands/ claws over my ears, wincing.

It has to stop.

The top of the beast's large head sways back and forth below me. Howling.

I can't take it. I have to make it stop.

With a barbaric yell, I jump from the ledge, clenching one claw into a fist and bringing it high above my head. The closer I drop to the beast's head the higher I lift my fist.

Until my yell ends as my fist smashes down on the beast's head. The moment my fist connects with its head there's silence.

Because it vaporized. It's gone.

Nothing.

I'm standing where it was standing. Bewildered.

The other demons are looking at me, eyes are wide and uncomprehending.

That was unsettling. I've never had a dream where I didn't look like myself.

After I take some time to accept this, I feel into what the dream meant. It feels like it had three meanings. One, I've decided to overcome my fear of my intuition and accept all the ways information can come to me: thoughts, feelings, dreams and any other form my intuition takes. Two, I have, on some level, accepted The Light's journey. Three, I've crossed a border into unknown territories in the spirit realm.

What I'm concerned most about is getting back, which is why I've taken so long to decide. It's easy to jump into something, but usually a lot harder to come back, and whatever this is I'm doing, this... journey - I have no idea how hard it'll be to come back from, or if I can at all.

Because one thing is becoming clear. Everything I've been taught so far is going to be a detriment: who I think I am, how I view reality, who I think others are, my values, my judgments of myself and others, my fears.

This journey will require I have an open mind and be willing to learn, which is fine; I like learning, but this, whatever this is that's happening, is something altogether foreign.

I start my morning yoga/meditation, knowing that I'll need to stay as calm as possible throughout this... journey.

Then I start getting ready for work.

***

I'm watching myself above and to the side in spirit form. Physical me opens my eyes and I'm standing in a basement suite. Leslie is standing about five feet in front of me. He looks surprised to see me.

I cock my head at him and then take in the details of the room. This basement suite has no doors that lead outside, or windows that I can see.

I look back at Leslie. He's standing shirtless and barefoot, wearing a pair of faded jeans. He's staring at me, his expression quizzical yet guarded.

Expressionless, I walk slowly past him into the kitchen area. There's a small butcher block/island in the center of the mid-sized kitchen. From above, a rectangular fluorescent light shines harshly down. The walls are a worn, pukey beige color. Dirty dishes in the sink. Empty boxes and discarded wrappers lay haphazardly on the countertops.

There's a hallway off the far side of the kitchen. I walk toward it and look down the hall. A wall seals off the hallway after six feet. Dead end.

Turning around, I start walking around the butcher block and walk past the sink. I notice Leslie has turned but stayed where he was standing when I arrived. His eyes are following me. The floor is linoleum, a seventies pattern of dark brown and caramel colors. I continue walking slowly around the butcher block, circling the kitchen.

All at once, Leslie strides quickly around the other side of the kitchen island, walking toward me. I continue walking slowly, as the corner of my right foot gently steps on the side of a piece of hardened toast on the floor. Crumbs explode and shatter.

He stops a foot in front and to the side of me and slams his arm against the wall, holding his arm straight with his palm flat against the wall.

Directly in front of me.

I stop walking, turn, and look at him. My face is expressionless. He's leaning forward with his eyes open, his face closing in on mine. He means to kiss me.

He's trying to see if I have romantic feelings toward him. I don't. As his face closes in on mine I close my eyes. Cold, closed, dispassionate lips press against mine. They don't stay there for long. Just long enough to gauge if I respond.

Which I don't.

His head moves back, away. I open my eyes and look at him. His eyes register incomprehension, yet he seems to understand I have no ill will toward him.

He drops his arm. I turn and, walking past him, continue walking forward, until I've circled the kitchen and am back at the area where I first arrived.

I notice a partially open door off the kitchen, revealing an unmade double bed, clothes, and wrappers on the floor. Leslie's room. To my right is another door down a hallway about fifteen feet away. I walk to it. The door is partially open. I look in from the hallway.

A thin man, about fifty years old with beady eyes, four or five days' growth on his face, balding and incredibly pale, is sitting mesmerized in front of a computer screen. His hand is poised alertly over his computer mouse. He's wearing a wrinkled gray t-shirt and jeans. A malicious look sits on his face as he stares at the screen. In front of him the room is filled with computers; old, new, desktops, laptops - piled high, one atop the other. There's no room to move in this room. There's no other furniture in the room, other than the chipped white with beige star Formica table he's using as a desk and a white plastic lawn chair he's using to sit on. The man doesn't notice me.

Turning, I walk back toward the spot I arrived in. Leslie's standing with his back against the cutting block, facing me. He's holding a hairdryer up and his hair is standing up in all directions.

I look around the suite again. No doors. No windows.

He's trapped here; there's no way for him to leave.

I look him in the eyes and wish I could help him.

Then I'm gone.

That was really odd. I haven't had a dream like this before. It felt like I dove really deep somehow, and in a way, it sort of felt like I was sharing it with Leslie too. Like maybe Leslie woke up and remembered the dream too? But I don't know this for sure. If he did, I wonder if he's upset. If I was supposed to do that, to go there. But how do I control where I go when I dream? Who I see when I dream? And who was that man in the basement suite with him and why were there no doors or windows? Why can't he leave?

I decide I need more information.

***

> *"Run from what's comfortable. Forget safety. Live where you fear to live. Destroy your reputation. Be notorious. I have tried prudent planning long enough. From now on I'll be mad."*
>
> *— Rumi*

I'm watching myself in spirit form as my physical self is walking purposefully through a field. It's an overcast day. Sparse, woody weeds barely clinging to life, hugging the ground, and dirt patches are prevalent. Occasionally there are dry, tall pieces of grass that seem to hang precariously.

A man in his early thirties is following me about three feet behind me. I look back and his head is down. The top of his dark brown, curly, short, unruly hair looks back at me. He's looking down at a camera he's holding while he walks quickly behind me.

I don't know him.

I'm walking toward a trailer. A single, solitary, unkempt mobile home in the distance. Pock-marked and sagging metal silently despair.

No trees, no roads, no other signs of life. The wind is silent.

I reach the mobile trailer door and turn the handle. It opens.

A worn, brown shag rug greets me. I walk up three metal steps into the living room of the trailer.

Sparse, cheap furnishings. A few lamps with seventies designs, orange and brown, a dilapidated, stained orange fabric couch, a faded pink floral lounge chair, a scratched-up, light blue plastic lawn chair. The place is clean, though. As clean as it can be.

A young girl stands looking out a window in front of me, her back to me. Her stringy, fine, dirty blond hair is tied at the back of her neck with an elastic.

She turns and looks at me. She has fine features; she's pretty. But her face looks tense, drawn, with dark circles under her eyes, and her eyes have a defeated look. She's also very young, maybe fourteen. About seven months pregnant. It feels like she's been spending a lot of time alone here.

I walk to the kitchen and open cupboards and the fridge. I seem to be looking for something. I leave the kitchen and start walking toward the bedroom at the end of the hall. Halfway down the hall I notice a small metal clasp in the floor. I pull on it and a square portion of the flooring rises. Inside the cavity is a metal box. I take the metal box out and place it on the floor. It's unlocked. I open it. Papers, writing. I put the papers back, close the box, put it back and close the lid on the piece of floor.

I walk back into the living room.

Leslie is there, talking with the young girl.

His hands are open, palms facing up as he's speaking to her.

She looks scared. He seems to be trying to reassure her. They don't notice me. Maybe they can't see me?

I walk to the door, open it and step down out of the trailer. I start walking back across the field, back the way I came. The man who followed me here is behind me again. I don't know if he followed me into the trailer or not.

Halfway across the field I hear angry shouts in the distance. Stopping, I turn around and look in the distance toward the yelling.

Leslie is running toward me. Okay, maybe he can see me?

As he gets closer I can see his complexion is ruddy, anger is blazing from his eyes, and a vein in his neck is standing out. His long limbs are screaming rage.

He stops five feet in front of me, his jaw pulsing.

I send him, "What? What's wrong?"

Angrily he points to the man behind me. He's pointing at his camera. The man who's been following me. His camera. Leslie wants the camera.

I turn and look at the guy behind me. "Give him the camera." He steps forward and holds it out to Leslie.

Leslie yanks at it violently, then sends it smashing to the ground. Pieces of plastic and glass jump through the air. He starts erratically stomping on the

main part of the camera; nothing exists for him except the immediate destruction of this piece of equipment.

In a way, this looks kind of comical.

I turn around and continue walking back through the field.

What did I learn? Well, obviously not to be with anyone with a camera when I'm around Leslie in dreams.

Can I control this? I don't know. I also wonder who these people are that Leslie is with in my dreams. So far, they've been angry young men who have drug addictions, an unhealthy older guy with a seeming computer addiction and a very young, scared, pregnant girl.

I'm not sure any of this information is helpful. What ***is*** helpful is understanding that whatever is going on, Leslie feels trapped, like he has to do what he does.

***

The next morning after getting ready for work, I grab a full green garbage bag sitting by my apartment door and leave, locking my apartment door, and begin walking down the two flights of stairs to the back door. The parking stalls are in the back lane and a large metal garbage bin sits next to the parking stalls.

Walking around my car I head to the big, dented, dark blue metal city garbage bin and swing the garbage bag a few times. It's a big heavy bag, so I'll need some motion to swing it up into the bin opening at the top. As I release it, it flies through the air and lands in the bin, but I don't hear a thud, which is odd. It must be full. I'm not tall enough to see into it. The bin is about six feet high. I'm about 5'5". Turning, I begin walking toward my car when I hear a cry from inside the bin.

"Aiieeeeeaaaaahhh,"

I stop and look back.

The head of a small Asian man pops up from inside the garbage bin, swiveling around, looking for who lobbed the heavy garbage bag into the bin he was in, I guess.

Shocked, I look at him as our eyes lock.

"Are you okay?" I ask.

Silently he looks at me, rubbing his head, a frown forming on his face.

Wait a minute, I think. What was he doing in the garbage bin? How did he get in it? How's he going to get out of it? And how was I supposed to know he was in there?

He doesn't look like he's bleeding or anything.

I turn around and walk to my car, unlock the door, get in and start the car, check my mirrors, and let the engine warm up for a few minutes.

As I'm waiting I look over to the garbage bin to see if he's still there. He doesn't seem to be.

Changing the gear from park to reverse, I step on the brake and then hear a knock on my driver's side window.

I turn my head and the Asian man is standing outside my driver's side door, looking in at me while he's holding his head with one hand and holding out his other hand with his palm facing up towards me. His eyes are squinting at me and the corners of his mouth are pulled back, somewhat pursed somehow.

The look in his eyes is accusing.

Stunned, I momentarily wonder what he's doing. What he wants? Then it dawns on me...

He wants money. Reparation. For the bag hitting his head.

Something bubbles up from way below, inside my lower stomach, travelling up through my upper stomach, my lungs, up my throat and then bursts out of my mouth.

Uproarious laughter escapes me. I can't stop it. I'm laughing so hard my eyes are closing, throwing my head back and forth.

The Asian man is still standing at my driver's side window, looking in at me.

Now he looks chagrined.

Which is making me laugh even harder.

This is awful.

I just can't stop, though.

But I know my laughing is bothering him.

You ever have one of those moments of laughter? When you know the right thing to do is to stop laughing but you just can't? The laughter is uncontrollable?

Eventually, I take my foot off the brake and shaking my head, smiling, I back up, driving down the alleyway, toward work, thinking to myself how incredibly ironic life can be at times.

***

A few weeks later, after I finish a yoga/meditation session I feel into, I sense what I need to do next in real life, "reality."

What it feels like is I need to be near a very large body of water.

Like somehow, I need to be close to this energy, the energy of a large body of water.

I don't know why.

I've never felt that way before so logically this doesn't make sense. But I've entered a realm where logic doesn't apply.

I've lived in Vancouver, B.C. before, so I've explored that part of the country. But I haven't been out East before.

I feel into that.

Yes, it feels like I'm supposed to go East. To the water.

I give my notice at work and start organizing myself for the trip. The cats will come with me, although I don't know how that'll go. I'm driving.

I took in Sabre, a stray, when he was four months old, and since I've had him I've taken him with me for car rides while I run errands, a couple of times a week. He loves car rides. He's about seven years old now. Bruce, a rescue I adopted to keep Sabre company while I'm at work during the day, doesn't like the car. At all. He howled a lot during the ten-hour drive from Vancouver to Calgary when I left my ex.

Well, we'll just have to play it by ear. The Light will give me signs, clues. I just need to have faith.

I'm not sure how long I'll be gone. It feels like about a year. But I don't really know.

I sell my furniture and donate or give away the non-essentials. It's surprising how little I actually need.

I let my friends and family know I'm leaving. They ask all kinds of questions. Why? Where? How? They seem excited for me, but also envious and resentful. This isn't really a pleasure trip, though. It's more like a serious work/fact-finding trip. I'll just have to make my own fun where and when I can.

I talk with my friends' children privately and explain to them I have to go away for a while, that I love them and that I'll be back. They seem to understand and don't ask me any questions.

I finish my online TESL course and earn a certificate.

I also spend some time online researching quantum physics, trying to gain a better understanding of what's going on. I'm not finding it helpful. It's too scientific. It says nothing about intention, creativity, imagination, intuition, meditation, sending thoughts, emotions, being able to share dreams with others, consciousness, or The Light.

So...

No help at all.

***

Finally, the day I'm leaving arrives. The car is packed; I've cleaned the apartment and am almost ready to start the drive. I've decided to take the long way to Eastern Canada. I have one final bag of garbage to take out and then I can load the cats into the car and start driving. It's early, about six o'clock in the morning, in the middle of August.

Carrying the bag of garbage down the stairs leading to the back-exit door, I push open the door and find a raven standing on the walk five feet in front of me, looking at me, as if it's been waiting for me.

I hesitate.

A bird waiting for me?

Smiling, I shake my head at my silliness and start walking.

The raven stays where it is until I'm a foot from it, then flies to the top left side of the cement wall, a part of the stairs that lead down to the parking stalls.

It perches and turns and looks at me again. Staring at me.

I stop and hesitate for a few seconds, looking back at the raven. Nah.

I keep walking past the raven and as I do it takes flight again.

Reaching the bottom of the stairs I turn and walk to the large, dented, dark blue metal garbage bin. The top lid of the side closest to me is closed; the far side is open. Walking up to the far side, I lift the garbage bag up and as I do I see the raven sitting on the far edge of the bin, close to me, staring at me.

I lower the garbage bag and cock my head at it.

Is this a sign? Is the raven trying to tell me something? What's going on here?

I stare back for a few minutes. It feels like it's some type of message from the spirit realm, letting me know I won't be alone.

I smile at the raven, then lift the garbage bag up and throw it into the bin. The raven flies away.

Chapter 6:

Tests, Allies, and Enemies

The drive takes quite a while, about twelve days' total. I drive about eight to ten hours a day. This gives me a lot of time to relax, sing, think, take in the different landscapes, and appreciate them.

I haven't been to eastern Canada before. I haven't driven across Canada before. Not that I'm particularly nationalistic. This is just the place I happen to have been born.

At night, I stay in motels with the cats. It's extra work hauling their food, litter, water, and food dishes in and out of the car, but they're great companions. After the first day Bruce really warms up to driving. By the third day he's standing on the passenger seat with his front paws up on the dashboard, looking out the front window, acting like a first-rate co-pilot. He's not howling at all.

I review what I've learned so far about my "reality".

So far it seems like whoever Leslie is, he has a lot of power and controls a lot of people, either with money or force. He has a lot of money and owns businesses. He's also unbalanced. The police seem to work for him? I'm not sure.

Sending thoughts is a real thing. It isn't a science fiction thing. I'm able to send thoughts and communicate with Leslie. So far, he hasn't sent any thoughts to me. Can I do this with other people? I don't know.

I may be sharing dreams with Leslie, I think, which if I have he mostly likely isn't pleased about. But I don't know if it's only some of the dreams I have where he's in them or not.

He seems to be trying to make me think I'm crazy. Kyler helped me by showing me I wasn't crazy.

Whatever Kyler did brought attention to others about what Leslie was doing, to me and to the child. And I know if Leslie could kill me he would, but too many people know now, and that would make me a martyr.

A martyr is more powerful dead than alive so he doesn't want me dead, which is good; I never had an intention of sacrificing myself. I'm just supposed to help/warn him and dying isn't part of my idea of doing that.

My yoga/meditation, food changes, changes I've made to what I have in my environment and use on my body have been helping me a lot. I'm getting signs from the natural world that I'm doing okay, to keep going. My dreams seem to be telling me the same thing.

I spend time thinking about what I want to accomplish in the future; getting a better understanding of how my intuition works, how my dreams are inter-related to the physical plane, or "reality," improving how to communicate with Leslie the importance of protecting the environment and stopping the lowering of energy of nature, and how to repay Kyler.

I wonder if I'll be able to send thoughts to Leslie from a farther distance.

I'm not sure. I think so, but I'm not sure. If I can't that's okay; I can use the time to experiment more and digest what's already happened anyway.

As I'm driving I'm also noticing I'm being followed across the country. At least this is what it feels like. I wonder again if I'm developing some kind of paranoid thing. But I know I'm not. And it makes me mad that I'm questioning myself. I've never had paranoid thoughts. I just don't operate that way.

At different times, loud motorcycles either pull out in front of me and drive ahead of me, or they pull out from behind me and follow me. Sometimes it's police cars. Most times when I stop at a motel, I either wake up to a loud motorcycle in the morning, or I hear one after I check into my room. It sure feels like I'm being followed. This must be Leslie.

I'm sensing that this trip is going to require that I refrain from dating anyone, from having sex. That if Leslie can, he'll use that against me. Which isn't that big of a deal for me. There's no one in my life at this point that I feel compelled to be intimate with. I've learned a lot so far about what I "think" I need and what I actually **do** need.

It's strange because Leslie for sure doesn't feel like a friend, but somehow not altogether like an enemy either. Although I do get the sense he doesn't like me very much. But I also sense that it really doesn't matter what I do, that no matter what, he just plain doesn't like me. It feels like my gender is the main reason.

I wonder about that. Why would he feel like that? Maybe because he equates all females with his mom, who apparently couldn't stop whatever happened to Leslie when he was a child from happening. Maybe because he's in a constant state of suffering? That's what my dreams are showing me so far. It doesn't seem like he experiences happiness, love or peace. Maybe because he doesn't experience those things in life?

I don't know.

What I wonder is, can't he change things if he doesn't want to suffer? He seems to have a lot of power. Why can't he use it to make himself happy? I don't know. I do sense I'm treading on thin ice, though, but I'm not sure how to carry out what The Light asked without trying to learn more information.

***

My drive eventually leads me to Halifax, Nova Scotia. I'm not sure what to do next, though. It feels like I'm supposed to stay in this area for a while. But it's the beginning of September and there's a one percent vacancy rate for apartment rentals. I didn't know there were four or five universities in Halifax. I decide to stay in a motel and patiently wait for the next sign from The Light.

I also decide to try something new.

I try contacting Kyler with my imagination. I don't know if it'll work, if my intention will come through, but it can't hurt to try, right? So, after my yoga/ meditation practice, when I'm totally relaxed, I use my imagination and...

I'm opening the door to a basement. I'm holding a wooden serving tray. The tray holds sliced fruits and vegetables, chocolate melted dip for the fruit and a vinaigrette dip for the vegetables, a pitcher of clean water, two glasses, a few napkins and a small vase holding a yellow and white carnation. Also, a thin wool blanket is tossed over one of my shoulders.

I have to set the tray down on the first step so I can close the basement door behind me. I wait a few moments to let my eyes adjust to the dim lighting. Once they do I pick up the tray and walk carefully down the wooden stairs.

The room at the bottom of the stairs is empty. It's an unfinished basement, with a cement floor. Kyler is sitting on the floor with his back leaning against the wall. He's alone. He's here a lot, I sense. He's looking down. Doesn't register my presence.

I walk toward him slowly, clearing my throat. He looks up slowly.

"Hey, thought you might be hungry or thirsty, so I brought some stuff," I send him. Gratitude washes across his face. The corners of his mouth lift slightly. He doesn't reply. Relieved, I set the tray down and pull the blanket off my shoulder.

"It's not good to sit on cold concrete; you can get sick from it," I send as I fold the blanket so it's a padded seat for two against the wall. I keep chattering on.

"Come sit on this... way more comfortable," I send. I touch his arm lightly and momentarily. He looks at me and reluctantly moves over, sitting on the blanket.

"So, what do you feel like?" I send. "Some fruit? Look at this chocolate dip!" I send as I dip a slice of green apple into the melted chocolate and wave it in front of him.

He's looking down at the floor again. I chomp on the apple, dip it into the chocolate again and eat the slice in two bites. Man, it tastes good! I look at him. He's still looking at the ground. I take another slice of apple and dip it into the chocolate again. I start waving it back and forth in front of his eyes.

"You know you'll like it," I send. He takes the wedge and starts nibbling on it absent-mindedly.

I continue chattering on as I hand him a napkin and pour him a glass of water.

He says nothing. But I can sense he's slowly pulling out of himself and he's starting to eat and drink, occasionally looking at me and nodding his head. It's okay he's not talking. He isn't alone. I can at least do that for him. I sense he feels alone, isolated, ashamed, and guilty most of the time. Which is why he uses heroin. Which makes it worse.

After this lucid dream, I review how it feels. Somehow it feels like Kyler understood and received my intention. But, I don't know for sure.

***

I'm in spirit form hovering above myself. It's night and the stars are winking through the clouds when they can. I'm standing in the middle of a paved street in a neighborhood that, in the not-so-distant past, was downtrodden, but has recently been given a facelift, a new retro look. The windows of the businesses lining the street house avant-garde restaurants, an organic furniture store and an exotic import store.

New, old-style black lantern light poles flank the road like soldiers, their glossy paint reflected by the odd, much thicker and taller city-provided green painted fluorescents. The windows in the apartments above the shops are all dark. Everything and everyone is sleeping. There's a tree halfway down the street, beside a soldier. It's healthy and its leaves are whispering to me.

Then I see them.

They're gathered around the outside of the tree about nine feet in the air, in a ball. They dance and glow in their own intricate, ever-changing pattern, delighting in the warm air and the darkness. Ecstasy in luminescence.

Smiling, I turn my head from side to side, looking to make sure no one is around.

That no one will see.

Satisfied, I will my feet to leave the ground and I start floating toward them slowly.

Reaching them, I open my hands and using my palms I run slow circles around the outside of their circle, watching as small, red reflections of light bounce off my palms.

I feel their energy.

They delight in the night, in play, in dance and in sharing their dance.

They flow and glow, glitter, and flitter.

Teasing the dreams of the sleepers.

That dream felt like a good omen.

I also can't afford to stay in a motel for very long. I have little savings.

I'm hoping The Light will give me a sign soon. The motel room I'm in doesn't have a kitchenette. The best I can do is buy some groceries, like broccoli and cauliflower, and place them in plastic bags on top of the toilet back lid, which keeps them somewhat cold. I have some fruit, oat grain bars and some bottles of water. About once per day I have to eat a bigger meal, though.

The next day I decide to have brunch at a breakfast cafe a few blocks down the road. I'm sitting in a booth looking at one of those one-page, double-sided, newsletter-type papers that only cafes seem to have.

I'm waiting for my order, an omelet, and have finished reading both sides.

I start looking at the pictures, the ads, on the borders of the paper.

My eyes stop suddenly on a picture. I squint at it. It's a picture of a small cottage. But I recognize the cottage somehow. I look at where it's located. I've never been there and I don't recognize the name. But somehow, I recognize the picture. I try to understand how I can recognize a picture of a cottage in a place I've never been before. I feel into this.

It feels like I dreamed of this cottage, but quite a while ago, so the details are fuzzy.

My omelet arrives. I continue looking at the picture of the cottage as I eat.

Something is going on with this. I decide this must be a sign. After I get back to my motel room I call the number listed under the ad of the picture of the cottage. It's a campground where you can rent a cottage, an RV space, or a tenting spot. The lady who answers sounds friendly and open. I ask if she would consider a longer-term cottage rental, a month. It's Fall and they have few people staying at the campground. She agrees and we agree on a price. She gives me directions and I drive there. The campground is near a place called Tatamagouche.

The cottage looks just like the ad, only better. It's clean, has a small kitchen, a living room, and a separate bedroom. Awesome. The cats love it. I find an out-of-the way place to put the litter box. I unpack the car and decide to walk down to the water. So far, it's turning into an Indian summer, the days are still warm.

Walking down to the water I look up at a street sign and see a familiar name. It's my last name. On the street sign. White letters against a green background.

Stunned, I stop. This is definitely a sign. I'm on the right path. I have to take a picture and send it to my family; they won't believe me if I just tell them. Why? I don't know. But I know they'll believe a picture.

The sand leading to the water is light brown and the temperature of the water is warm and comforting. Colorful sandstones are littered everywhere, smiling playfully up at me from under the water.

After spending some time walking in the water, picking up and inspecting sandstones, I return to the cottage. I'll need some groceries. I make a shopping list. The nearest store is in Tatamagouche, a ways away, so I'll need to drive there.

The first street sign I see after I leave the campground shocks me. It's my first name. On a street sign. I just saw my last name on a street sign. What are the chances of that? This is definitely going to be different. Getting used to living life like this.

I'm out of my comfort zone, but I'm also delightfully surprised at these unexpected happenings.

And the days roll on in a therapeutic way. I spend a lot of time on the computer, looking for and applying for jobs. I spend time down at the beach in the water, looking at seashells and sandstones. I read, write a little and visit with the manager of the campground. Mostly I'm trying to wrap my head around what's happened these past few years. And how different living life like this is.

I'm trying to process what I've been learning and how my dreams are related to the physical realm. Thinking about how I'm going to convince Leslie without losing my life, my sanity, or my soul.

I'm continuing to do my daily yoga/meditation practice. I've also cut back to eating meat to once every few months now.

***

I'm lying down on a solid surface. It smells like wood. There's a rocking motion. I smell salt. A gentle breeze tickles the hair on my body and weaves through the hair on my head. I can hear fabric moving above me. The sun is kissing me, warming my pores, relaxing me. My breathing is deep and rhythmic.

A mist of water cascades onto my skin after a splashing sound occurs beside me, water hitting wood. I slowly open my eyes and a rainbow is waving above me.

No, it's not a rainbow. It's a rainbow-colored sail.

I sit up and look around me. I'm sitting in the middle of a one-person wooden sailboat on a smooth, wooden plank. The plank is just wide enough to hold my frame and runs vertically down the center of the sailboat.

I look around me and my eyes drink in deep blue water, gentle waves rolling across its surface as far as my eyes can see, in all directions. Oblong white clouds drift slowly, easily by in the otherwise clear, light blue sky. I taste algae in the air. The sailboat moves unhurriedly through the water.

A mischievous, errant wave occasionally slaps the side of the boat, sometimes sending a mist over me, and sometimes refreshing droplets of water that quickly evaporate on my skin.

I lie back down on the wooden plank, closing my eyes, and smiling, losing myself in the gentle rocking.

This was a great dream. I wonder if I'll ever have this dream again. I'd like to.

> *"You are not a drop in the ocean. You are the entire ocean, in a drop."*
>
> *— Rumi*

***

A month passes and I haven't heard back from any of the jobs I've been applying for online. I've been making follow-up phone calls to ensure my resume is being received. I arrange to rent the cottage for another month.

For the past few weeks it feels like Leslie is physically hanging around. Guess I won't need to wonder about having to try to communicate with him over a long distance. I haven't been able to determine what the next step is with him, so I haven't been trying to communicate with him or find out any more information about him. At least this is why I think I'm not having any dreams with him in them.

***

I'm watching myself in spirit form above me and I'm also me, sitting across a table from Kyler. He's smiling at me. I look around and realize we're on a moving train. The ground blurs but the sun and sky do not. There are plates of food taking up all the space on the table. Fried short ribs, veggie platter, chicken fingers. Pub fare.

Kyler is gnawing on one short rib after another, talking while he's chewing, and smiling. Thoroughly enjoying himself.

"Eat, eat!" he sends, cajolingly.

I don't eat, smile back, or reply. I watch him. He's acting different. Gregarious. I'm not used to this side of him. It's almost like a fake front, though. It doesn't feel right, as if he's forcing himself. The train is slowing down to a stop. Once it reaches a full stop Kyler bounces out of his seat and strides off the train. We're stopped next to the top of a circular ridge.

I turn in my seat and look out the window. Kyler is standing on the edge of the ridge looking down. He's shouting and waving his arms in the air, whistling with one hand to his mouth. I can hear rock music start to play, muted through the window. It's a concert. There's a band playing in the basin below the ridge.

I watch as Kyler starts dancing. He looks funny, his arms and legs jabbing out, not seeming to match a beat. But his eyes are closed and he has a huge smile on his face. I turn around, pick up a piece of broccoli and start slowly chewing on it.

Time passes and after a while I can't hear any muted music. I walk off the train and go looking for Kyler. He isn't where he last was when he was dancing. I'm walking along the ridge when I see a group of young men, some heavily tattooed, some not, wearing baggy, dark blue jeans, and white tank tops. They're sitting in a circle, about fifteen of them. Most of them are looking at Kyler. He's sitting with his knees up, spread out in front of him, his arms resting on his knees. His hands are moving back and forth as he animatedly talks. He pauses... they laugh.

I stop about ten feet from their circle. Kyler sees me looking at him. He stops talking. He looks down. His body language looks as if he's contrite, apologetic.

I'm not sure how I can repay him. The way he's been living his life is all he's known. He doesn't have either the confidence or will, or maybe both, to break out of it. Or maybe he just doesn't know how good it is to not live life like he does. Plus, he has his addiction to deal with.

I don't know how, or if, the fact that there's some kind of connection between the spirit/dream world and the physical one will make a difference when it comes to figuring out if I can repay him. Help him. And again, I don't know if he shared that dream with me or not.

***

Another month passes and I'm still not gaining ground finding a job here. I figure I'll give it another month and if nothing turns up I'll move on. I use the Internet to find a room to rent outside of Halifax, in a place called Mahone Bay. The house is over a hundred years old. I can sense a lot of different energies.

I decide to register at some temp agencies in Halifax. One calls me back and I'm given a temporary, three-month assignment working for a large company in Halifax. The woman I'm renting a room from gives me the name and number of a woman who commutes into Halifax every day. She's interested in carpooling.

After carpooling with her a few times, I learn she works for the military, an executive-type position. What's strange is the way our conversations go. It's as if she's trying to get information from me, while acting like a "friend," but more like a psychiatrist or something. It feels odd, off, not quite right. After a handful of times I stop carpooling with her.

***

I'm enjoying going for walks on a trail nearby. It's Fall and every day I watch the trees slowly changing color, getting ready for their winter retreat. The air smells crisper, cleaner. The woman I'm renting a room from has two large dogs. I've been taking them on the walks with me. We usually go for about an hour and a half. The dogs smile the whole time.

One day we're walking back on the trail when ahead I see a man with a dog walking toward me. His dog looks very old and out of shape. As the man approaches I can see he's in his mid-fifties, thinning hair, about sixty pounds overweight. He's wearing a dirty sweatshirt and a black pair of sweatpants. He has a few days' growth on his face. He doesn't look clean or fresh, as if he doesn't wash daily, or look after himself.

He looks... I don't know, like life is missing from him, somehow.

He slows as we get close to each other and calls out a greeting to me. I return his "hello" and he stops in front of me, asking me a question. I stop and notice as I do that one of the dogs I'm walking has positioned itself directly between me and the man.

A protective gesture.

Huh.

Then, as I'm looking at and listening to the man talking, the strangest thing happens. I'm seeing a big, fat black worm crawling out of the side of the man's mouth and across his cheek, leaving a slimy trail behind it.

Then a black beetle escapes out one of his nostrils, crawls a few paces and then drops off his face. These insects sort of look real... solid, but they also look ghostly in a way.

I'm stunned. And I have a bad feeling about this man.

I've also never seen or experienced anything like this before.

I cut the man's monologue off, wishing him a good day. He holds out his hand to shake mine, and because I've been taught to be "nice," I shake his hand, then continue on my way, unsure of what just happened.

After about ten paces I feel the strong need to shake my hand vigorously, the same hand I used to shake the man's hand. It feels like I'm trying to shake off bad energy or something.

Huh.

Definitely strange brew.

***

Using the Internet, I finally find an apartment to rent in Halifax and move there. My length of stay is indefinite but I like plants, so I decide to get a few plants, a secondhand kitchen table and chairs, a few secondhand pots, pans, dishes and cutlery and a new futon couch that folds out to a bed. That's all I need. And that's all I can afford.

After a few weeks, it feels like Leslie is living in the apartment above me.

So, he's above me.

Again.

Sigh.

This time he seems to have someone else with him a lot. It feels like a young female.

And it feels like I again need to try communicating with him the importance of the lowering of energy in nature.

Honestly, it feels like this really annoys Leslie. But to me, it feels like it's the only reason our paths crossed. The only reason I'm supposed to deal with him. He's incredibly unbalanced, though, so I need to be careful, but at the same time, I also need to try to do what I've been asked.

I've met a woman who lives in the same apartment block as me. We hang out from time to time, going for walks together or visiting one another's apartments. I tell her how I'm trying to watch what I eat and am making homemade salsa, salads, humus, and samosas. She tells me she trained as a nutritionist. She doesn't look really healthy, though, so I'm not sure about that.

On one of our visits she tells me about genetically modified organisms (GMOs). She also tells me who owns this company. I don't care who owns the company. But I haven't heard of this before. I look up more information on this on the internet. Turns out it's a way of genetically altering a natural seed so it won't produce seeds, and pesticides are added to the seed.

I think about that for a bit and decide maybe that's why the pot I'd been smoking was having those side effects on me. It had been genetically altered. The last ten years or so, before I quit, there were no seeds in the bags.

Huh.

I also read how this has been done to common seeds, like wheat and corn. This isn't good. These two ingredients are in just about everything. I can tell that if I don't eat natural foods, my intuition will be negatively affected. Makes sense to me: my body is a natural organism.

Instinctively I know my body and brain will function best if I consume natural organisms. For the most part I'm eating a lot of fruits and vegetables, and this is helping. But I'm going to have to look into this more, make sure I'm eating and drinking things that'll be helpful for me.

***

Work is going well and the people are friendly. I've been doing some dancing at home at night after work. I've gotten hold of some workout dance videos. I haven't tried this before. It's quite a lot of fun. The cats get the funniest looks on their faces when I do this.

I talk on the phone with a friend, who encourages me to take up Tai Chi. Meet new people, get out a bit more.

Okay.

I look up a local class and join it.

It's a small class, there's only about ten or twelve of us.

Mr. Wing, a Chinese man, teaches the class. He seems pleasant and patient. We practice Monday, Wednesday and Friday from five in the afternoon until seven. There's a drop-in class on Saturday too. We practice outdoors in a local park. Even in the winter.

The people I end up spending some time with are Anna, a young woman in her late twenties who tells me she works for an Internet design firm as a coder. She's getting out of an unhealthy relationship. She's thin with long hair. Then there's Sophia, a woman in her late fifties, from South America, with a charming Spanish accent. She tells me she's divorced and visiting her daughter in Canada for a time. She's not that tall, about five foot two inches, and not thin. Not heavy, but not thin. Healthy. Then there's Mark, a man in his early sixties. Single. His wife died of cancer some years ago. He tells me he works with troubled youth. I also meet another man, John, but... I don't spend much time with him. John tells me he's retired from the military. That was his career. He tells me he suffered a head injury. He's single.

They seem like all right people. But something is feeling off about the situation. I can't put my finger on it but something feels off.

But I decide to keep an open mind, give these people the benefit of the doubt. After all, maybe what's been happening in "my" world has nothing to do with them. I'm having a hard time doing this, though; the feeling that somehow the situation is a setup keeps overriding everything. I'm not a particularly distrustful person, though, and I don't like the fact that I'm being distrustful of the situation. So, I decide to push that feeling away and continue going to Tai Chi classes.

***

Sometimes after Tai Chi practice a few of us go to a nearby cafe and hang out. One time, after a Saturday morning Tai Chi class, Sophia and Anna and I visit a nearby cafe.

We're sitting at a table drinking hot chocolate and visiting. The table nearby is empty until a man in his mid-forties sits down next to us.

He isn't reading a book or looking at an electronic device. He's alone. He sits down and closes his eyes. He appears to be resting. His chair is the closest to mine, facing the same direction as me. He's wearing jeans, a dress shirt, a sport jacket, and comfortable, relatively new shoes.

As I'm listening to Anna talk I begin feeling something. It feels strange, like tendrils of energy creeping through my brain...

Searching. Digging. Invading. It feels like the guy who sat down next to us is doing this. And I realize he isn't resting, he's concentrating—concentrating on invading my mind!

This realization pisses me off and I decide to concentrate on mentally/ psychically sending him the equation of a not-too-gentle drop-kick to the head. I notice after about a minute that the creeping tendril feeling begins fading away.

A few moments later his eyes pop open, as if he's startled, then he gasps and he somehow manages to jump back in his chair.

Then he quickly scrambles to his feet and leaves.

Confused, I think about this for a moment. That was strange. I thought maybe I could've been imagining that "invading" feeling. But when I sent him a psychic/mental drop-kick he acted like he somehow physically felt it, which is weird, because it means a few different things.

First, he **was** actually invading my mind! Second, my mental/emotional response actually affected him physically. But my drop-kick was only a thought. You can't drop-kick someone with a thought, right?! And you can't consciously dig into people's minds with your own mind, right? Because even though my dreams are showing me stuff, and I'm not entirely sure if I'm sharing them with the people I'm dreaming about or not... and I'm not sure if what my dreams are showing me is, like, real—you know?

This is odd.

I think about this some more and conclude it must be possible to invade someone's mind or he wouldn't have tried to do that on me. Then it brings up more questions... Why would he do that? Who was he? Does he work for someone or something? Has this happened to me before and I didn't know it? Before I decided to go on this... journey?

The fact also doesn't escape me that this happened when I was with Sophia and Anna.

As I think about it more I wonder, *is this how Leslie feels when I have a dream with him in it?* ***Is*** *he actually sharing that dream with me?* ***Does*** *he feel like I'm invading his privacy? So, he sent someone to show me this?*

The problem is I have no other way to find out more information about him in order to communicate with him. He doesn't talk to me, sending thoughts or otherwise. And if I'm supposed to warn him about the environment I have no other way...

Eventually, I decide I don't know what to think or do about this.

But for now, I find it unsettling.

Next, I decide to look at the ingredients in my store-bought deodorant. I do some research. It looks like there are harmful chemicals in it too—chemicals I don't want to put on my skin to be absorbed into my body. I notice that women's deodorant and men's deodorant are different. Women have more harmful chemicals in their deodorant, more chemicals that affect the natural production of hormones in the body. I decide to stop using deodorant and try to find an organic, natural product to replace it.

***

Anna calls me after work one day. She invites me to meet her and John at a park to hang out and practice Tai Chi together. Warily, I accept and meet them. We hang out for a little while, exchange small talk, practice some Tai Chi. And I can't shake the feeling that the people in my Tai Chi class have ulterior motives toward me.

I'm in spirit form hovering above myself, watching as my physical self opens my eyes. Then I'm in my physical self too. I'm on a moving object, sitting, holding a child. I look around and see it's a round-type boat, motor-less, with a raised deck.

I look at the upper deck and John is standing on it, holding a large spoked wheel with two hands. He's wearing a blue and white naval captain's hat. It's covering his eyes, as if he doesn't want me to recognize him. But I do. I recognize his energy, his body type, his facial shape. The boat seems to be shaped like a ball with the top and bottom cut off, flat. So, it somewhat bobs on the water.

I look down at the child in my arms. It's my friends' child. The one that was being assaulted. The child is sleeping.

We seem to be spinning around haphazardly as we're dropping through caves of water. There's a steel rail behind me. One rail rests against my lower back, another across my upper back and I can see still another rail just above my head.

"Hold on!" John yells, as he forcefully turns the wheel and we careen through an entrance to yet another cave, drop in and spin around. Thankfully the caves all seem to be large enough and rounded also. I use one arm to reach behind me and grasp the rail behind my back. With the other arm, I hug the child closer to me.

The child groggily opens his eyes, lifts his head heavily and sleepily says to me, "Too bright; make it darker, okay?" then closes his eyes and at the same time drops his head heavily back onto my shoulder.

There are two large floodlights on the upper deck, next to John, one on either side of him. This is the only light we have in this watery, cave-like, boat slide. I use my feet to brace myself against the rail, raise myself slightly, untie a white rain jacket tied at my waist and drape it over the child's head.

Good grief. I'm trying to make sure we don't go overboard, hit our heads against the side of this boat or a cave wall and drown. Each time we drop into a new cave the boat whirls drunkenly and rocks precariously. The shape of the boat allows it to bob in the water, although at times, waves careen across the lower level where I'm sitting and I have to raise the child higher. My lower body is soaked.

We pass down and through about eight of these caves and each time before we drop John yells, "Hold on!"

I wish he'd quit doing that.

Finally, I don't hear a waterfall-type sound below us so we must've reached the end. The boat settles and stops turning. I can see a walkway jutting from the side of the cave out to an opening. Beams of natural light stream into the cave from an opening. The boat rests against the walkway, fully stopped now and only slightly rocking. I use one hand to grab a rail behind me and hoist myself up to a standing position. I re-position the child and his head flops sleepily on my shoulder. Cautiously, I step off the boat onto the walkway and stand for a moment. Somehow, I seem to have sea legs, because I'm not veering around on solid ground. I walk through a tunnel leading out of the cave into daylight.

That didn't feel right at all. It felt like John invaded and took over my dream. It felt like a psychic-mind-game-kind-of-dream, as if John knows the about the child Leslie was assaulting and/or was having assaulted and he's attempting to make me think I was responsible for it and that, with his help, I "saved" the child.

Which is all baloney. First, I'm not responsible. Second, he didn't help anything; if anything, this was about him trying to confuse me, and third, the child isn't "saved."

Aside from trying to bring up the subject with the child's parents, I talked with the child, letting him know I knew what was happening to him, that it didn't matter what was going on, I loved him and that what happened to him was a result of someone else choosing to not heal themselves and instead choosing to pass along their pain.

That isn't to say he may or may not struggle with what happened when he gets older. So, he wasn't "saved." He'll have many opportunities to heal and bring an incredible amount of positivity into his life, just as we all do. What's most important is that he knows he's accepted and loved.

And I review what I know about John. John was in the military. Does the military have something to do with this? What's with these people I'm meeting who are connected with the military? First it was the carpool woman, and John said he was retired from the military... are these people associated with Leslie somehow? Because I don't normally meet people who are connected to the military. At least I haven't in the past.

I decide in future, I'll limit the time I spend with John. A lot.

Because that was bizarre.

***

I'm watching myself in spirit form. I'm standing guard, close to a fence, in a schoolyard. Children are yelling, laughing, and chasing a crimson ball across green, freshly cut grass. I can taste the chlorophyll in the air. Another adult is walking toward me, spelling me off for a break.

I walk into the red-brick, sharp-edged school, down a low-ceilinged hallway to the gym and open a door. Eight chairs have been placed in a wide semi-circle. I start walking toward the farthest chair then stop and turn my head to the side. My back is to the door. Something is going to happen. I decide to sit in a chair parallel to the door. I close my eyes and place my palms face down on my thighs.

With my eyes closed I see them walk through the door. The first one is a man, in his late twenties, about 5'9", slender, long tapered fingers, handsome in a boyish way, wearing a black bowler hat, black jeans, runners, t-shirt, and a long, dark trench coat.

Hat. Hiding something. Not a good sign. Behind him lumbers another man, much, much stockier, taller, 5'11", broad facial features, short, dirty blond hair. His protector. Another bad sign.

Hat guy approaches me, his shoes soundless on the floor. He's trying not to startle me. Opening my eyes, I slowly stand and once he's close enough I strike out. Grabbing his wrist and using his body weight and the energy in my lower stomach, I propel myself up and at the same time kick him hard and down in the stomach, as I release his wrist. The next moment I grab the chair next to me, flip it and position the back of the top of the chair under his chin, against his neck. This happens within seconds.

Out of the corner of my eye I've been observing stocky guy. He looks alarmed. He's not too quick though. He moves towards pinned hat guy. Looking at stocky guy, I push the chair slightly against pinned guy's neck. Pinned guy gurgles and, wide-eyed looks imploringly at stocky guy. Stocky guy stops and looks at me.

I look back down at pinned guy. His eyes look apologetic. He nods slightly and holds both his hands up, palms facing me. He turns his head to look up at stocky guy and motions with his head and eyes to back away. Looking at a space between the two guys I see stocky guy hesitate, then back up three paces and look down.

I look back down at pinned guy. A few moments pass.

I flip the chair away from his neck and return it to its proper position. Then I sit cross-legged in front of him.

He props himself up on an elbow, looking at me for a few long moments, then sits cross-legged in front of me, facing me.

I look at him expectantly, eyebrows raised.

He reaches into an inside pocket of his trench coat, which I now see is made of thin wool, and pulls out a light brown, worn leather wallet. He gives it to me.

Puzzled, I look at the wallet, then at him. Then I understand: he stole it. He's a practiced thief.

His eyes urge me to open the wallet, look at its contents. Perplexed, I take the wallet and open it. It has ID in it. A few bills. Two pictures. This is Leslie's wallet. One picture is of his mother, black and white. One picture is of me, in color.

The thief is saying a few things, without saying anything. He doesn't agree with how Leslie is behaving toward me, feels I would be in the right to take something that means something to Leslie, and he wants me to take something from Leslie.

I sigh.

I give him back the wallet. Using my mind, I send him thoughts explaining that I don't want to take anything from Leslie; I'm trying to understand how to communicate with him and build trust. If I take the wallet, then Leslie won't trust me. Plus, it'll mean I share Leslie's fears. Which I don't. I'm not trying to take anything from him. I'm trying to help him understand, so he can help himself and others.

As I'm sharing this information with him his eyes widen.

After I finish he stares at me for some time, gauging my sincerity. I continue looking him in the eyes. Slowly he nods his head in understanding. We stand in unison. I give him a hug and wish him well.

That was a different type of dream. It felt valid, though, not like the one with John. Not a mind-game-psychic kind of dream.

But I don't know those two guys. I haven't met them before in real life. Was that another test? He was a thief; that means he's closer to Leslie's world.

So, it could've been a test.

Did Leslie put him up to that?

Did Leslie put John up to the boat dream?

This is getting a bit confusing. And why am I so on edge in my dreams?

I **really** have to calm down.

***

Early in the morning a few days later, I'm quickly walking to my car in the parking lot. I'm going to be late for work. As I'm unlocking my car door, I notice a man's legs underneath the car parked next to mine. He's wearing black jeans. As I open my car door the man pulls himself out from underneath his car and jumps to his feet.

"Hi!" he says to me, smiling.

This is the thief from my dream. I look back at him. I'm stunned.

I blink.

A few moments pass and I'm noticing I'm mentally detaching from this situation.

This isn't happening.

Wordlessly, I get into my car and drive to work.

That hasn't happened before. I haven't had a dream with someone I don't know, and then met them in real life after I've dreamed about them. And it's as if he knew he shared the dream with me. Meant to. Like he felt he knew me.

This is a bit unnerving. It makes me question "reality."

What the hell is reality, anyways?

***

At work, a few co-workers and I have started going to for walks on our lunch break. Today I'm walking with Amanda. She's a single mom, in her late twenties, a sweetie. We walk down a big hill to get to a pathway that's surrounded by foliage. We visit as we walk, laughing and giggling. At one point, we both stop when she asks what time it is. We have to make sure we give ourselves enough time to walk back to work. We only have enough time to walk back now.

Stopping, we turn around and hear a grasshopper chirping loudly. We both look down and notice a grasshopper sitting on the pavement a foot in front of Amanda. Something about the way it's sitting there reminds me of how a challenger looks at its opponent, like the grasshopper is sizing us up, sending us its challenge.

Amanda and I look at each other quizzically then back down at the grasshopper. Then Amanda playfully pats her shoe on the pavement just in front of the grasshopper and we laugh. We must look like giants to the grasshopper, and it's funny that it thinks it can overpower us.

Then about eight crickets chirp loudly all around us.

We're being warned.

> *"Strength does not come from physical capacity, it comes from an indomitable will."*
>
> *— Mahatma Gandhi*

Amanda's eyes widen in surprise and we both begin laughing. She's laughing in surprise and I'm laughing at her response, her awareness of the natural world, and how playful it is. How wonderfully surprised she is to recognize she's connected to the whole. Then, chuckling, we step around the grasshopper and continue walking back to work.

But silently I think about how I've read that, historically, whole nations have starved and died due to locusts, a species of grasshopper, eating the food crops.

That evening I'm at Tai Chi practice. A young man has joined the class and has been practicing a lot, which pleases Mr. Wing greatly. He's constantly encouraging us to practice all the time during any spare time we have. Me? I think Tai Chi is okay, but I prefer my daily yoga/meditation, and then walking, hiking or biking in nature. I find Tai Chi interesting, but I doubt I'll continue with it.

After class Mr. Wing asks the young man to demonstrate to the class what he's learned so far. Mr. Wing seems proud of him. The young man shows us the first ten moves. He moves gracefully and he's picked up the moves in detail. He's definitely a good student for Mr. Wing. After he finishes I clap my hands lightly, smiling and nodding at the young man.

I look around and notice no one else is clapping, smiling, or saying anything. I look at Mr. Wing and he's looking back at me with an agitated look on his face. Then he tells the young man, while looking at me, that the young man is **not** to listen to others who encourage his progress, that those others are trying to impede his progress by making him think he doesn't need to improve.

What? As in, what the hell?

It's like Mr. Wing is insulting me or something. Which is weird. I've gotten along with Mr. Wing so far, so this abrupt change of behavior is unsettling and hurtful. As if he meant it to be hurtful.

As I'm driving home to my apartment after class I'm feeling frustrated, angry, and sad. It feels like I'm trying the best I know how to deal with everything. Everything feels like a moving target; just when I think I'm beginning to start to understand it, it changes, or I learn something I didn't know or that I'm made to feel bad about not knowing.

I'm feeling more upset as I drive. Thankfully it's only a ten-minute drive from practice to get home.

I walk into my apartment and as soon as I do the tears are running down my cheeks.

I don't cry often, but obviously, the stress needs to have an outlet. All of this has been a lot to digest and I decide I'm going to have a good cry for the next ten or fifteen minutes and let it out.

Then I can feel Leslie's presence directly overhead me in the apartment above me.

I sense/hear him sending me a thought, in a concerned, prying, needling, annoying way...

"What's wrong? Are you okay?"

This instantly pisses me off. He doesn't communicate with me in person at all, never responds to me in any way when I try to warn him about the lowering energy, assaults and/or has my friends' child assaulted, seems to be sending strange people to my dreams to confuse me, is following me around everywhere harassing me, and the only time he does want to communicate with me, using thoughts, is when I want privacy?

Just because I'm trying to warn him doesn't mean I like or want him following me around and hanging out above my head all the time, invading my life. The fact that we could be having a normal, respectful conversation, either using thoughts or in person, but he refuses, has been a huge detriment to the whole communication thing. And at the moment I'm not feeling very magnanimous about the whole thing.

"LEAVE ME ALONE!" I scream the thought at the ceiling.

I hear footsteps staggering backward and then someone's back hitting a wall.

Stunned, I think about that for a moment.

Did I do that? Did whatever I sent have that strong an impact?

Really?

No... it can't be. It was just a thought...

But maybe? If so, then cripes. I'm going to have to learn how to take that down a few levels. I don't realize how strong it is.

Which pisses me off again, because I was in the middle of looking after my own emotional needs, of venting and releasing pent-up stress and frustration in the form of tears, and he intruded on that.

Again, turning the attention to himself.

Not going to happen.

I push him out of my mind and place myself back in the same frame of mind and heart as when I walked in my apartment door, and let my emotions have their say for the next ten minutes.

Then, relieved, I start making dinner.

Later that night I'm woken up by screaming.

I look at the clock. It's 2:30 in the morning.

A man's voice is outside the building, and he's screaming, "Faggot!" loudly, repeatedly.

He sounds really upset.

It sounds like Leslie. I think about this for a while. He's living with a young woman—his girlfriend—above me. I've felt that. The odd thing is it feels like she's upset Leslie is following me around. As if she's jealous. Good grief.

I don't understand what's going on, though. He sounds like he's in a lot of pain. Does he think he's gay and it upsets him? Does he not want to be gay? Does it bother him? Is that something you can choose? It's dawning on me that maybe he's confused about his sexuality. That whatever happened to him when he was a child affects how he identifies with himself. Which makes me feel sad for him.

I wonder if what happens to a person when they're young needs to impact the rest of their life negatively.

I decide no, it doesn't, but that the person needs to want to heal, love and understand themselves. Which is why I don't think I can help him with this, though. He doesn't want to do this and I don't have any experience dealing with someone who doesn't want to do anything about their own situation.

Maybe that's why he hangs around me, though. I don't know. Because I don't care what his sexuality is, or what happened to him. I accept him as a human being and treat him as my equal. Which seems to also piss him off, me treating him like an equal. He believes he's smarter than I am. And who knows? Maybe he is in some respects.

But he isn't in others.

And the problem is, his behavior is pretty disrespectful and malevolent toward me. But I'm learning this has a lot less to do with me, and more to do with how he feels about himself.

I'm also not particularly comfortable with this situation.

At all.

And I fall back asleep.

Waking up to my alarm clock, I start getting ready for work. As I'm showering and dressing for work, images are flashing through my mind.

Blood.

A knife.

Blood on walls.

Blood on the floor.

Rage.

It feels to me like something very violent happened in the apartment above me after I fell back asleep.

The young girl who was living with Leslie...

I think she's dead. It feels like he killed her in his state of I-don't-know what-to-call-it last night. Like he had some sort of rage fit or something.

But that couldn't be… could it?

It feels like it, though.

But people don't just do things like that. They can't do things like that and not have to go to jail for it. Right?

I think about that for a moment.

Yes. Yes, I think people actually do things like that. People who have power and money can do whatever they want, it seems. I feel into this.

Is this the first time Leslie's done this?

No. It isn't.

He's done it many times before.

He's a professional widow/er.

That poor girl.

***

I feel vertigo as I begin opening my eyes.

Concrete stairs pass underneath me and I'm at an angle. Concrete walls are on either side of me.

My hands and feet are tied behind me and I'm tied to a pole.

Lifting my head, I see plain black shoes peeking out of a black swirling fabric as they step up and toward me.

Once at the top of the stairs I'm taken to a wooden bench of some sort and unceremoniously dropped onto it. In anticipation, I lift my neck.

I hear the sound of a wooden pole being pulled through rope.

Looking to my side I see a tall, wiry, gaunt, balding man in a loose, long sleeved, draping black coat. Something about him resembles Leslie. I think it is Leslie. He's staring down at me. His mouth is shaped in a grimace. His brows are furrowed.

A little person is standing the wooden pole against the wall. A little man. He looks angry. Then they both leave the room using the stairs they just brought me up. I sit up with some difficulty. My hands and feet are still tied.

I look around the room. Behind me on the wall hang various sharp instruments.

Saws, blades, knives.

The concrete floor looks as if blood stains from centuries past refuse to be forgotten. There are two large, circular, smooth, concrete columns in the room. Now I can sense my spirit self and can see myself through her eyes. She/I am looking down over the room.

Then I see another physical me.

The second physical me materializes from behind a column, strides purposefully over to me/me and unties my hands and feet. Then she/I turns, and strides back to the column, moving behind it.

I'm looking after her/me, somewhat confused, and rubbing my chafed wrists. However, time feels short so I quickly begin looking for doors or other escape routes. I have no idea if they plan to torture me or something. The look of the instruments on the wall in the room doesn't bode well. I walk to the center of the room, unsure what to do next...

Suddenly I hear footsteps running up the stairs two and three at a time. Jumping to my feet, I quickly move to the center of the room. The man who looks like Leslie runs into the room, looks for me, runs toward me and then stops three feet in front of me. Second physical me peers around the side of the column, watching us.

Not knowing what to do, I instinctively I cup my hand in front of my lower stomach and throw energy at the man. He jerks back as if he's been physically struck by an energy force. Then he mimics me and throws energy at me. He's strong. We volley energy blasts at one another, one after the other, about eight times. I can feel his energy diminishing. Mine isn't. I know he'll lose. I don't want to hurt or kill him, though; I just want to exhaust him to the point where I can leave.

My second physical self smiles at me from behind the column and somehow, we exchange places. I'm now standing behind the pillar watching the other me throwing energy at the man.

I turn and run down the stairs. Reaching a heavy wooden door at the bottom I turn the cold iron door knob and forcefully push the door.

A biting wind takes my breath away as the door flings wide open.

The ground is covered in a two-inch, dry, brittle snow, the kind of snow that looks as if it'll blow away but instead doesn't and crunches beneath your feet. An icy snow. The sky is an ominous swirling mass of grays. Flecks of hard snow bite at my face and hands.

I'm standing at the top of a hill in a residential area. Rented, moderately-kept suburban middle income homes line the street across from me. There's a small blue car with rust stains on the roof parked on the street, facing downhill, in front of me.

I run to the car, looking back at the door. No one coming. Yet.

As I yank the door open it begins creaking in protest. Jumping in, I can see keys in the ignition. I try to start it. It burps and gasps, refusing. It's an automatic. I release the parking brake, shift it into neutral and jump out beside the car, knees bent, one hand holding the wheel while my other hand starts pushing the car. I'm bending low, sending energy from my lower stomach to my thighs, knees, arms and back. Furtively I look back at the stairs. No one.

As the car begins moving and then gaining speed rolling down the hill, I jump in, close the door, and turn the key, my breath sending plumes of white out in front of me. The motor catches and I shift into drive. Cold. The air is so cold here.

What the hell is with Leslie? Why is he always trying to harm me? Or scare me? How does The Light expect me to communicate with Leslie? All he seems to know is violence, or the threat of violence, and drama.

The Light must be teaching me patience.

Obviously, Leslie isn't used to dealing with someone like me. He's used to dealing with people like himself. Fearful people. How do you communicate peacefully with someone who seems intent on being violent?

This is difficult.

Patience, The Light softly whispers. *Patience.*

***

A few weeks later, I'm sitting in my living room at night on a weeknight watching a documentary on my computer. I haven't watched television for quite a long time now. I'm enjoying this commercial-free way of learning. Sabre is lying on my legs and Bruce is lying on top of the futon couch behind me.

Suddenly, Bruce lunges at the window at the same time I hear a large thumping sound against the window behind me. Bruce is batting, spitting, and snarling at the window erratically.

What was that? I try to see what Bruce is so upset about but it's so dark outside I can't see a thing. I try something new. I close my eyes and open my mind - it was a flying squirrel! I didn't know they had flying squirrels here!

Bruce continues sitting in front of the window and a half hour later I hear more erratic thumping on the window in front of where Bruce is sitting. Bruce gets upset again, howling, spitting and scratching at the window vigorously. And I know. The squirrel is teasing Bruce.

Laughing, I close the curtains.

The next morning at work I ask my co-workers if they know if there are flying squirrels in Nova Scotia. All of them reply no, they don't think so. Most of them look confused, like they haven't heard of an animal called a 'flying squirrel'. I Google it and there are four different species of flying squirrels in Nova Scotia.

That night, sending my thoughts, I try to tell Leslie about the flying squirrel incident. How the squirrel was teasing Bruce. And how people seem to be so detached from their natural environment they don't feel, see, or understand what's going on. That it's important to recognize how important it is to us, as a species, to understand that the energy level is lowering in nature.

I'm not sure if he heard me. As usual I get no response. If he did hear me he's probably annoyed. What I'm learning is he doesn't like to hear me talk about this.

No matter what, he's not pleased about me, which I can't help. This is the job The Light gave me. I can't say I'm particularly thrilled about it either, because I'm not.

But I am trying.

***

I'm slowly coming to the realization that most people are basically how I was before I took up the challenge of this journey. I just wanted to "be normal," to get along, be happy. Avoid pain. Keep to my lane. But I had some access to my intuition. There were barriers to using it before this, though.

Mainly I was afraid of my intuition because I was taught to be. I was taught to "get in line" and **want** to be like "everybody else."

That's where Leslie and people like Leslie come in. I think they handle the things no one else wants to, because people want to be fed answers; they don't want to forge their own paths, find their own answers. They don't want to understand or experience any type of pain or confusion, to have the patience to teach themselves and learn how to move through it to the other side. They don't want to figure out for themselves what works for them.

They want to be "fed" answers. They want the easy way. Because they've been brainwashed to believe they don't have the power to make choices that give them the freedom to choose what works best for them. Which is an incredibly powerful tool for Leslie and people like Leslie. A tool that gives them a lot of power, money, and control.

You have pain? Leslie or people like him can give you drugs, or alcohol, or sex. You want to know how to look and talk so you fit in? Watch TV. You don't want to exercise and eat healthy? There're pills. You don't want to figure out what your gifts are, what you brought to this world to share with others? Well, just take up a job, any old job, and it'll do.

I'm understanding more how difficult it is for Leslie and people like Leslie. Most of us don't want to look underneath things, so we put all the responsibility on people like Leslie. They're the bad guys. It's their fault, not ours. They're the ones to blame.

The collective subconscious.

***

I'm in spirit form watching down over physical me. I open my eyes and I'm in a dark room. I can't see anything. But I can feel a dark energy attacking me. It's swirling and whirling around me, then it seems like this dark energy is stabbing toward me, at me, intermittently. I don't feel like I'm bleeding or anything but it doesn't feel pleasant.

Suddenly, a very bright, blinding white light flashes into the area and the darkness goes away. In my mind's eye in the dream I see Mr. Wing's face, my Tai Chi instructor.

Another one. This dream didn't feel right either. It felt like another psychic-dream-mind-game. I'm not sure how much longer I'll go to my Tai Chi lessons.

***

About a week later I'm at work first thing in the morning. A young man who works in the same department as I do opens the door and walks in. We smile and greet each other. He turns the corner and begins climbing the stairs to his office, stumbles and falls on the stairs. I can't see him but I hear it.

Then I only hear silence, instead of someone picking themselves up and starting to climb the stairs again. I wait a few moments. After another few moments, I call out, "You okay?"

A moment of silence, then, "Yeah," he calls back, embarrassed. "Kind of stupid to fall up the stairs." A weak laugh.

"Nah," I say, "you just found a more creative way of climbing the stairs." I hear him chuckle and then feet climbing up the stairs.

I'm standing in a dimly lit room. My spirit self is watching over me from above. A soft light shines above somewhere, the only light. It's slowly swallowed up by darkness five feet away.

Lying a few feet in front of me is the young man I know from my work—the one who tripped going up the stairs. We're acquaintances only. We've never eaten together, shared a conversation. We've shared polite greetings. Yet here we are.

He's lying still on his back with his eyes closed. I watch as slowly his spirit form rises out of his body and begins to walk away into the darkness. I wait, remembering my great-aunt.

After time passes I hear his voice, frightened, calling out, "Help! I'm lost! Where am I?" I wait for him to pause and then shout calmly into the darkness.

"It's okay, you're fine, just follow my voice," I say. "If you keep following my voice you'll start seeing some light." I keep talking and soon I can hear footsteps quickening, getting closer.

I see his spirit self, smile, and look down at his body. He follows my eyes and looks down too. Relief spreads across his face. He visibly relaxes and begins walking toward his physical self. Once he reaches it he looks up, smiles at me, and then melds back into his physical form.

This felt real. This didn't feel contrived, like the other ones with John, the thief, and Mr. Wing. This one was authentic, like the one I had with my great-aunt. I wonder, *did that guy share that dream with me?* I'm never clear when someone I know in reality is in one of my dreams. In how many of my dreams is there a direct relationship to the physical realm? Again, I'm not sure if it's okay to ask them. So, I don't.

***

A month later I'm offered a six-month contract position for the same company but for another department, at a different location. I accept the offer and let the people I'm working with know I'll be changing offices. The next day I find an envelope with a Thank You card from the young man I dreamed about, the one I work with who tripped going up the stairs.

This is a good sign. He's telling me he shared the dream with me and appreciated what I did. It proves to me that what happens in the spirit/ dream world **is** somehow connected to the physical world. But I'm not sure if it's all the time with my dreams. It also shows me that my intuition is correct when it's letting me know a contrived-head-game-dream from an authentic one. I still don't know what kind of control I have in where I go, who I see, or what I do in the dream realm, though.

Sophia, Anna, Mark, and I have planned to hang out for an afternoon. I haven't decided what to think of these people yet and I'm wondering if I can learn something from them, if maybe I'll get a better understanding of what's going on if I can somehow learn something from them.

We're going to a beach I haven't been to before. We've all contributed to the picnic lunch and carpool to the beach in Mark's car. The beach is packed and finding a parking spot is near impossible on this Saturday afternoon in the summer. Eventually we do, and spend a few hours playing cards in the sand and chatting. It's an enjoyable day.

I get the feeling Mark has wanted to get to know me better, romantically. Of course, I'm in no position to do this. First, I have too much going on trying to figure this other stuff out and warn Leslie at the same time. Second, even if I didn't, I'm not attracted to him romantically. He's a great guy and fun to visit with but that's it.

I've been trying to let him know I'm not attracted to him without hurting his feelings. He's been dropping hints for a while now. He doesn't seem to either understand or accept my polite declines in response to his advances. A week later I learn from Sophia and Anna that Mark has a drinking problem, alcohol. Maybe this is why he isn't getting the hints I'm dropping. I'll have to find a more direct, but gentle, way to let him know.

Sophia texts me at work a few days later. She's agreed to foster a female cat and her litter of kittens and wants to know if I want to come for a visit over the lunch hour. I text her back, saying sure. After I arrive we're watching the kittens wobble over each other while eating our sandwiches. I ask her where her husband is and if they get along. She says she's divorced and her ex-husband works for the military in Canada. She says she doesn't get along with him.

***

Sophia and Anna are sitting on either side of me. I'm in spirit form watching myself and also am myself in my dream. We're sitting cross-legged with our palms facing up on our thighs, our eyes closed. We're meditating together. Deep, calming breaths as our shoulders rise and fall slowly in unison. My spirit self notices Mark arriving. Instead of sitting and joining in the meditation, he sits behind me. Then he reaches his arms forward and around my shoulders, his hands clasping in front of me and squeezing me. This doesn't feel like a hug. It feels like a cling. An invasive cling.

Which pulls me out of my calm, meditative state. And that annoys the hell out of me. I open my eyes and bring my hands up between my body and his hands, and with a loud "Ahhhhhhhh!" I break his hands open. My mind sends, "Get off me!"

I hear Mark whimper and pull back.

Anna and Sophia open their eyes and without moving their heads, turn their eyes toward me. I close my eyes and take deep breaths, because what I feel like doing is using Mark's body like a football and punting it across the universe. Mark seems to understand the energy. He curls up and moves back farther.

I close my eyes again and begin to concentrate on the stillness, my breath, on nothingness. On peace.

So far, I'm becoming more distrustful of the people in my Tai Chi class and the dreams I have with them in them. They feel fabricated. I don't like the feel of this one.

***

A few days later I show up for Tai Chi class. Our instructor, Mr. Wing, isn't teaching today. Today one of the students is leading the class. This has happened quite a few times before. We get no notice that he won't be teaching the class and he doesn't seem to think there's a problem with this. I'm wondering why I'm paying this man to teach a class he doesn't show up for half of the time.

After the class I say as much to Anna. She agrees with me and says she heard some people say they thought Mr. Wing was a spy.

The word surprises me.

I've never heard anyone say the word "spy" in a real life conversation before.

I go home and think about it. Is that what this stuff is about? These people with ties to the military, the people in my Tai Chi class and Leslie? They think I'm a spy?

I can't help it and double over laughing for an entire five minutes, tears streaming out of my eyes. The irony of this situation is unbelievable! They're confused because spies do spy stuff for their own benefit, money basically. How can I be a spy when no one's paying me, and what I'm doing isn't for just my benefit? Good grief. Plus, aren't you supposed to have multiple fake passports, expensive clothes, fast cars, and buckets of money when you're a spy?

Because I don't have any of these things. I'm barely scraping by. Plus, my car needs some work and I have to find a mechanic. And I don't feel like I'm making any headway with Leslie. What I do know is that people who ***are*** spies are playing head games, wasting my time, trying to confuse me.

Which isn't working.

But it is trying my patience.

***

I'm watching myself sleeping on my side, on my futon couch in my apartment. I am myself. Someone quietly climbs onto the bed next to me and lies on their back, folding their hands over their stomach. My back is facing them. I turn my head and, with half-opened eyes, look over.

"Sophia? How did you get in here?" I ask groggily.

"Through da door," she says.

"I didn't give you a key," I reply.

"Oh. Jes. I came in through da weendow," she says.

"Oh," I say, and turn back on my side and fall back asleep.

What was that about? It doesn't feel right.

Sophia seems to be showing me she also knows how to access dreams. But it feels like the other dreams, with Mark, the thief, and Mr. Wing. Fabricated. Invasive. It feels like more of the psychic-mind-game-thing. Which I'm reticent to feel about Sophia. I'd like to like her.

But... facts are facts.

***

I decide I have to get some much-needed work done to my car. The plates are expiring soon, which means I'll have to register it, which means the car has to pass an inspection before I can insure it. It's over ten years old. I call the mechanic I took my car to when I first arrived in Halifax and needed new brake pads and make an appointment. He tells me that if I drive my car to his shop early the next morning, he can arrange to have me driven to work and then picked up at the end of the day.

The next morning after I drop my car off at the shop, I'm being driven to work by one of the guys who works at the mechanic shop. There's something familiar about him and I try not to look at him too often or for too long.

Finally, I realize what it is. He reminds me of Kyler. Same face shape. Roughly the same body type. I ask the guy where he grew up and he tells me he grew up close to Halifax. He tells me he used to catch, kill, roast, and eat frogs when he was a kid, which means he grew up poor, which also means he had a rough childhood. This is also why he's reminding me of Kyler. I still haven't thought of a way to repay Kyler.

I'm standing in a crowd and watching myself in spirit form from above. The energy of the crowd is uneasy, fragmented, confused, murmuring. It feels like suppressed anger, lacking confidence. The crowd sways like a tormented organism. There's an invisible line no one breaches, although I can feel some very badly want to. The sky above is gray and colorless. The air tastes rancid.

I sense timing will be crucial if I want to breach the line and leave. Tentatively, I step out of the crowd, across the line and stand alone, crossing my arms over my chest. The murmuring continues. This is a good thing. Moments later a man in his mid-twenties circles me, a sneer on his face, "Want some drugs?" His flat, black eyes pierce mine.

"No," *I reply loudly and calmly. He melts back into the crowd. So, these are all drug addicts. Some have stopped using, but they don't know how to leave here. Is this why I'm here? To see if I can leave and if I can, they can follow?*

I wait a few moments more, then uncross my arms and join the crowd again. I can feel them moving toward me. They're nervous, apprehensive, and fearful but have also allowed themselves to feel a little hopeful, which means courageous.

After it feels like the ones who've stopped using drugs are close by, I begin walking forward, out of the crowd, again crossing the invisible line. There's an open concrete tunnel about fifty feet away, its black maw beckoning. I continue walking toward it, only looking forward. I can feel them behind me. There's about fifteen of them.

Once at the tunnel I dig my lighter out of my pocket, flick it and peer in. A small stream of tepid, rank-smelling brown water sits idly on the bottom of the floor. Eight feet high and eight feet across, the rounded tunnel's walls boast graffiti, symbols and signs that speak a foreign language. I notice them behind and beside me. I sense their confidence growing, their fear ebbing away, which is great. I don't know where this tunnel leads, though.

Wordlessly I walk into the tunnel and choose a steady pace. The tunnel goes on for a few miles. It seems an eternity. It feels like slogging through waist high wet mud. Relentlessly, I continue. At one point one of them starts singing. Her voice is beautiful, strong, melodic, and upbeat. It makes me smile and lifts everyone's spirits. I'm thankful for it, because the weight of responsibility I'm feeling is heavy. It's nice to have a break. Even for a few moments.

As we reach the end of the tunnel, sunlight streams toward us, lighting up the inside of half of the tunnel. I step out of the tunnel and am blinded temporarily by the sunlight. Shielding my eyes with my hands, I turn around and watch them exit out of the tunnel, one by one. All fifteen. Good. We didn't lose anyone.

They range in age from about twelve to twenty, a mix of females and males of varied ethnic backgrounds. They look worn out. They need food, water, and rest. I check and have a five-dollar bill in my front pocket. I look back at them, meeting their expectant eyes. I purse my lips.

Turning around, I see a large, flat area littered with train tracks, then a small hill rising to an industrial area where a row of buildings looks down on the train tracks. I start walking again, toward the buildings, at a slower pace now. After crossing the tracks, we climb, slide, and stumble up the mostly dirt hill, fist-sized rocks partially hidden in the dirt.

At the top of the hill I look at a nearby building. There's a cheap "Cafe" sign above a door on the top floor. It's a tall, three story building with a faded white painted staircase hugging the side of the building, leading up to the top floor. Walking up the staircase I hear them climbing behind me. I'm wondering how I'll be able to give them all sustenance with only five dollars.

We climb the stairs slowly, methodically. A steel door with a small wire meshed window greets us at the top. I open the door. The Cafe is small, with five small round metal tables with two cheap wooden chairs to each table. It smells amazing, though—garlic, vegetables, bread baking. I walk to the counter and an older man, in his late sixties, exits the kitchen and slowly walks toward the till at the counter.

"The soup smells good," I say.

"Aye-ya, it is. She makes it homemade fresh every day," he replies noncommittally.

"How much for a bowl?" I ask.

"Five dollars," he replies.

"Do you have day old or week old soup for cheaper?" I ask, looking back at the group.

"Nope. She only uses fresh, organic ingredients every day. It's expensive," he replies.

Resigned, I nod my head. I walk to the cooler and buy bottles of water we'll share. I pay the older man, thanking him, and we leave the cafe and climb back down the stairs.

That felt authentic. But was it really a place? Does it have anything to do with the "real" world? How did I find that place? What was I doing there? Maybe I was looking for Kyler, hoping he'd be one of the ones who'd be ready to leave. That I'd be able to repay him. But he wasn't there. The mechanic's helper reminded me of Kyler, so I must've been working on that problem subconsciously. Huh.

Then I wonder, again, how much control do I have over where I go and what I do when I dream? It always seemed like before all of this stuff with Leslie, I was just somewhere random. Now it feels more like I'm somehow directing where I'm going in my dreams. Sometimes. Somehow.

***

A few days later I'm driving to a store with Anna. I'm trying to find a wok so I can try my hand at cooking authentic stir fry meals. We park in an open parking lot next to the store and get out of the car. The parking lot is large; half of it is filled with cars belonging to people who are visiting the same store as I am. The other half of the lot is empty. It has a large "Private Property" sign on the building on the other side of the lot.

After I close my car door, and as I'm turning around to start walking to the store, a man calls out, "Hey!"

I stop and turn around and notice a man who was standing by a truck, the only vehicle, parked on the other side of the lot, is quickly walking toward me. I notice as he's walking toward me he's wearing jeans, a black leather jacket and his hair is mid-length and messy. He has a few days' growth on his face. His eyes look empty. He stops walking six feet from me and then points at a spot near my front fender.

"You crossed the line," he says.

Confused, I reply, "What?"

"You crossed the line," he says again, exasperated, pointing at something in front of my car.

I walk closer to him, toward the front of my vehicle, to see what he's pointing at. When I get there I still can't see anything on the ground where he's pointing.

I look up at him.

"What line?" I ask.

He moves closer to my car and is pointing straight down toward a very faded yellow painted line, almost invisible, separating the two lots. My front tire is sitting on the line. So, the nose of my car is technically "over the line."

"Oh. I didn't see it. It's pretty faded. I'll back up," I say. And I do.

As I walk into the store I wonder if that conversation has something to do with my dream the other night. Did Leslie somehow know about that? Is he annoyed about that? So, he sent the guy in the parking lot to send me a message? Hmmmm. Well, that's his business, or one part of it as far as I know, I think, based on other dreams I've had about him, so he might be annoyed.

This is a rather difficult situation. It's not my intention to interfere with Leslie or his business, but then again, those individuals in my dream had stopped using and wanted to leave.

That's free will. Everyone has free will.

If he is annoyed, then that means that what I did in that dream had an impact in "real life" or "reality."

Which is confusing.

Do all my dreams have an impact with this "reality?" Or just some of them?

I don't know all the rules yet, but it doesn't feel like I've crossed any lines.

To me anyway.

Then I start thinking about the words "crossing a line." Which reminds me of the word boundaries. How much do I really know about boundaries?

I think about this for a while.

Well, after trying to steal when I was a teenager and it didn't make me feel good, I learned that boundary. But what about other boundaries? I'm pretty sure my childhood wasn't a great training ground for learning boundaries. Which is no one's fault. I'm no different than anyone else in that regard; much of our behavior, the way we are, is a result of what's passed down to us.

Nevertheless, I want to take advantage of all learning opportunities, so I need to look at this more. Because this is causing me to feel guilty, ashamed and confused, like I'm supposed to know something really basic that I don't know.

And it takes me back... to a memory.

I was child, about seven years old, and often I'd be woken up in the middle of the night on a school night, and be told to play the piano for my parent's drunken guests. This happened quite a lot. After I'd finished playing for them, I was then told to give these guests a hug good night.

These people were strangers to me and I didn't want to. But I felt pretty much forced to. My parents provided me with food, clothes, and a roof over my head. And they wouldn't tell me to do something that was bad for me, right? And after all they did for me, it was the least I could do, right? And besides, what else was I supposed to do?

I also saw other people's boundaries being crossed regularly. Seeing my mom with black eyes, broken noses, broken arms and once a broken leg taught me that it's acceptable and normal for others to cross the boundary that separates one human being from another, one's physical well-being from another.

So yes, I have to agree, on a personal note, I probably do need to work on boundaries. I don't know how to do this, though. It must have something to do with my dreams. How do I not cross boundaries when I'm dreaming? Which brings me back to the same question: How do I control this?

Also, what bothered me most about this last dream was that there was no healthy food for them once they left. How are they supposed to get strong without healthy food?

Which gets me thinking. Organic fruits and vegetables are expensive. Yet they cost next to nothing to grow. So, I start doing some research on the Internet.

I find information on hydroponics. I find information about NASA using hydroponics to grow food in space. I find information about growing food using no soil and very little water, with heirloom seeds, connecting vertical tubes, with hemp baskets hanging from holes inside the tube, connected to a fish tank, which provides water and fish feces, an excellent ingredient for growing healthy food. A very small tube is inserted inside the larger tube with holes throughout it.

If you connect a pump to the fish tank, along with a timer, you can pump the water from the fish tank through the tube in five-minute intervals, whereby the tube sprays the water onto the seeds sitting in the hemp baskets. You can also attach a solar battery to the pump so the sun's energy can be used to grow the food indoors.

This is hugely interesting to me. I'm not that great with building things, though. I think of who I might know here who would be good at building something like this, experimenting. The mechanic's helper. I think about this for a minute.

It's been about a month since the dream with the kids and the tunnel and getting the roundabout message that I crossed the line, so it might be okay if I call the mechanic who looks like Kyler to see if he'd be interested in helping me.

He's good with his hands and I know he's like Kyler; he can create things and he has a good imagination. I call him and ask if he'd be able to meet me. He agrees and we meet at a local park.

After I explain what I want to do, I ask the mechanic's helper if he thinks it'd be hard to build. He says he doesn't think so. I've drawn a sketch of what I think it'll look like and labeled different parts.

I'm not sure if he can read. His eyes squint when I move my finger under the labels sometimes. At one point, he tells me he's not that good at reading. He wasn't good at school. I tell him that's not a problem; he's good at visualizing and building things, and that's a gift.

I ask if he'll help me with it. He says yes. I tell him I think I know the parts to buy so I'll start doing that and will call him when I think I have everything. I'm going to need to buy as much as I can secondhand. He has tools, or access to tools, so that won't be a problem. I'm not sure where it'll be built—we don't discuss that—but I'm excited. I thank him and we go our separate ways.

Afterward a feeling comes to me that his mind turns the symbols on the paper around. Something like dyslexia, but it isn't dyslexia.

When I get back to my apartment and am parking my car in the parking lot I hear a loud noise. It sounds like a motor being revved very loudly. A feeling comes over me that Leslie is mad about me meeting with the mechanic's helper. I'm not sure why. Then I wonder, *Is the mechanic a drug addict too?*

I open my eyes and find I'm sitting on a small two-seater couch. My back is straight and my hands are resting on my thighs. I sense someone sitting next to me. I look to my left and see it's the mechanic's helper. He looks strange, though. He's looking straight ahead, but he looks disoriented, like he doesn't know where he is. His eyes look unfocused. He's leaning back, sort of slumped, against the back of the couch. His hands are resting on his thighs and his head is mildly weaving from side to side.

I peer closer at him. I can't see any blood or bruising. Physically he looks okay. But something is wrong with him. I sense someone standing in front of me. I turn my head and see Leslie standing five feet in front of me.

His face is blotched with red spots, the tendons in his neck and forearms look like they're going to split apart like an elastic that can't stretch any farther, his hands are clenched into fists and he's standing with his legs apart. He looks like a volcano about to explode. I calmly look back at him.

*"C**T!" he screams at me, spittle flying from the sides of his mouth.*

I blink, take a deep breath, and then exhale.

Then stand up and begin walking away.

Well.

That didn't go very well.

Okay. The mechanic's helper is a drug addict and Leslie doesn't want me talking to him. Doesn't want the mechanic's helper to stop doing drugs and thinks he might if he hangs around me.

All right. I decide that, for now, I'll experiment with creating a solar-powered indoor food grower later. I can also do some research on other ways of growing food.

It's more important for me to focus on trying to communicate with Leslie about the lowering of energy in nature.

I'm not making any headway figuring out how I can repay Kyler, though.

The mechanic's helper calls me a few days later, telling me he's leaving town. He isn't sure where he's going but he wants a change. And I wonder. Did he share that dream with me?

***

A few days later Sophia calls me and asks if I'd like to go to Cape Breton for the upcoming long weekend. This sounds like a great idea so I agree. I haven't figured out what the deal with Sophia is yet. I've stopped going to Tai Chi classes. I ask her if she'd like to go kayaking there; she says no. She wants to explore the Cabot Trail.

She suggests we book a hostel to stay in. I haven't stayed at a hostel before. I look up and make a booking for us in a hostel in Cape Breton for a few nights.

Sophia picks me up at six o'clock in the morning that Friday morning and we drive from Halifax to Cape Breton. Once there we drive the Cabot Trail. I thought it was a walking/hiking trail. It isn't. It's a road.

At one point on our drive, I see a sign for a hiking trail called Waterfall Trail. I want to stretch my legs and ask Sophia if she'd like to go for a walk. She agrees and we start walking the trail.

The foliage is amazing. Ferns grow on the ground everywhere. There's a type of tree that grows in Nova Scotia that doesn't grow in Alberta, called a Witch Hazel tree. It's quite different from any tree I've seen before. After walking on the trail for a few hours Sophia complains she's getting tired. We walk back to the car and drive to the hostel. We don't arrive there until later in the evening, about eight o'clock.

I'm exhausted and immediately jump in the shower, planning to go to sleep right after my shower. It's been a long day and I have kayaking booked early the next morning. As I'm leaving the bathroom and walking toward the living room I stop and watch a laughing little girl haphazardly running across my path. She's about three years old. I wait. An older man, perhaps her grandpa, walks across my path calling after her.

Once he passes I see a coffee table. A black bowler hat sits on the table. I recognize that hat. On the other side of the coffee table is a couch. There's a pair of legs in black jeans sitting behind the black bowler hat. My eyes travel up as I look at the person sitting on the couch behind the hat.

The thief who stole Leslie's wallet. He's looking at me. He nods his head at me.

I blink, then continue to my room, where I fall asleep soundly.

Sophia drives me to the kayaking business the next morning. The guy who owns the business asks me if I can wait about a half hour. An older couple called him and asked if they could join us. Sophia and I aren't in a hurry so I agree. The couple arrives and we set off. We paddle to an island where we stop and have a snack and visit. The couple are British. The man invented The Pill. He spends most of his time going to court because other manufacturers try to copy his patent. They seem like a nice couple.

My own point of view about The Pill is it's a bad thing. Synthetic hormones cause cancer. There are natural plants that can accomplish what The Pill does without causing harm to a woman's body. Plus, the synthetic hormone is leaving the body as urine, which then meets with water, which then meets with our natural environment, mixing unnatural chemicals into the natural world.

On top of that, if mass media stopped promoting sex, I doubt unplanned pregnancy would be such a problem. More focus on individuals developing their own creative gifts and interacting with themselves and others in healthy, beneficial ways would be a step in the right direction, information I wish I'd had when I was young.

But that's just my opinion.

As we paddle back to our starting point I notice eagles flying above and a nest very, very high in a tree. They're a family of eagles. The mother is the largest of this breed of bird. They almost seem to be following us as we paddle. Swooping and swerving in the air above, they look majestic. Looking up at them, I temporarily ground myself in my kayak. Laughing, I use my paddle to push myself into deeper water.

After we get back to the hostel I boil some water, squeeze some lemon into it and sit on the front porch. A ruby-throated hummingbird flies close to a flower near me and hovers as it feeds on the flower's nectar. I've never seen a hummingbird before. It's beautiful. I call to Sophia and she manages to get a look at it before it flies away.

The rest of the weekend we explore other parts of Cape Breton and go on a birding tour on a boat. The fresh air and change of scenery is wonderful.

During the trip, here and there, I try to ask Sophia questions about dreams, thoughts, and feelings and how they relate to consciousness and reality. It feels to me as if she might know more about these things, things that I'm groping with trying to understand. Sophia doesn't really say much to me about it, which ends up making me feel like I'm the only person in the course of history who has these kinds of experiences.

It's an odd, solitary, lonely feeling.

After we get back to Halifax, Sophia sends me a video clip. It's a woman talking about how she's visited in her dreams by a man who does terrible things, violent things, to others in real life that negatively affect a lot of people. But that it's okay. That's the gist of the message I get from the video.

So, what is Sophia saying? She understands what I'm trying to figure out and that it's just my lot in life to deal with someone on a personal level who does things like this? That doesn't feel right to me. It feels misleading, which is about what I've come to expect from the people in my Tai Chi class. The people I'm coming to regard as "spies".

To some extent I'm learning I can or do have some control over what I dream, and what information and energy I access. I haven't figured it all out yet, but I do know that. The video clip Sophia sent me? It doesn't feel like it has anything to do with my journey, what The Light has tasked me with or what The Light has in store for me.

***

After I get back I send thoughts to Leslie about the Witch Hazel trees, the ferns, the eagle family, and the hummingbird; how it feels like nature is trying to gently reach us, to play with us, to show us how important the natural world is to our well-being, our survival.

Of course, no response. But I'm pretty sure he heard me.

Chapter 7:

Approach to the Innermost Cave

I'm watching myself in spirit form as my physical self is climbing stairs. The stairs are off-white and made of stone. The edges have been rounded by time.

So many stairs.

I've been climbing for a long time.

I don't look up to see where the top is because I'm not sure I'll make it and really, the effort and the journey can only be taken one step at a time.

Sometimes, one agonizingly slow step at a time.

I keep climbing.

There's no sense of time.

I don't look back to see how far I've come.

I don't look to see what's on either side of the stairs.

The stairs are seven feet wide, not steep, but not shallow either.

I'm aware of a blue sky above me.

It wouldn't matter what the weather was.

The stairs.

All that's important is climbing them.

At a certain point, I stop to rest, sitting down on a step.

My spirit self takes a more solid form and joins me.

We sit on the steps together, side by side, marveling at this and that. We laugh and share jokes and memories.

For some time, we amuse ourselves and pass the time this way, while I rest.

Then we hear voices and look up.

A small group of people are climbing the stairs below us, toward us.

There are eight of them.

None of them look related. Each is distinct in their own unique way: eye color, hair color, skin color, age, and the way they're dressed. Yet they're together in the same task as me. Climbing the stairs.

They stop a few steps below us.

An older man with a wrinkled, tanned face smiles up at me with sparkling, azure blue eyes.

"Keep going!" he urges as his hands flow up and toward me.

"Keep going!" he says again.

"Yes," the group says, "keep going!" They're all smiling, encouraging.

I want to rest more.

I stand and move to the side, ushering them to go past me.

They refuse.

They won't go past me.

"Keep going," they smile encouragingly.

I sigh and nod my head.

Resigned, I stand and turning around notice I'm only five steps from the top. At the top are two large white pillars, creating a doorway.

I climb the last five steps to the doorway and walk through it. Now I'm in a foyer facing three heavy, ornamentally carved doors made of a worn, warm-colored wood. The ceiling is fifteen feet high and wooden.

To my right is a doorway with no door. I turn right and walking through the doorway, find myself in a small, windowless concrete room with a dirt floor. In the far-right corner of this room is another doorway. I begin walking to it and stop in front of it.

Looking through the doorway into this room I notice its size, that of a football field. It's ceiling-less and it also has a dirt floor. The sky above is cloudless and the sun is shining brightly down into the room. A six-foot wall, made of the same worn, off-white stone as the stairs I'd been climbing, surrounds this room. The door I'm looking through is close to one end of this ceiling-less room, where I can see a large mound of dirt, about four feet high and six feet wide, sitting in the middle, like a goal post. It looks like a massive gopher hole. I look across the room and notice there's another mound of dirt at the opposite side of the room.

Suddenly a healthy young adult lioness leaps up and out of the mound of dirt closest to me and charges full speed toward the opposite mound. Powerful muscles undulate gracefully under her coat. As the lioness nears the opposite mound she leaps through the air, as if pouncing on prey, and disappears effortlessly down and out through the mound.

I look to my left and this time a young, healthy male lion leaps up and out of the mound, racing across the room, leaping, and then disappearing down and out. I watch as hundreds of these young, healthy lions and lionesses leap up through the mound, race across the room and then leap to disappear through the opposite mound.

As they run, the sun kisses their coats, revealing silken threads of gold.

I soak in the beauty and majesty of these creatures.

Eventually, I turn and walk back to the foyer and stand in front of the three wooden, heavy, ornamentally carved doors. Each door has a doorknob with an antique black lock, the kind where the key is five inches long and has few teeth and the teeth are square shaped.

A small, wizened old man materializes to my right and holds up a large key ring three-quarters full of keys. The keys are antique looking, black iron, thin, with four-inch long handles and thick, square, teeth. He holds the key ring up at me, eye level.

Then, smiling at me, he sweeps his other hand toward the doors. He seems to be asking me which door I'd like opened. I point a finger at the middle door and we walk to it together. He chooses a key, inserts it into the lock, turns the key, looks up at me, smiling and turns the doorknob.

The door opens and I begin walking forward, stepping through.

This was a different type of dream. It feels more like a prophetic dream. I'm not sure, but I don't think I've had a prophetic dream before. At the same time the dream seemed to be a message, where The Light is telling me to keep going; I'm doing well. I'm learning. I don't know about that; it feels to me like I'm fumbling around in the dark, helping some people but also pissing off other people. Probably a lot of other people.

"The Prophets accept all agony and trust it,
For the water has never feared the fire."

— Rumi

But it doesn't feel like I'm making any progress with Leslie. The Light wants me to get across to Leslie the importance of our natural environment, how we need it.

I wish The Light would give me some more concrete clues on how to go about doing this.

In the meantime, it seems like Leslie seems to feel we have some kind of personal relationship. I don't think he understands I don't really feel that way. I may understand him, somewhat, only because I need to in order to understand where he's coming from, to understand his point of view, his motivations.

I'm agreeing to this type of communication, the odd time through thoughts and the rest of the time through dreams. But for me, this is business. Nothing personal. The fact that I have to get to know him personally somewhat—and even then, I'm hesitant to—is because of The Light. The business of The Light. Because really, I wouldn't have this life if it weren't for The Light and in the end, that's where I'll be going back to.

But more importantly, to me, Leslie represents the collective subconscious, the fears of all of us collectively. And the dangers of living unconsciously and unmindfully (like I was before I started this journey). Understanding the fear(s) is helping me understand what we'll need to do in order to ensure the survival of our species.

This is important to me. I believe in the afterlife, and I believe we experience many lives, many forms in this plane of existence, this place we call Earth. Whatever it is we need to learn, we come to this place to learn. I don't know about everyone else, but I know I want the chance to learn again, and for that, I'll need an environment that allows me to do that. The majority of us need many, many, many lives. It's a difficult place to learn, this place. Confusing. And it's supposed to be. If it were easy, we'd all be enlightened beings and wouldn't need to come here, right?

But just because it's important to me doesn't mean it's important to Leslie. That much I'm aware of.

***

As time moves on it feels to me like consciousness is never-ending, that when our physical experience is over here, we move on to a different state of consciousness. Our energy continues. In this different state of conscious we're given the opportunity to continue with our learning. What we do here determines what happens after our physical experience here.

That must be why some people who have near-death experiences, who behaved in ways that were unloving towards themselves and others, have negative near-death experiences and usually change a lot after their near- death experience. Most people have some type of positive experience with The Light.

But it doesn't matter.

The Light has a funny sense of humor. It uses people, no matter what their behavior, to teach others. Maybe that's what The Light is trying to teach me too. To not just see Leslie in a business-type way, to have more compassion for Leslie, but in a detached way. If that makes any sense.

Because I pick up on energies so much I tend to feel "too much" and want to help, when really, if Leslie wants joy, peace, and acceptance for himself, of himself, he's going to have to work on that for himself. This occurs to me but it doesn't really sink in. It doesn't sink in because I can sense the energy of Leslie's pain. And in the past when I've felt someone else's pain it affects me, in that I notice that energy and want to help in some way, mainly because I don't want to pick up on that pain.

So, what I'm learning is that I don't know how to manage my own energy. I'm learning. But slowly. Too slowly, it seems to me.

***

I'm in a bedroom, but I'm not **in** *the bedroom, neither in physical form nor spiritual form. It's like my eyes can see into this room. There's a man with very short, mostly gray hair sitting in a chair with his hands tied behind his back. He's wearing light blue cotton boxer shorts and dress socks. That's it. He's in fairly good shape. On the bed is a white dress shirt and some type of military dress jacket. There are a lot of colored bars and whatnot on the breast of one side of the jacket. This jacket belongs to the man.*

In front of the man is a woman. She's standing facing the man sitting tied up in the chair, wearing black patent, five-inch-high heels, a black leather thong and a spiked dog collar around her neck. That's it. In her hand, she's holding a cat-o'nine-tails whip.

Neither one of them knows I'm there.

I haven't had a dream like that before. I'm either in the dream in spirit form and physically in the dream, most often, or I'm in spirit form only, not as often. In that dream I was neither, which is surprising to me.

Huh.

It was as if I was looking through a window that the people in the dream didn't know was there. It felt as if that was really happening, in real life, which is creepy. A creepy scene, and creepy that I was there. I don't want to have a dream like that again. I get the feeling that dream has something to do with Leslie. Did Leslie "give" that dream to me? Can something like that happen? Or did I access it because of Leslie? What could the dream be trying to tell me?

I think about that for a while.

Leslie's main vice is power, and power, to most people, comes in the form of money. Leslie's good at finding ways to make a lot of money. He doesn't care how. Which is why drugs are a good business for him. So, blackmail and providing sex to people must be also.

So, Leslie is trying to say that it isn't his fault that people want to do the things they do. He just provides what they want. If what they do can be used against them, it doesn't bother him to do that. If it weren't him providing what people want, it would be someone else. He didn't create this system, he's just good at using it.

He has a good point.

To a large extent, I have to agree with him. Our current system is set up like a Survivor reality TV show, where the people who lie, manipulate, steal, and backstab win the prize, which is insanity. Humans are born to work together as a unit, combining each person's unique gifts to strengthen the whole. But it isn't Leslie's fault our system is set up like it is. He's just going along.

Which reminds me of the saying, "If everyone starts jumping off a cliff, do you follow them?"

Plus, there's also the other side. Leslie is involved in big business, which means mass media also, which promotes sex and drugs. He's addicted to power, so it's in his best interests to ensure the media is drowning with sex and drugs. The media is used as a form of brainwashing, thereby ensuring people use these things as outlets, instead of healthier, more balanced outlets. Which means he makes more money. Leslie's main fear is not having power/money, so, to him, he's only doing what he ***feels*** he needs to do to survive. It feels to me like it doesn't matter how much money or power he has, he'll feel he needs a lot, lot more.

I don't know what to do other than try to keep talking with him about the importance of the environment, though, and finding any way I can to illustrate this to him.

It's like telling a child if they put their finger in the fire it will burn and hurt them. They don't really believe you until they burn their finger. But in this case humanity is the finger, and the environment is the fire.

It isn't like we haven't been seeing the signs that nature has been giving us. Earthquakes from drilling oil. Oil spills polluting water we need to survive. Declining bee populations. Declining wildlife populations. Air pollution. These are warning signs. Something much bigger is going to happen if we continue this way. After it happens it'll be too late. Nature, the earth, will be fine. It will replenish. But civilizations have gone extinct before, when their arrogance has gotten out of control.

And I wonder, *Why did The Light ask me to do this?*

This is an impossible task.

I'm feeling overwhelmed most of the time, like it's a constant companion.

***

I'm hovering above myself in spirit form, looking down at me. I'm in my current apartment sitting in the corner on the parquet floor. The apartment is empty. Replacing the entryway to my door is a different entryway, a sunken entryway separated by three steps and a foyer in front of the door. From where I'm sitting, it looks and feels like there's a set of stairs that lead to a lower level.

I'm quietly sitting with my legs up against my chest, my arms loosely hugging my legs, facing the door that leads into my apartment from the hallway.

After some time, I hear footsteps climbing the stairs toward the foyer in front of my apartment door. A pair of hands sets a small wooden stool down beside the door. A small ghetto blaster sits on top of it. A finger presses a button on the ghetto blaster and upbeat classical music streams out of the speakers, tickling the air.

It feels like whoever put the stool and music there is giving this to me—a gift.

I wait, enjoying the music, a smile growing on my face.

After some time, I tentatively stand up and walk toward the music. Once I reach the ghetto blaster I stoop down and pick it up by its handle, carrying it back with me to the far side of the room. I set it down and sit next to it, placing my hand on top of it, feeling the vibrations moving through my hand, up my arm and travelling through my body. I close my eyes and enjoy the sensations.

When I open my eyes, I see something else on the stool on the far side of the room.

It's a huge gift basket! A large, light brown, woven basket is brimming with things. A large red bow is tied to the top of the handle, floppy and funny. So, the music was a gift and now they're giving me this! Wow! How nice! Who are they? I wonder.

Excitedly, I stand up and retrieve the gift basket. Then I realize, I have nothing to leave them. No pen or paper for even a Thank You note. I try sending them the thought, mind-to-mind, while looking down the stairs and concentrating on the words "Thank You."

Then I take the basket back to the corner of the room, sit cross-legged with the basket in front of me, and, listening to the music, slowly take it apart. Fruit, chocolates, crackers, a few specialty water bottles. Wow! I pick up a green apple and start munching on it while exploring the contents of the basket, lifting the items out one by one, and after reviewing each one slowly, laying each one on the floor around me. I can't get over what a nice gesture this is.

I sense some movement over by the door and look up. An older woman, in her mid-sixties, with long brown hair tied into a bun at the nape of her neck, is standing in the foyer. She's wearing a pair of plain brown pants and a beige and pink floral, long-sleeve, flowing top. She smiles at me and then looks down at the stairs close to her and smiles again, as if encouraging others. Two people shyly join her in the foyer, a man, and a woman; both look to be in their mid-to late forties. They are the older woman's children. I look down at the floor around me, at the all the gifts they've given me. Then I think, I'll share the gifts with them!

When I look up they're gone, but now there's someone standing there. He's a clean-cut man, in his early thirties, with short, dark brown hair, wearing pressed black dress pants, shiny black dress shoes, a white starched shirt with a black bow tie. He's holding a large silver platter in one hand, his arm bent at the elbow so the platter rests at his shoulder height. I can see champagne glasses and the sides of colorful crinoline paper cups on the platter.

He walks up the stairs to my living room, smiling at me. Other waiters are following him, interspersed with people wearing black-tie dinner attire. I stand up and look down at myself. I'm wearing an elegant, floor length, purple satin evening dress. On my right wrist is a fine silver bracelet adorned with small diamonds.

I look up and the room is filled with people milling about exchanging hand- shakes, kisses, laughter, and low, animated conversations. The classical music is still spilling out from the ghetto blaster, a calming symphony playing in the background. A waiter stops in front of me and offers me champagne and hors d'oeurves. Smiling, I choose a small hors d'oeuvre from the platter, thank him and pop it into my mouth.

As I start chewing I turn to my right and the wall separating the living room from my bedroom is gone.

Instead there's a cave water park, complete with two waterslides made of the same rock material as the cave, a smooth, dark brown rock. Everything's smooth. No sharp edges. There are large white candles lit and sitting in crevices and on top of rocks throughout the cave, lighting the cave with a warm, consistent glow.

Children and adults in bathing suits are splashing and playing in the pool at the bottom of the slides. Intermittently, someone catapults from one of the slides into the pool, laughing. Their laughter is staccato as they collide with the water.

Now I'm in a one-piece bathing suit, running down the cave steps into the cave and then up the steps to one of the slides. Next, I'm laughing as I turn from my back to my stomach and back again, going down the slide. Warm water films the slide. Crashing into the pool, the water tingles my scalp and caresses my face.

I'm treading water while staring at a nearby candle, flickering and flitting, while echoes of play are bouncing off the cave walls.

I look up what certain items mean and I feel into the feel of this dream. It felt authentic. I didn't recognize the woman and her grown children, though. That was really nice, though. Refreshing. Helpful. I'm thankful for this dream. It takes away some of the stress I've been feeling. It gives me faith that some understand what I'm trying to do, some that aren't "spies."

***

A few days later I'm driving back to my apartment from running errands. My turn signal is on and I'm waiting for a break in traffic to turn into the parking lot of my apartment building. I look at the sidewalk and see the woman and her two grown children from my dream. They're walking on the sidewalk toward me. By their eyes, I can tell they recognize me too.

This is the second time this has happened, where I meet someone first in a dream, and then later either meet or see them in real life: the thief and now these people.

The shock has worn off now, though, and I'm realizing that, just like in the physical world, there are all kinds of people that travel in both planes. I think they were letting me know that. I was beginning to think it was only people who were unbalanced, or confused, or who had ulterior motives.

I find this both reassuring and comforting. And I'm very thankful to and for them.

***

A few days later I receive an email, an invitation from Mr. Wing to attend a farewell dinner at a local restaurant. Mark is leaving Nova Scotia. I thank him for the invitation and let him know I'm not sure if I'll go. Next, Anna calls me and asks if I'm going. I'm not really partial to it and have, in fact, decided I want as little to do with these people as possible. These people aren't my friends; I know that.

Again though, I've been raised, programmed, trained to "be nice," but I underneath I feel angry and resentful. Regardless, after she encourages me, I agree. Because somehow, they're connected to Leslie and I know in his own way he's trying to be patient with me. Like I'm trying to be with him.

I find a card for Mark that I find hilarious. It's a boat with a cartoon guy wearing a sailor hat sitting in a wooden boat on water waving goodbye, with a huge bubble saying, "Bon Voyage!" on it. It seems to suit the occasion, seeing as I dreamt of him steering that boat and all.

I meet Anna at the restaurant. It's an Asian restaurant and we're sitting at a very large, round table. I look across the table and I recognize the man sitting across from me. It's the military guy involved in the S&M situation in my dream the other night.

Good grief.

After arriving home from dinner that evening I wonder about consciousness and what I've been learning. I try researching it online and can't decide if maybe it was a precognitive dream I had about the military guy at dinner or if I was experiencing remote viewing. I'm not sure. I don't know enough about either of them to say one way or the other.

I decide to go to one last Tai Chi class. I've paid for it so I might as well. After the class, Mr. Wing approaches me and starts talking about a well-known story in his culture. He's talking about a lone warrior who fought enemies for a long time, who had little to eat, but fought valiantly. Eventually the warrior was killed and somehow his opponents learned the only thing he'd been eating for weeks was grass, which made him more honorable. Then he tells me I've fought well, and there's no need to fight anymore.

I listen to him and say nothing except goodbye.

Afterwards, when I get home, I think about what he said and conclude I don't know what he's talking about. I'm not trying to fight anyone. I have, in fact, been trying to defend myself. The only things I've been trying to do are warn/help Leslie, while at the same time trying to learn more about this dreaming/consciousness stuff and see if there's a way I can try to repay Kyler. The fact that Leslie keeps attacking me and I have to defend myself is just part of the deal, it seems.

Besides that, there's nothing healthier for you than dark greens.

And finally, I stop when The Light lets me know it's time to stop. Not before. And I conclude Mr. Wing is confused and is, most likely, a spy.

A few months later I'm surfing the Internet and I come across a piece of anime artwork. It shows two females; one looks like me and the other looks like Anna. She's holding a plastic bag and I'm holding a paper bag. It seems to be some sort of environmental statement.

Mr. Wing created this piece of artwork.

So, he's an artist. And he doesn't understand my journey. What's more, instead of using his own life, his own experiences, to explore—use his own life as his muse, he used mine.

Which is a shame. There's so much to learn here. I thought I had learned a lot before I agreed to this journey, but I've been learning so much more than I could've imagined! I'm learning to question "reality," who I am, what I can do, how I can learn more about situations and people, what's possible, and my own fears. And with each new discovery I learn something new about myself I didn't know. Another facet. A lot of it has to do with de-brain- washing myself.

Which is difficult. Kind of painful. No wonder so few people attempt it.

***

The business I'm working for has offered me a full time permanent position. I wasn't planning to stay, though. It feels like I'm supposed to leave soon. The company has offered me $10,000 less a year, according to the temp placement agency that placed me there, than the current going rate for what I do, which makes it easier for me to decide it is time to leave. I thank them and turn the position down.

A few nights later, after work, I'm walking on a sidewalk down a street that leads to a path in a nearby park and notice a man in his mid-fifties walking toward me on the other side of the street. He seems to be staring at me and he has a grimace on his face. That's odd. I take a breath and feel into this. It feels like he's the owner of the company I was working for. It was a large company.

"Bitch," I hear him mutter as we pass one another. Huh.

Now why would he say that? I don't even know him. I didn't take a sick day while I worked for that company. Well, then. A friend of Leslie's perhaps. Doesn't matter.

I dismiss this.

It really isn't any of my business what someone else thinks of me.

***

Before I leave I want to go whale watching in Fundy Bay. This is an experience, an opportunity I don't want to miss. I make my way there, driving and crossing bodies of water, using three ferries, to eventually arrive on an incredibly small island. Less than two hundred people live on this island.

I try to imagine what it must feel like to grow up on and live in an area with so few people living around you. It must feel like a big family in a way. I grew up in the city and have lived in cities my whole life. I think it would be a refreshing change for me, one day.

I book myself on a whale watching tour and am told, along with the rest of the group, that you don't always see whales and they can't control that, so to keep our expectations realistic.

I know we'll see whales, though. I can feel it in my bones. The sturdy boat we set out on is painted white. Iron railings surround the boat. The day is sunny and bright and the waves lap against the boat playfully.

After an hour or so, the Captain excitedly points at the water a few hundred feet from the boat and we see the top of an adult whale head and then water shooting up out of its blowhole. The head of the whale is enormous. I can only imagine how large this creature is.

For the next hour, we watch it swim beside the boat, slowly getting closer. At times, it dives down and its tail bursts up out of the water, powerfully slapping down and then disappearing beneath the surface. After another hour, another adult whale joins it and then a much younger, smaller whale.

The Captain seems really excited by this. The whales gradually swim closer and closer to the boat. I keep changing positions from a viewpoint at the top of the boat, then climbing down a steel ladder to the main part of the boat, then back up again. This is incredibly exciting!

At one point one of the older whales turns over on its belly and I can see more of the length of the creature. It is fantastically huge! At another point, the youngest whale is swimming about twenty feet from the boat, when it blows air from its blowhole and I can smell it! It smells like seaweed, fish, water, salt and rancid all at the same time.

An hour later, I'm standing on the lower level, holding the rail, when I see one of the larger whales' head come to the surface, swimming beside the boat, in the same direction as the boat, no more than eight feet from me. As I look at the whale, its eye is directly across from mine.

For several suspended moments, we stare at each other. I can see in its eyes how intelligent, gentle and loving it is. With one powerful movement, it could throw the boat I'm standing in on its side, and it knows this. But it would never do this.

It reminds me of The Light and how The Light is reflected back to me in the living, natural world. The moment seems to stretch on for an eternity.

After the whale goes back under the water it feels to me as if the living, natural world is wise beyond words. They show us everything through their actions.

Their instinctive, playful, patient actions.

***

After I get back to my apartment from whale watching I excitedly try to convey how incredible it was to Leslie. How do you convey this, though? I just can't do it justice with words. I can't do it justice with feelings.

It's frustrating. I'm feeling incredibly frustrated.[6]So instead, I set about donating my furniture and packing. I won't be keeping in touch with the people I met at Tai Chi. Maybe Sophia. Probably not. My friend and co-worker, Amanda, cries when I tell her I'm moving. I let my other friend, the lady who managed the campground I stayed at when I first arrived, know over lunch. I'm grateful to have met these wonderful people.

I think about the cats. I have a feeling I'll be doing more travelling and all this moving around isn't good for them. I decide once I arrive back in Calgary I'll give them up. It's too difficult to look after them while I'm on this journey. And I don't know when it'll be over. Which is difficult. They've been wonderful companions and I've been very lucky to have them these past ten years.

And I'm not given my damage deposit back. This hasn't happened to me before. I always clean my apartments well when I leave and receive my full damage deposit back. I attempt to get it back by using a government agency, where I have to attend a hearing, where they decide in favor of my side. But I'd have to take the company who owns the building to small claims court to get my damage deposit back. What's the point of the government agency, I wonder? Small claims court will cost me more than my damage deposit in time and effort.

And I know, this has something to do with Leslie.

And I decide to let it go.

***

After I arrive back in Calgary I feel like I need to spend a little time in the Rocky Mountains. I need to feel the energy of the mountains. It's winter in Alberta. I decide to try work-sharing, where you stay at a place and work a certain number of hours to pay for your accommodations. I haven't done this before. But I find a trail riding company offering work-sharing and arrange a short stay, a week or two.

I drive there and am greeted by a horse, a large, healthy, mahogany-colored horse with white feet and a white stripe down its nose. The people I spoke with on the phone aren't home. I hide behind a tree and play hide and seek, peeking out at the horse, playing. After a few minutes of this, he trots over and lets me pet him. Whiskey Jacks fly from tree to tree. I can see squirrel tracks in the snow. The mountain air smells crisp and clean, much different from the salty air of Nova Scotia. After a while the owners arrive.

The wooden cabin I'm staying in is the main cabin where they live, an older couple. The winter is a slow period for their business. I enjoy my stay there, helping them feng shui the main house, clearing away junk and clutter that's no longer useful.

I also help them castrate three male horses, which I haven't done before. My job consists of mainly laying across the mildly sedated horses' heads, while a woman in her late twenties, experienced with castrating horses, removes their balls and something else—I can't remember what, but it's important when you're castrating horses.

Leslie is around too. I mostly notice this at night. There's an angry, pained presence around. I'm not sure what my next step is with Leslie.

***

One day a friend of theirs arrives for a visit, a young woman. I'm sitting and reading on the couch in front of a wood stove. The older man is outside working around the cabin and the woman is getting coffee ready to serve her friend. I look up from my book and see their friend standing in the kitchen, facing me, a contemplative look on her face as she regards me.

The older woman is standing in front of the sink, her back to the young woman. She's talking to the younger woman, but I can tell by the younger woman's expression she's only half-listening. She seems to want something from me. I quietly read for another ten minutes, while also attempting to gauge her energies, then climb up the ladder to my room.

This would be a good time to practice consciousness. I decide to concentrate on the young woman's energy. She didn't look upset but I'm feeling an energy underneath that she is. She's agitated, worried, concerned, frustrated.

Something is bothering her and she wants to ***do*** something about it. She doesn't know what, though. I feel into that then let that energy go, pick up my book and start reading again.

About an hour later I must've dozed off, but I'm not in REM sleep. I'm at a level of consciousness that's between REM sleep and lucid dreaming. And I see the young woman's face and then her body and she's standing ten feet in front of me. Her expression reveals she's asking, pleading with me.

I take a deep breath and using my mind say, "Rest easy," and send her waves of calm and peace. I watch as she receives the message. The lines on her face relax. Her neck muscles and eyes soften.

I slowly wake up.

Later, I climb down the steps of the ladder and have supper with the couple and their friend. The young woman is laughing and joking with the couple. The couple seem surprised, relieved, and happy with their friend's upbeat mood.

After the young woman leaves, I'm washing the dinner dishes and the woman tells me that their friend has been going through a difficult time and describes her young friend's situation a little more. I nod my head and appreciate how difficult her situation is.

Afterwards I think about the message I instinctively sent her: "Rest easy."

And I'm pleasantly surprised I could do this.

It means I've learned how I can use what I understand about consciousness and energy and can apply it to healing for those who are open, able, and willing to receive it in a more directed way, in real life, as opposed to in the dream state, where I've learned I can show people's spirit selves back to their physical selves. This is highly interesting to me.

But I also feel exhausted in a way. It feels as if trying to understand how the spirit world and this "reality" work has been taxing on me, that I'm having to learn a lot in a short period of time. At least it feels like a short period of time for me, but it's actually been years. But in the process, I've been adjusting to all of this information and building on it by experimenting, which then changes my perception, and I need time to adjust emotionally, physically, physiologically, psychically, and spiritually.

For me, it's a lot to take in. I'm pretty sure I've been screwing up a lot, but I've also been learning. A lot.

***

I drive back to Calgary and register at a temp employment agency. I'm given a temporary contract office position as an Office Manager for an educational organization in an office downtown.

I have no idea what to do about the situation with Leslie at this point, so I haven't been doing anything.

But I've kept researching ways to grow healthy food. I stumble on a concept called permaculture. I decide to take a weekend introductory course and learn more about it.

During the course, I learn permaculture is a natural nature-based design system that includes all life forms in a way where all life forms, plant, animal, insect and human, cohabit in a mutually beneficial way that provides food, medicine, and other essentials for humans. It includes the natural forms of nature available to us, like, wind, water, sun, and the slope of the land. Pesticides and man-made chemicals aren't used.

Intrigued, I decide to continue learning more about this. I sign up for a "perma-blitz". This is where a group of people get together and transform someone's yard into a food forest. A designer has worked with the homeowner, created a plan, and then a "perma-blitz" is held to transform a regular yard into a food forest that supports the homeowner's food wishes.

Pretty cool.

***

I'm hovering above myself in spirit form watching my physical self standing with Kyler on an old, cobbled, windy street. The sun is shining directly overhead. Large, smooth round rocks have been built up into three-foot-high walls of the houses lining the street. I look around and see a magnificent white castle, with bright blue turrets, a mile away.

"Whoa!" I exclaim to Kyler. "Look at that!" and point to the castle.

Kyler turns and looks at what I'm pointing at.

"Whoa," he says slowly. The wind mildly blows around his brown hair.

"Let's check it out!" I say excitedly, looking at him.

"Okay," he says slowly, "but hang on, we gotta do something first."

There's a motorcycle parked nearby. I follow him as he walks over to it, kicks up the kickstand, straddles it and starts it.

"Get on," he says loudly, over the din of the chugging motorcycle.

I climb on behind him and grasp the bar on the seat behind me as he changes to first gear and slowly turns the handle to give the motorcycle gas.

Next, we're weaving through the cobbled streets, the air cool and refreshing against my cheeks, parting my hair, and tickling my scalp.

He slows down and then stops in front of a shop with a "Closed" sign perched in its window. He pulls the kickstand out with his toe, turns the motorcycle off and dismounts. I follow suit. He stands in front of the door of the shop for a moment, then looks back at me and opens it. I follow him in.

Three very rough-looking men, in their late twenties and early thirties, are in the shop. Their eyes appraise us. A reptilian feeling washes over me. The shop is in disarray. Boxes of various sizes and colors lay strewn about shelves, some half open. There doesn't seem to be an order to anything, as if it isn't really a shop for customers.

Warily, I position myself close to the door. I'd rather be exploring the castle.

Kyler approaches them, his back to me. He starts speaking to them in a low voice. I can't hear what he's saying.

One man is leaning against the counter facing us, a toothpick jutting out of the side of his mouth. His elbows rest behind him on the counter. Another man is behind the counter; his head is down and he seems to be concentrating on using his calculator and marking things down in a small wire-bound notebook. The last man is sitting on a plastic lawn chair in front of the counter, his legs splayed out straight in front of him, crossed at the ankles, his hands folded in his lap. They're looking at and listening to Kyler.

After a few minutes, Kyler stops talking. Then slowly, the men's eyebrows draw closer to the bridges of their noses, their eyes squinting. The meaning of what Kyler said is sinking in. It appears they don't like whatever Kyler said or asked them.

Then the man using the calculator stops looking down at his calculator and looks up at Kyler, the man resting his elbows behind him on the counter steps forward menacingly, clenching his fists, and the man sitting, stands up and takes a step toward Kyler while snarling, "Come back tomorrow."

Kyler nods, turns and we leave.

I'm looking at Kyler questioningly as we mount the motorcycle. He's silent as he starts it and we ride away. I look back at the shop, then forward at the back of Kyler's head. What was that about?

Overall, I don't like it. The people Kyler talks to in my dreams seem to be dangerous and connected to the world he operates in—in reality. Which means he isn't trying to stop doing drugs and being involved in that world.

And I'm slowly becoming resigned to the fact that I may not be able to repay Kyler.

***

I continue with my daily meditation/yoga practice and thanking The Light for guidance and get ready for work.

Later that afternoon, I'm taking a break at work, standing outside my building and to the side. I watch as three white feathers swirl around in a circle in front of me.

This is a good sign.

***

A few weeks later I'm at work on a weekday. The phone rings. I answer with the standard polite greeting. There's a pause on the other end of the line.

A feeling comes over me that this call, this connection, is important to whoever is on the other end of the line. I cautiously wait a few moments and then say, "How can I help you?" ready to hang up if the silence continues.

Then I hear an elderly woman's voice say calmly, slowly, and clearly, "I'm not afraid to die."

I freeze and look at the phone, bewildered.

I don't know what to reply. There's a finality to her words, as if she's decided something very important related to her life, to her living life or not, and is simply informing me of her decision.

She doesn't want to talk about anything, or to discuss anything. She's simply stating a fact for her. But there's a loaded amount of energy, meaning and feeling behind this statement...

What.

The.

Hell.

Is.

Going.

On?!

I don't know this voice, or this person.

I feel uneasy.

Something feels very off.

I wait for her to say more, but after a few more moments she cuts the connection.

I hang up, confused, trying to make sense of the call.

Why would someone ***do*** that? ***Say*** that? Out of the blue? To someone they don't even know?!

I don't know.

What's more, I don't want to know. Because what I felt into leaves me feeling really uncomfortable, uneasy.

I'm hovering over myself, watching myself standing in a yard. Through the gate, I can see a body of water. My surroundings are foreign, a different geographical area. I don't recognize it. The air smells different and there's different foliage.

I watch as three children walk out of a building together. I understand intuitively that they are a parent-less family who look after each other.

Their eyes are wise, too wise, beyond their years.

They notice me looking at them, look back at me and stop walking. And I realize in that moment, the elderly woman who called me and said she wasn't afraid to die did something to help these children. She was well off financially. Not wealthy, but well off. And she made arrangements for them. Helped them. Whatever was going on, she wanted to give them a better, happier future. This place is new to them.

I don't know these children and I didn't know the elderly woman who called. How can I have dreams and have some sort of understanding of what's taken place with people I don't know? Of situations that don't have anything to do with me? Why is this information coming to me? Am I supposed to do something with this information? I close my eyes and ask The Light. The answer is no; I'm not required to do anything.

Yet I'm perplexed.

I still have an uneasy feeling about the situation.

I'm hovering above myself in spirit form, watching myself. I'm standing in an abandoned warehouse. Sawdust litters the floor. Sunlight is filtering through dirty, broken windows high above. Dust motes gently fall through the air, weightless. The air smells dank, old, stale. The warehouse is mostly empty.

A man is sitting in a chair in front of me. He's silently cleaning his fingernails with a knife.

The blade is six inches long, curved and very shiny.

He's about five feet eleven, and has a somewhat thin frame, except I sense wiry muscles beneath his clothes, as if he's fast. His shoulder-length, greasy, dirty blond hair lays limply on his head. His jaw is clenching and unclenching as he examines his fingernails. A thick, jagged scar runs across his right check and sears down to the corner of his mouth.

Then the following information comes to me as an instant download. This man has something to do with the elderly woman and those children. And he's angry. She did something. She permanently found a way to get those children away from this man. He killed her because of it. He's still angry.

He's angry and believes I had something to do with it. I don't.

I take a deep breath through my nose.

"Why am I here?" I ask him calmly.

He looks up. His eyes are dead. Then he goes back to cleaning his nails with his knife.

After a few more moments, he slowly says, "They always ask me that," his voice flat, but somehow also sing-song at the same time.

"But you know," he continues unconcernedly, "I've gotten bored answering. So, bored with the stupid question."

He stops cleaning his nails and looks at me.

Dead.

Flat.

Eyes.

I take a deep breath. Wait a few moments.

"Why am I here?" I ask him again, firmly, and calmly.

Because I know he can't hold me responsible for what she did. She exercised free will. And none of this has anything to do with me.

He squints at me and the corners of his mouth turn downwards, causing creases to run down his chin.

It feels like the dreams I'm having are having more to do with real life than they used to. Or maybe they always did? I'm not sure. But I definitely have to figure out how to ***not*** access information that has nothing to do with me. How does this work? How does a person control what information they access?

I really wish there was a course or something on this stuff.

So far, I'm learning consciousness, information and energy are accessible to anyone at any time. Anyone, because I don't think I'm particularly special; I just think I've been willing to try to figure this stuff out.

But right now? The phrase "Everything and everyone is connected" is taking on new meanings.

I also feel exhausted, as if I was dragged into a highly charged, emotional situation that had nothing to do with me. Which isn't great. I'm already having a difficult time balancing my energy and trying to figure out how to warn/help Leslie. Somehow, I have to figure out how to limit what information/energy I pick up on.

I have to keep experimenting. Patience.

A few days later I'm sitting on the train going to work. I think about the man in the cafe in Nova Scotia, how I caught him wheedling into my mind, digging, searching. I wonder, if I could feel him doing that, can I do the same thing as him?

I don't know.

But I wonder.

I decide I won't know unless I try.

So, I empty my mind and then with my mind, take in the energy of the people sitting and standing on the train.

I pick up a lot.

A lot.

Details from and of each person. I pick up their fears, their hopes, their frustrations, the pain they're holding onto. I keep my eyes open and watch to see if anyone feels or notices what I'm doing.

Nobody does.

Huh.

So, it's possible for anyone to do this.

I'm learning, though, that in doing this I've accessed energy, a lot of it lower energy, negative... so afterwards I concentrate on releasing any information I picked up on, because I don't want to dream about anything I did pick up on. And if I don't, then I'll know that to some extent I ***can*** control what I pick up on.

After I get off the train and as I'm walking to work, I feel into how that made me feel.

Mainly I feel like I intruded on them. I feel like I took something that belonged to them, and them alone. I didn't have their permission.

I also didn't enjoy it. What's the point of knowing this information if you can't do anything to help? It isn't fun, learning what people's fears are. Most the people weren't thinking thoughts based on hope, love, fun, or creativity.

I decide I didn't like that. Usually, when I'm riding the train or bus I like spending my time imagining myself flying beside the train. Why? Well, I suppose it's my main respite, a way I use to escape from the seriousness of what I've been learning, the information that feels like a heavy burden I've been carrying around, thinking about, wondering about, trying to figure out solutions for.

Because whipping around, turning, zooming over cars, around light poles, somersaulting, diving through the air, and dancing all the while feels good. I'm usually listening to music while I'm doing this. And I don't ride the train often, so it's a wonderful respite when I do.

And it feels so much better than diving, without people's permission, into their consciousness.

***

I review my dreams over the next few weeks. None of them have anything to do with any of the people on the train, or the information I picked up on and released.

Okay.

So, that exercise taught me ***I can*** control the energy I pick up on.

Thank God.

***

A few weeks later I'm at my desk in the downtown office I'm working in. Three middle-aged Caucasian men walk in and approach the counter/my desk. They ask a few questions about the institution. I sense they aren't here to learn more about this educational institution, though.

One of the gentlemen sits down, facing me, while another is standing behind the third man, who is leaning on the counter in front and to the side of me. Out of nowhere the man leaning on the counter in front of me starts talking about fracking.

At length and in detail, he starts passionately describing the process while walking back and forth in the lobby, gesturing with his hands, and looking at me.

I watch and listen to him. Not his words, but his energy. He seems fearful.

Arrogant.

Greedy.

After a few minutes, I look at the other man standing. He's raptly listening to his friend. My eyes move to the man sitting down. He's watching me. I watch his expression and after a moment he looks ashamed and drops his eyes.

Unsure what to make of this, I start ignoring the man speaking, put one of my MP3 earphones in my ear, and start listening to a song as I begin working on a project I've been assigned.

About five minutes later, the man who was explaining the fracking process in detail approaches the counter again. He asks for directions. I politely provide him with directions.

They leave.

A few hours later I get the feeling Leslie sent those men. It feels like Leslie's showing me the type of individuals he deals with; thereby how difficult it is to convince these people of the importance of preserving and promoting our environment. He's also showing me that he shares their viewpoint, which means I'm not doing a very good job of convincing him.

As I'm leaving work at the end of the day I receive a thought communication from Leslie.

One word.

"Political."

That's it. He's telling me all of this is political, and he isn't in charge of it. Which means, maybe, just maybe, he understands what I'm trying to warn him about, but that he can't do anything about it?

I'm not sure. Leslie is arrogant and self-serving, so this is also a word he can use as an excuse. But it's also the only thought, or word, he's sent me so far that has anything to do with what I've been trying to warn him about over these past years. I think about it. This word may or may not represent progress. Maybe I ***am*** making progress. He communicated with me.

I think about this.

The only thing stopping our civilization from moving from dirty energy to clean energy is greed, which is one of the faces of fear. Collectively we've all agreed to some extent that this space we inhabit on earth is ours for the taking, not ours to responsibly look after. At the same time, though, a lot of people are beginning to choose other, more nurturing ways to live connected to and responsibly with nature.

I go back to thinking about the word Leslie sent. He met me somewhat in the middle. He understands what I'm saying. Of course, it could also be a mind game; Leslie seems to like playing mind games. I'm not sure he's even capable of an honest interaction.

But it does make me wonder, am I pressing this point too far? Am I being too polarized in my viewpoint? I mean, obviously, I am, but I'm simply the other side of the scale. Clearly a more reasonable stance to take would be to invest energy in the solutions. I am doing that, though, by learning what's holding us back as a species.

And for the purpose of warning Leslie, I've had to take the complete opposite stance. Could I be over-emphasizing the importance? Could my intuition could be off?

It doesn't feel like it, but it also feels like Leslie doesn't hold much merit in my intuition. But if he's willing to send me a word, to illustrate what he believes the problem is, to show me one of the reasons why, I'm willing to give him the benefit of the doubt.

The thing is, I feel I've been pretty patient so far—with the, for lack of a better word, spies he arranged in Nova Scotia, the child he was assaulting, the constant stalking, the way he's been under-the-radar bullying and attempting to scare me, and the overall way he's disrespectful towards me.

The problem with this situation is first, there's no face-to-face speaking but, on second thought and because I'd like to actually live through this, maybe that's okay, but I know it always helps to talk with someone directly (if they're relatively balanced), and second, because of his fear of losing power, i.e., less money, he doesn't want to entertain other options, other creative options—where he can still have his power and the environment can be protected and the energy of nature re-vitalized at the same time, thereby ensuring the survival of our species.

Patience.

Again, The Light is teaching me patience.

After work, I'm walking down the city street to the bus stop where I catch my bus.

As I'm walking I'm looking straight ahead and can see something at the far end of the block, in the air. Its energy draws me. Its graceful shape moves in the wind within the air, white flashes of feathers. I watch as a magpie flies six feet above the sidewalk, heading toward me. I continue watching as it flies closer and closer, landing on a pole three feet from where I'm standing. Our eyes are locked. It has messages for me.

Then the magpie starts speaking... quickly. Using its voice, it changes tone and pitch, a secret language. In my peripheral vision, I see an older man, in his late fifties, standing under the pole. He's looking up at the magpie, listening, and then looking at me. I'm keeping eye contact and listening to the magpie, ignoring the man.

After about five minutes of listening, with my mind I send a message to the magpie.

"Ok, it's okay."

The magpie stops talking, blinks at me, cocks its head, continues looking back at me for a few more moments, then flies away. Speaking with animals, wild or not, means you have to be open to their energy. This magpie provided me with a lot of information and energy. And I need time to digest it.

I also decide that this was a sign to investigate if my intuition is off, whether I've been over-emphasizing the issue with Leslie. Because the magpie doesn't seem to think so. I decide I need to gather more information about my intuition and how it's linked to nature/the environment, to test and check its validity.

So far it seems to be pretty good, but I'm open to being wrong. People make mistakes. I make mistakes. I've been making mistakes. I could be over-reacting. I don't think so, but I have to make sure.

***

I've been working for a temp agency at the company I'm working for. The educational institution offers me a full-time position. I thank them and turn it down, opting instead to go to Alaska. Somehow some of the answers I'm looking for will be found there. It just ***feels*** like that. I don't know why.

Of course, again, how do I explain this to my friends or family? Obviously, I can't.

***

Using the Internet, I find a farm in Alaska looking for people interested in work/share opportunities. The last experience I had with work/sharing was positive, so why not? I've never worked on a farm before. I call and speak to a woman who gives me directions to the farm. I pack some clothes, a First Aid kit, sleeping bag, pillow, clothes, toiletries, extra toilet paper (I don't know why), cell phone and my camera and choose a route using secondary highways. I'd like to see as much wildlife as I can on my drive. It should take about three days.

I leave during the last days of May. The drive is spectacular. A falcon flies across my front window, its wingtip almost touching the window. I see a brown bear, and I see a grizzly bear and her cubs feeding off the side of the highway. At one point, I notice cars stopped ahead of me on the highway and as I'm slowing down I can see why the cars are stopped. A herd of bison are walking on and alongside the road. The cars are pulled off to the side of the road and stopped. I continue driving, but very slowly, by the parked cars, keeping an eye on the bison on my left, not three feet from my car, and the bison ahead and on my left. They're gradually moving to the sides of my car.

A motorcycle loudly pulls up on my left side and rides alongside me for a moment. A young bison, startled by the loud noise, is walking on the left side of the motorcycle, and begins to hurry its step while moving toward the center of the road. I look to my right and can see another bison, an adult.

It feels like it's the young bison's mother walking with its head turned toward the younger bison. I slow down more so the motorcycle moves ahead of me and then I stop. The young bison stops, looks at me and then begins crossing the road in front of me. Its mother has stopped on the other side of the road. Once it reaches its mother, they touch noses. I watch them for a moment as they look back at me.

I continue driving until I reach Destruction Bay. I'm not sure what time it is. Destruction Bay is a lake surrounded by tall hills, like a basin.

When I drive into it the sun is setting and brilliant oranges, pinks, reds, and yellows are reflecting off the surface of the water and the red soil of the hills surrounding it—a firework of warm, vibrant colors.

I have no idea how long I've been driving... I haven't been looking at a clock. I usually gauge what time it is by the position of the sun in the sky. It feels like I've been driving for a really, really long time though. After I pass through Destruction Bay I look at my eyes in my rearview mirror. My eyes are super bloodshot.

I dig out my phone and look at the time. It's midnight and the sun is still quite high in the sky. I've been driving for seventeen hours! I think about this for a minute. In the summer the days get longer and the farther north you go, the more pronounced this is. I haven't been this far north before and I had no idea the sun would still be so high in the sky at midnight!

I'm about an hour from the U.S./Canada border. It's dangerous for me to keep driving at this point. I'm basically punch-drunk tired. I decide to look for a place to sleep. Once I pass the border it's only about eight hours to the farm I'll be working/staying at for the summer.

There are a few places to pull off but they're full of vehicles. I keep driving and end up finding a spot. There's a gravel road leading off the highway that dips down beside the highway. There's enough room for one vehicle. I decide to park there and catch some sleep. A meadow lies to the right of where I park. It's raining lightly when, exhausted, I quickly fall asleep. Before I fall asleep I hear a man laughing on the road above where my car is parked.

It sounds like Leslie.

***

HOOOONNNNNK... HOOOOOONNNNNK... HOOOOONNNK

Waking, I look at my cell phone and see it's about six hours later, and I'm hearing a horn blaring and men shouting. Dazed and with a great deal of effort, I start sitting up and look out my window. I can tell my less than shoulder-length hair is a bizarre mess and sticking out all over the place.

Looking around and then up, I see two men standing on the highway above me, looking down at me while shouting and pointing toward my car.

I look where they're pointing and see a pond out the window on the right side of my car. Huh. It wasn't there before. It's still lightly raining.

Then I look down at the floor of my car… and see it's filled with water!

Up to the bottom of the seats!

Jumping into the front seat, I hurriedly begin turning the ignition key, praying the car starts.

The key isn't in the ignition!

Jumping back into the backseat, I dig up my car key and jump back into the driver seat.

I turn the key and the engine turns over!

I heave a sigh of relief and place the car in drive, driving out of the small pond, where I park the car and, leaving it running, I start using a plastic container to begin bailing the water out of the car. This takes quite a while and it seems like it's slowly filling back up as I'm emptying it.

Once I'm satisfied I've done the best I can for the time being, I decide to brush my teeth, wash up and then find a gas station where I can buy a hot drink and relax for a minute.

Ten minutes down the road I find a gas station, buy a coffee, and look at the floorboards again. They still need to be sopped up.

I open my trunk and pull out the sixteen-pack of toilet paper and drop the rolls onto the floorboards. They soak up a lot of the water. Then I chuck the soaked toilet rolls into a garbage bin.

I notice my purse was on the floor in front of the passenger seat. It's soaked. My wallet, cell phone and the rest of the contents are dripping.

Huh.

Well, not much I can do about that.

I continue driving and reach the border. The border patrol man sitting in the kiosk asks me for my passport. I pull it out of my purse and apologize that it's a little wet. The man gingerly takes it with his thumb and forefinger, holding it like a very tiny miniature skunk.

"And how did it get like this?" he asks me, admonishingly.

I tell him how I didn't realize how long the days are in the summer up north, that I haven't been this far north before, and that I usually use the sun to gauge the time. I didn't realize I'd been driving for a long, long time. I pulled off the side of the road to sleep, it was raining a bit, and when I woke up I was in a pond and the car was somewhat submerged.

While I'm telling him my story he's looking down and concentrating on using tissue to wipe the outside and inside of my passport.

When I finish my story, he looks up at me.

"Is thaaaaaat riiiight?" he asks me, slowly and sarcastically, one eyebrow raised.

I look at him like he's crazy.

"Yeah… it is."

Why would someone make up a story like that?

The right side of his mouth turns up slightly, and he hands me back my passport and wishes me a good visit.

I thank him and continue on.

***

Finally, I arrive at my destination and discover… it isn't really a farm. There are about six chickens that lay eggs. There's somewhat of a garden that the owner wants help with, growing raspberries and potatoes, and an orchard. There's an old heritage homestead house that the owner rents out, as well as two other cabins. I'll be cleaning the cabins, collecting eggs, and working in the gardens. And other duties the owner assigns. I ask if anyone needs paid help and she mentions a nearby restaurant looking for a dishwasher; one of their dishwashers recently quit.

So, I begin my summer of washing dishes at the nearby restaurant four days a week for ten hour shifts and working on the "farm" about four hours a day. I ask the owner if there are native, edible plants I can use to make salads and the owner points some out for me. Pesticides aren't used at the farm.

I haven't had a job as a dishwasher before, and the work is strenuous. Really strenuous. A spike in tourism during the summer means the restaurant is busy. I gain a newfound respect for dishwashers.

I meet some of the other people who are work-sharing at the farm. Most have been to Alaska before. All of them are from the U.S. Most only stay for a few weeks. Only a few have agreed to stay for the summer.

One day I'm working in the garden and a man rides up on a tall, pale Clydesdale horse. He says hi and we exchange polite conversation. The horse's light blonde mane waves at me. There's something about this guy, though—it feels like somehow this guy is connected to Leslie.

And I know if I want to learn more I'm going to have to hang out with this guy.

Which I'm not overly enthusiastic about, because this guy is like Leslie-not much respect for himself or women. He's the playboy type, which means he really doesn't like women. And he most likely has a drug addiction.

But I need to learn and understand more. He invites me over for a beer and I accept. He lives close by; is a neighbor of the owner of the property I'm working/staying at.

***

The owner of the property I'm working/staying at invites me to go mushroom picking and I join her a few times. At one point a particular mushroom is ripe and after it's been fried in olive oil and garlic it tastes citrus-like. It's delicious. I help the owner collect mushrooms and sell them at the local Farmers Market a few times over the summer. Out of curiosity I go mushroom hunting on my own and end up collecting fourteen different species of mushrooms. Determining which ones are edible is difficult, though.

Sand hill cranes often land elegantly in the meadow in front of the trailer I'm staying in. Their flowing movements as they walk through the meadow remind me of ballet dancers. They choose one mate and mate for life. If one of the pair dies, the other one will call for it forlornly, day after day, and will not choose another mate for the rest of its life.

***

I try using an outdoor shower. I haven't done this before. It's amazing to smell fresh air and have fresh air surrounding me while showering. The water runs cold after five minutes, though, so the showers are quick. The owner collects their water from rain barrels and we use this water for cooking, washing dishes and hand washing ourselves.

When I'm not washing dishes at the restaurant or working at the farm, I start hanging out with the man who owns the Clydesdale horse, the neighbor. We sleep together. It feels to me like this had to be done. And I never said I was a nun. Of course, the sex is crappy. But I'm attempting to show Leslie I have nothing against the people he knows.

And I learn in a roundabout way this guy does indeed have something to do with hard drugs and he runs his own "crew." That he's violent, although he does nothing to me. His particular thing is meth. Nasty drug, that. I hang out with him a few times a week. When I do I drink beer, which I'm not particularly fond of, and smoke pot occasionally, which is very strong and, of course, has no seeds.

***

At one point during the summer I'm cleaning one of the cabins. A helicopter pilot had been renting the cabin for quite a few months. As I'm cleaning the cabin I can smell propane. Strongly. The owner drops by and I ask if they can smell the propane. The cabins are heated by propane tanks. The owner can't smell anything. I ask if they can bring someone else along to double check. The smell is overwhelming to me.

The owner does, and their friend can't smell anything either. I'm insistent, though. And I don't understand why they can't smell the propane.

The three of us use water and dish soap around the nozzle of the hose connected to the propane tank. Rapidly forming bubbles tell us there are two large leaks in the hose connector. The propane is leaking. They seem surprised. I'm relieved. Sometimes I'm not sure if I'm smelling, seeing, hearing, and understanding things that my senses are warning me about. I have, after all, been told I have quite an imagination.

***

I learn that the moose have been hunted almost to extinction near the populated and even outer reaches of denser populations in Alaska, and three historically common species of fish here have been categorized as endangered.

I spend my summer this way, learning new things and trying new things, like planning two by ten pieces of wood, sanding the inside of a cabin, cleaning cabins, washing dishes at the restaurant, exploring the beach and noticing the different plant life, insects, and animals... and collecting information. Lots of information. I continue doing my daily meditation.

***

I welcome the opportunity when the man with the Clydesdale horse I've been hanging out with about three times a week invites me to go salmon fishing. It isn't the type of fishing I've ever heard of, though. They use spears and hooks.

Intrigued, I accept. I've noticed he has erratic behavior, probably because of the meth he does. He's about the same age as I am. He doesn't seem to have a routine. He says he picks up odd jobs. I sense he's seeing a much younger female. I think this younger female is someone he uses to sell his meth. Of course, she doesn't think she's being used. She thinks he cares for her. And she seems threatened by my being around him. Good grief. This is the life of someone like this, drama. They crave drama.

I couldn't care less about all of it; the only thing is I know that somehow one or two important facts about nature, our environment, are going to be uncovered by me interacting with him.

That's all I know.

It's the middle of the day in mid-August. We're traveling by boat to an island renowned for its salmon. There're about eight of us in the boat, people who are somehow business-related to the man with the Clydesdale horse. The neighbor. It feels like they each have their own "crews". Again, I couldn't care less about what they do. Not what I'm here for.

On the way there, one of the guys on the boat tells me that there's a fish farm located at the top of the falls we're heading to. He tells me all the salmon are farmed, which means there aren't wild salmon in Alaska anymore. I nod to him.

This information is important. I don't know how, but it is.

I stand up on the boat to look at the island we're heading toward and notice to my right, fifteen white birds flying in the same direction and beside the boat, in sync with the boat's speed, about ten feet from the boat.

This is a good sign. A sign from The Light I'm on the right track.

It also unnerves a few of the people in our group who notice, but there's nothing I can do about that.

We reach the island and climb up the rocks beside the falls until we're at the top. Once at the top, I see there's a beautiful pool of water. The current is strong so only an adult can stand still, with some difficulty, while using their spear to stab a salmon. I watch as the people I traveled in the boat with take turns spearing salmon.

I smile encouragingly when they victoriously hold their speared salmon in the air. They look happy. After they reach their quota we climb back down to the bottom. At the bottom of the falls a fast-running river runs out to the sea.

Then, standing on the sides of the river, they wait for a salmon and are using a really thick fishing line with a massive hook on the end, and they throw the hook at the salmon, hoping the hook catches on some part of the salmon's body. If it catches on any part of the salmon's body they yank viciously on the line to bring the fish closer to them, so they can hit it on the head.

The fishing is frenzied, fast and barbaric.

These are forms of fishing I've never witnessed.

I'm used to fly fishing in rivers and spin casting on lakes. The type of fishing where you relax as you enjoy nature and the experience as a whole, taking your time. Where the type of fly you use is chosen carefully (based on the weather, time of year, condition of the water, the bugs in and around the water), and you use patience, cunning and an understanding of the water currents to determine where the fish are likely to be.

I decide I'm partial to the way I've fished and not so much to these ways.

Afterwards I thank the neighbor and head back to the farm I'm staying/ working at.

I'm in spirit form, hovering above myself, watching me. I'm sitting, balancing, on top of the post in the center of a red, painted, merry-go-round, the kind you find in a children's park. The merry-go-round is spinning very fast. I look and the neighbor, the one I recently went fishing with, is standing on the outside of the merry-go-round with one of his friends, who also went on the fishing trip. Both have malicious grins on their faces and they're bent forward, using the strength in their arms to push the merry-go-round faster. I'm not sure why they have those looks on their faces.

"If you keep making it go faster, I'll jump!" I shout cheerfully at them.

Their grins grow more malicious and they work harder to push the merry-go-round faster.

I use my hands to lift myself to a position where I can move my feet underneath me, and balance myself on the small top of the center piece of the merry-go-round. I wait a moment and then push forcefully with my legs.

Next, I'm diving through the air and as I'm getting closer to the ground, I tuck my head in. As I make contact with the ground, I use my hands and arms to pivot me forward into a front somersault. I realize halfway through the first somersault that I'm dealing with a lot of velocity, so I do another five somersaults to slow myself down and end up lying flat on the ground on my back.

I put my hands behind my head and smiling, look up at the sky. It's a beautiful day.

Huh. So, the neighbor actually has quite a lot of malice towards me. Well, I suppose it's not that surprising actually.

The merry-go-round thing reminds me of the boat dream I had with the military guy in Nova Scotia.

What's with these guys and spinning around?

I'm not sure if the neighbor shared this dream with me or not. I decide to visit the neighbor and let him know I'll be heading back to Canada soon. He smiles at me, the smile never reaching his eyes, and tells me to drive safely.

In the meantime, one of the other workers on the farm talks to me about how he wants to try gold panning. He says that there are places in northern Alaska you can go and legally gold pan.

I haven't been gold panning before. It might be something interesting to try for a few days before heading back to Canada. He doesn't drive. I tell him I'll think about going for a few days, and if I decide to try it, he can come with me. He's ecstatic.

***

I decide it'd be fun to try gold panning. I let him know and we plan the date we're leaving. He lives in the U.S. but he wants to drive back to Canada with me, after gold panning, and then catch the bus back to his home in the U.S. afterward. We'll be gold panning for two days.

While driving I get to know him better. He's about fifty years old and a little rough around the edges. I get the feeling he experienced trauma as a child. I'm starting to wonder how many people haven't?

We listen to music, enjoying each other's company, and appreciating the scenery. He likes sipping on beer as we drive. I suspect he's an alcoholic but his moods don't swing erratically and he seems fairly calm.

We arrive in a place called "Chicken," so named because when the town was first formed the townspeople couldn't agree on how to spell ptarmigan. We stop and enjoy a drink at the only bar in Chicken. There's one restaurant, one store, one gift shop and a small bar. For some reason people's driver's licenses are pinned to the walls of the bar. Hundreds of them.

We leave and find a campground where we set up, gather our gold panning gear, put on our rain boots and hike to find spots to gold pan. The sun is shining, the sky is clear, and there's a cool crispness to the air, gently warning of Fall. Leaves have started to turn and the trees are changing their clothes. Reds, golds, yellows, oranges, and greens dot the landscape.

We arrive at a somewhat wide river. There's a small creek running in front of us, separating us from a piece of land that's closer to the river. I tell my companion I'm thinking of gold panning on the other side, across the creek, closer to the river.

He studies the creek for a few moments, then looks at me and says seriously, "We can't cross it. It's too deep."

I look in the water. It's about five inches deep. The water is clear. We're wearing tall rain boots.

"Sure we can!" I reply enthusiastically.

He looks at me astonished. "No, we can't! Look! It's too deep!"

Perplexed, I look back at him and then look back down at the water. It's still only five inches deep. I decide not to say anything. Instead, I start walking through the water and across to the other side. I don't look back.

We end up gold panning in that spot that afternoon and the next day. We find some gold, not a lot, but the experience and the area is amazing.

He thanks me for bringing him and I thank him for the idea. It was fun. I decide to take the Top of the World highway back to Canada.

As we're attempting to cross the border, a border patrol person asks me to pull over, park and wait. They ask my companion to step inside the building, into an office.

Apparently, there's some problem. He isn't allowed to cross the border. He tells me he lost his license from drinking and driving. I tell him no problem, we'll go back the way we came and I'll drop him off at a place he can catch a bus.

After I drop him off and continue driving back to Alberta, I start noticing wildlife. Bison, birds, elk, moose, bear, swans. Then it occurs to me, the four days I spent with that guy? Not once did I see or have an experience with wildlife. Which is very unusual for me. It's normal for me to see wildlife when I'm in nature.

Huh.

As I'm driving back through Destruction Bay, I decide to stop in the middle of the bay. There's a road that circles the inside of the bay and there's also a road that crosses through the middle of the bay. I drive on the road that crosses over the water, stop and take a few pictures.

I get back in my car and look at the pictures. There are five ghostly white forms in one of the pictures. They're hovering above the water, about five feet tall. The forms are indistinct and spirit-looking, see through-ish. But they're there. This is another sign. Higher beings are watching. They stay close to me. This is a good sign.

And it reminds me of a story I once read. A tribe of aboriginal people were gathered around their medicine chief. The medicine chief had called them to the top of a cliff overlooking the ocean. In the distance the medicine chief saw ships heading toward their land. None of the people could see the ships because they hadn't seen ships before. So, their brains couldn't process what was physically in front of their eyes. Once the medicine chief began explaining what the ships looked like, the people began to see them.

And it occurs to me, this is what the spirit world is like.

I continue driving into the night, hoping to make some time. I'd like to get back in two days, not three. At one point, around two o'clock in the morning, I pull off in a gravel parking lot next to a cafe/gas station. It's closed. I need to fill up. I don't want to chance it and keep driving, as gas stations are sometimes few and far between this far north. I decide to park and sleep for four hours. The cafe/gas station opens at six in the morning.

I'm hovering above myself in spirit form, looking at myself. I'm sleeping across the back seat of my car, in the parking lot I just parked in. My blanket is pulled up under my chin.

My spirit form sees the man, the neighbor to the farm that invited me fishing, creeping up to my car door, the one closest to my head. The man pulls a long, flat piece of metal from his back pocket, quietly slides it into the crease between the door and the frame of the car, and gently pops the door open.

I wake up, in my dream, as the man is reaching in and grabbing me. He's a large, stocky man and easily pulls me out of the vehicle. He has a leather belt he's wrapped around one of his fists and he's trying to use the belt to strangle me.

One of his hands is in front of my mouth. I open my mouth and bite down. Hard. He screams, then releases me.

Well, I knew that even though he acted as if he was friendly toward me, he wasn't. But to try to kill me? A little over the top, if you ask me. I mean, I didn't do anything to harm him, so I'm not sure what to make of it.

It was unsettling, though.

I start my car and move it closer to the only streetlight there is, then turn the car off and fall back asleep for another hour. Then I use the gas station to wash up, brush my teeth, buy a coffee, gas up and keep going.

On the rest of the drive back I think about the clues I gathered while I was in Alaska.

The main one that keeps standing out to me is the discovery that there are little to no wild salmon left.

This is important, but I'm not sure why.

***

After I get back to Calgary I research this. I find out that a scientist who's been researching the main forest that runs across Canada, studying the bark of trees, has found alarming evidence. The main forest that stretches across Canada is connected by a mutual root system and the growth rate of the forest has diminished by half over the past twelve years. The reason?

Wild salmon.

Bears catch and eat wild salmon. The mother bear will catch fish for her young, and once she does the young will take their fish farther into the forest to eat in seclusion. The cubs don't eat all of the fish and their leftovers, the remaining portions of the fish, break down, becoming nutrients, and feed into the soil. The nutrients are then collected by the roots of the trees in the forest, which are all connected by their root system.

Farmed salmon doesn't contain the nutrients the forest needs to grow at the rate it used to. The nutrients aren't as rich as the wild salmon. This fact has, in fact, cut the growth rate down by half, making it weaker.

Everything and everyone is connected.

So, my intuition was correct.

The energy in nature, our environment, is lowering - decreasing.

And I'm relieved, very relieved, that my intuition has been giving me correct information all along. I wasn't crazy and I wasn't imagining it.

It is happening and it is cause for concern.

And I also think about the guy I went gold panning with. He was an alcoholic. So... fearful. And the whole time he was with me we didn't experience nature to its full potential. And it occurs to me. Nature is on a higher energy plane and will naturally stay away from lower energies.

Leslie is fearful, so lower energy. Maybe this is why I'm having such a hard time explaining and trying to get Leslie to understand. He hasn't experienced any beautiful moments in nature because he isn't connected to it. Isn't connected to himself, because of his fear.

Okay.

That was helpful to determine. What can I do about that, though?

I decide to let that sit for a bit.

It was a very worthwhile trip.

***

In the meantime, I look into permaculture some more and join another "perma-blitz". Each time I do this I learn something more about permaculture and how incredibly amazing it is. It isn't at all like traditional gardening. There's little to no weeding required. And

I volunteer and participate in a few more perma-blitzes over the summer. I learn how to use the slope of the land, how the land is positioned in relation to the sun, how to capture rainwater to feed the plants, what plants, when planted close to one another, promote more growth, and the importance of design when first planning to transform an area of land into a food forest. Most the hard work is in the planning and initiating the forest.

I also take some books out of the library and learn more about native plants. Many of them are edible and some of them medicinal. I read about how a local farmer found a large cache of walnuts in a hole by a stream on his land. The walnuts were over fifty years old and still fresh. Native American Indians used the land before the farmer. They dug a hole close to the stream, filled it with walnuts and then covered the hole with leaves, branches, and sticks. This preserves the nuts naturally for years.

And I wonder to myself, *why didn't I learn things like this in school*? After spending twelve years in school I was only able to read and write. But being able to grow healthy food, identify edible wild plants and learning how use natural plants medicinally—these are life skills. Survival.

Then I start thinking about how relaxing and therapeutic growing food in nature is. How beneficial it is to our environment. And I wonder, *why aren't there programs where incarcerated people can grow healthy food for themselves and their communities? Why are we shipping food in from other countries, when we can be growing it for ourselves within our own country? Why aren't churches growing food for the needy on their properties? Why aren't food banks growing food? Why aren't schools teaching children how to do this?*

Because based on what I've noticed, the benefits are incredible. Peace, enjoyment, and exercise for the person doing it, healthy food for those enjoying the harvest and a general increase in higher energy for our environment.

I'm hovering above myself in spirit form, watching myself. I'm walking on a concrete path that weaves through a field in an industrial area within a city. The field is large, about as large as three football fields. It rolls and undulates around me, wild grass growing. There's a cloudless, powder blue sky above. A wire fence borders the field to my left.

As I'm walking I'm noticing people sitting or lying in the field. Each person is about three feet from the other. There are hundreds of them. I keep walking but start looking closer at the people closest to me as I'm walking past them.

Most of them are between the ages of sixteen and fifty. The odd one is well dressed. Most are wearing regular street clothes, jeans, t-shirts, runners, or sandals. They seem to be frozen or something. They aren't moving. All of them have blank looks in their eyes and slack mouths, unaware of themselves or their surroundings. Like they're in a state of diminishing.

I stop and look closer at a young man close to me. There's a discarded needle lying close to him. He's a heroin addict. They're all heroin addicts. I start walking and notice ten feed ahead of me someone is standing in the middle of the path facing me.

Leslie.

Abruptly I turn left, walking off the pathway onto the grass. I plan to climb the fence. I reach the fence and find it's twenty feet high. At the top are three steel rods running above and horizontal to the fence, about a foot apart. Three rows of barbed wire run horizontally between the steel rods. I notice a gate cut into the fence a foot away. A thick padlock hangs, locked, connecting the gate to the fence. As I walk in front of it to inspect it, a small man materializes and unlocks the padlock. I open the gate and leave.

Another dream of Leslie and hard drugs. Why am I still looking for information about Leslie? Why?! I must be somehow still trying to figure out how I can reach him. So, I feel into this.

It feels like Leslie is a drug addict too. Not heroin but some other hard drug. Cocaine, maybe? Yes, that feels about right. So, in order of addictions/ illusions, Leslie's first one is power, then drugs. Illusions of fear. That can have very real effects in the physical realm. I determine Leslie isn't equipped to make an informed decision whether my intuition is on target or not.

I appreciate that, in his own way, he's been trying to understand, but in the end, he doesn't. It would require him to make changes to overcome his own fears, and it's difficult to overcome fears. It is freeing, though.

The tricky part is you won't realize how freeing it is until you've done it.

Then I wonder, just how far has it gone? If I've noticed it here in Canada, how much has the energy, nature, deteriorated, or is it deteriorating, on the rest of the planet?

I take another temporary office position in an office downtown and work there for three months while I feel into what my intuition wants me to do next.

***

After some time, I decide I'm going to the earth's lungs, the tropical forests of South America.

I sell my car and buy a plane ticket. I'll have to figure things out as I go once I get there. I don't speak Spanish.

Chapter 8:
Ordeal

"Not only the thirsty seek the water, the water as well seeks the thirsty."

— Rumi

I arrive in Quito, Ecuador where I first stay in a hostel. I take a week to acclimate and get my bearings. There's an older man, in his late fifties, who works at the hostel I'm staying in who suggests I take a certain herb. I get a good feeling from him. He's a healer and knows a lot about plants. He doesn't speak English very well, though. I use a translator on my laptop to communicate with him. I take the herb he suggests, because, again, I'm exhausted by all I've been learning and doing but it feels important to keep learning, keep trying to understand.

I feel a marked improvement in my energy level.

I also, during this time, think about Sophia. She was from South America and was also interested in plants and their healing properties. I really want to think the best of her.

I decide to clear my mind, be objective, remove any expectations I have of her, and speak with her over a video call one last time to determine, if we are, in fact, friends. She's the only person from my Tai Chi class in Nova Scotia I've kept somewhat in contact with. And I've only had contact with her twice since leaving Nova Scotia.

I ask the man if he can talk with my friend Sophia about the herbs he's been talking with me about. Sophia can translate to English for me. This will give me a chance to objectively decide if she is my friend. I call her on video, explain to her about the herbs the man is suggesting for me, that he doesn't speak English, and ask her if she can translate for me by speaking with the man. She agrees to.

I watch her face, her eyes, her body language, during the call. Five minutes into the call I know she isn't a friend. She is some sort of spy. I say goodbye to her and it feels like she knows I know. She looks ashamed. And the situation reminds me of Alice in Wonderland, where the dog who was the Queen's servant had to betray Alice, because otherwise the Queen would harm his family.

Well, what do you do? She did what she thought she needed to do.

In the end, I have to do what's best for me. Plus, it proves to me once again, my intuition was accurate in the past. I need to trust in it more, instead of believing what I want to about someone.

Be objective. Have no expectations, and listen to my intuition more. Be thankful for it.

Then I think about Mark, how it feels like he knew what a difficult situation I was dealing with when I was living in Nova Scotia. It feels like he was trying to add to my confusion. So, I send him, "You're a jerk!"

In some way, I'm wondering how far a thought/feeling can travel. Not that I don't mean the thought I'm sending him, because I do, but I also wonder if it matters.

Later that evening I wake from a dream. I was dreaming of a snake and the snake bit me. It feels like the snake was Mark; that he received my message and was sending me back his response.

Huh.

Ok, it seems even halfway around the world you can send and receive energetic messages to and from people.

Then I think and feel into it more. If Mark is an alcoholic, then that means he's in pain, pain he hasn't been willing to deal with. So, addiction. So, fear which covers pain he hasn't healed. Which means his pain is festering inside him.

And it wasn't kind of me to send him that thought. I consider this some more. He's confused. Then I decide to send him a thought of hope. Hope that he uses his courage to heal and live a healthier, happier life for himself.

And I conclude, once again, I need to be more mindful of my thoughts. They are powerful.

***

I decide to look for some type of work while in South America—teaching English, maybe, or finding a work/share opportunity. I'm not rich by any means. I find a few places to send my resume to and begin visiting the local art exhibits, parks, and shops. There's something to learn here that's important about the environment too, but I'll have to feel into it, recognize the opportunities and go by feel.

I receive an email back from a Birding Tour business. They have three locations: one in Quito, which is an arid area at a high elevation, the second is located in the cloud forest, and the third is located in the jungle.

Their website describes them as eco-friendly. They're looking for someone who speaks English who can assist their English-speaking customers. Most of their employees speak only Spanish. I'm expected to provide my own food, except when I'm asked to eat with the guests, and work approximately six to ten hours a day, although there will be slow times when I'll have more free time. I accept the offer.

The man who owns the Birding Tour business picks me up from the hostel. He's Ecuadorian and in his late forties. He seems friendly. We drive in his van to his secured, wealthy home where his wife, mother and three grown children live.

He asks me to wait in the living room. I can hear him having a heated conversation with his wife in the kitchen. It feels like the argument is about me. I hear his wife say the word "political." I don't speak Spanish but something feels off about this. Then I think about Sophia, who is linked to Leslie.

This feels like Leslie. Leslie has something to do with this arrangement.

So, Sophia alerted Leslie about where I was. Makes sense.

But it also makes me wary.

The owner eventually enters the living room and introduces me to his resigned-looking wife, his three children and his mother. He then drives me to the central operating place of his business in Quito. On the drive, I remind myself what I came here to do.

I came here to learn, find clues for my intuition, determine what, actually, is the current state of our natural world in the rain forests near the equator, and what factors are influencing our ability, as a species, to survive into the future.

The grounds of the place I'm staying used to be an old colonial-style hacienda of a wealthy person. There are walking trails, a pool, a banquet building, an office with an attached restaurant/billiard/game rooms, a large conference-style meeting building and a motel-like building. I'm staying in a room in the motel-like building.

I'm not sure why the business represents itself as "eco-friendly." So far, I've learned they don't compost or grow any of their own food. It doesn't seem like they even recycle. Maybe "eco-friendly" doesn't have many guidelines at this establishment, or maybe this is the state of what eco-friendly means in South America. I don't have enough information to make an accurate conclusion. I consider eco-friendly to mean they try to leave as little of a carbon footprint on the natural environment as possible and are constantly striving to improve.

As I'm walking up the trail to the motel the smell of eucalyptus fills my nose. I notice large, different-looking seeds on the ground. I pick one up. It reminds me of the buttons on a sweater my great-aunt gave me. She wore the sweater often in the winter and I've brought the sweater with me. I ask about the seeds and am told these are eucalyptus seeds.

The next morning I'm thinking about my great-aunt, and I wonder if she's trying to tell me something. I turn on my MP3 player and Elton John's "Your Song" begins playing.

This is my great-aunt's spirit sending me love.

***

I spend my time helping out in the office. The owner is asking me if I know computers very well. I know a little, I tell him, and ask him why. He tells me he's landed a contract to publish a birding tour book for the city of Quito and he needs help creating the book. I tell him I know something about desktop publishing software. He asks me if I'll help create the book and I agree to.

In the meantime, I've been asked to hostess a wedding taking place on the grounds. I'm to direct people to their dinner tables and offer assistance when needed.

I bring along my camera and because I'm bored most of the time, I film parts of the wedding, which goes on for the better part of the day and night. The photographer the couple hired seems to keep getting in the way of the footage I'm taking, but I'm also quite far away from the proceedings because the zoom on my camera is good.

Later, I edit the video footage and put together a seven-minute video of the highlights of the wedding and add music, including the bride's favorite song. I tell the owner of the business what I did, show him the video, and he encourages me to call the couple. I do and they're eager to view it. Once they arrive the woman tells me the photographer they hired canceled at the last minute and sent his uncle, who isn't a photographer. She tells me the photos they received were terrible; people's arms and heads were cut off in the photos.

I show them the video and after a few minutes, look at the woman to see she has tears rolling down her face. She's ecstatic with the video. The couple offer me a bottle of wine and I give them the video. I haven't made a video for anyone before.

***

After a few weeks goes by I'm asked to go to the cloud forest location, which is at a lower elevation than Quito. There are two buildings located on the property there, the main building which houses the rooms and a restaurant. There's a local Ecuadorian couple that work and live at this location. They manage the grounds, the restaurant, and the accommodation building. The wife looks after the cooking and cleaning, while the husband serves the food, looks after the grounds, and takes guests on birding tours. They're a nice couple. Neither speak English.

The first night in my room I look out the window at the stars. I don't have any lights on in my room. Outside of the city the stars are bright, winking and twinkling in the sky. It's pitch black outside and there's no light except from the stars in the sky. Except... in the far distance on top of a high hill I can see a light.

Then, as I'm standing at the window I sense an energy right outside the window... I close my eyes and feel into this energy.

It's small. It's afraid, and very, very sad. It feels like a baby monkey. I can see its face and body in my mind. And then I hear whimpering. The baby monkey is whimpering. It feels as if it's calling to me, wanting and needing me to pick it up. Hold it. Console it.

Keeping my eyes closed, I concentrate and feel into this energy more. The baby monkey's mother was taken from it and the baby is on its own. That's why it's afraid. It doesn't know what to do. Instinctively, I want to go outside and pick up the monkey. Hold it. But that would be the wrong thing to do, especially to a wild animal. Not because it would hurt me; it's too young to, but because it would create an image of what humans are like to the baby monkey. That humans are safe. And some humans aren't.

I don't want to interfere with the monkey's ability to survive in the wild.

I take a deep breath and send to the baby monkey, "You are very, very loved. You need to go away from here... deep, deep into the forest. Stay away from humans. All humans. They are bad and will hurt you. Avoid them at all costs. Find others like you. Be aware of what's around you. Your mother is with you in spirit. She loves you very, very much."

I open my eyes. I don't hear whimpering, but I know it's still there, looking at me. I can see it in my mind's eye, what it looks like. Its eyes. It understands what I'm sending.

I keep standing at the window. After some time, I sense it moving away, deeper into the forest.

After I get back to Quito I research monkeys. The baby monkey I saw in my mind's eye and communicated with was a dark brown woolly monkey, a type of monkey found in the region I'm visiting.

An endangered species.

Also, a species of animal critical to spreading nutrients, in the form of seeds, throughout the forest.

The next morning, I'm somehow able to communicate a question to the groundskeeper. I'm asking what the light was on the hill in the distance I saw from my window last night.

He tells me an oil rig.

***

A week later I'm asked to help the groundkeeper with a re-planting project. I have leather work gloves and work boots. I help the groundskeeper transplant plants from one location to another. At times, I'm by myself and I listen to my MP3 player and sing as I'm digging.

But "by myself" isn't really accurate. At times, I sense Leslie's around.

After a week of this the tops of my hands are covered in bites, even though I've been wearing gloves. The bites are very itchy and an inch high. I ask the groundskeeper if there's any medication on site for this. He nods at me and wordlessly asks me to join him on a hike. I follow him down a trail for some time.

At a certain point, he steps off the trail and using his machete, swings it at a tree. He looks at me and says, "Dragon Tree" and using his finger, beckons me to come closer.

When I do he points to the sap running from the tree. It's red and runny, like water. It looks like blood. He pulls out a small container and collects some of the sap. Then he uses some moss at the bottom of the tree to fill in the gash he just put in the tree.

We sit down on a log and he lifts the sleeve of his arm, revealing a large, ragged scar, running from his shoulder down to just past his elbow. He points to the sap. He's communicating that he used the sap from the Dragon Tree to heal his wound. He encourages me to rub some on my insect bites.

I do, and as I keep rubbing the watery, red sap turns into a creamy, pink cream. And the itching goes away. It reminds me of calamine lotion, what my mother put on me when I had the chicken pox as a child. Now I know, calamine lotion is a very watered-down version of the actual sap of the Dragon Tree. I thank him for sharing with me.

Within two days the bites are completely healed.

***

I go for a walk with him a few days later and am talking to him about permaculture, how the slope of the land can be used to capture the water running down the property, and off it and, using my hands and pointing to the water running off the property, tell him how beneficial it would be to build areas on the hill to capture this water, for the birds and other wildlife. I explain it'll also prevent the land from eroding due to water. For some reason, I'm not concerned that he won't understand me, even though I'm speaking English and he doesn't understand English.

Because somehow, he does understand what I'm saying; his eyes tell me he understands and he's nodding his head.

After the re-planting project is complete I spend most my time in the restaurant working on the bird book. The restaurant consists of a small enclosed building with an attached wall-less building.

In front of the tables are about ten hummingbird feeders. I keep my camera close to me and intermittently take pictures of the hummingbirds feeding while I work on the book. There are many species of hummingbirds. They're the jeweled delights of South America.

I learn a lot about these tiny, amazing creatures. I shoot video of them and try to take clear pictures of them, which is difficult - they're extremely fast.

One day I'm leaving the restaurant area after working on my computer. I'm walking on the path beside the bird feeders, heading back to my room. I sense something to my right and look to my right as I'm walking. A hummingbird, a male Buff-tailed Coronet, is flying at the same speed and in the same direction as I'm walking and turns to look at me at the same time.

We continue walking/flying in the same direction for about six paces, then we both stop, cocking our heads while looking at each other and thinking, *are you copying me?* at the same time.

Then we realize we're two completely different type of animals and at the same time we think, *Nah!* look forward, and start on our paths again.

As I'm walking away I can hear the groundskeeper and his wife laughing. They must've witnessed this interaction.

It doesn't occur to me until a few moments later that that hummingbird might've been having fun with me.

This makes me smile. This is what the natural world does: it delightfully surprises you in unexpected moments.

***

The next day I sense Leslie is around, and this feeling continues for several days.

In the meantime, some guests have arrived. Most the guests are wealthy Americans. At dinner, I'm asked to eat with the guests. I learn an elderly man, in his early eighties, is a seed geneticist. He's accompanied by his daughter, in her mid-thirties. His daughter seems to have taken an instant dislike to me, which is fine; not everyone gets along with everyone.

Later in my room I feel into the energy of the man. He has something to do with GMOs and being a part of creating them and profiting from them. This is why his daughter dislikes me.

It appears she feels that the way I feel about GMOs is harmful to her father. I'm not clear how I, one person, can affect anything related to her father or his business. Personally, I think her father is brilliant. I just think his brilliance can be used in a different way. But I understand she loves him and feels the need to protect him. But I don't understand why she feels the need to protect him from me.

Then I understand. This has something to do with Leslie. Something he's told her.

And it isn't as if I'm unaware that Leslie has been talking negatively about me to many people. I haven't looked online to check this because I know what I'll find. He's been attacking my character, ridiculing me, digging into my past, and basically doing everything he can to attack me.

What he doesn't seem to understand is, I don't care. It isn't that I'm oblivious; I simply don't care.

***

The daughter is trying to steal my wallet. I end up getting it back.

I wish these people would knock it off. It's my choice to determine what's good for my body and what isn't.

It's also my right to have an opinion. I wonder, maybe they haven't taken the time to experiment with the foods they eat and decide objectively for themselves how their body feels?

***

A few days later, the owner of the birding company asks me to go to the jungle location. It's at the lowest elevation in Ecuador. I agree to.

The next day I catch a ride into the nearest town and am waiting at a bus stop for the bus to arrive. A black helicopter flies into view and then hovers above and in front of me.

For five minutes.

Leslie.

After another two weeks, while in the jungle, I finish the birding book and the owner is pleased. He's asked me to create a second, much more detailed birding book. I agree to, but for a fee. He isn't happy about this, but I'm also working a lot more hours than I anticipated.

The jungle location includes an accommodation building and a separate restaurant. The owner is building another, much, much larger building on another piece of the property. All the properties are large, with many walking trails.

The first night, as I lie in my room reading, I hear monkeys in the surrounding jungle, talking and screeching to one another. I leave my room and stand on the balcony, looking out into the darkness of the jungle.

Then I see it. A small red firefly whisks artfully through the air below me, zigzagging up towards and past me and out into the jungle night again.

This is a good sign. It's also the first time I've seen a firefly in real life.

***

The owner seems to be hanging around a lot. He also seems to be acting like he wants to have an intimate relationship with me. This isn't going to happen, for a variety of reasons. Number one, he's married, and number two, because I know his behavior has something to do with Leslie. I'm not sure why Leslie keeps trying to do things to make this a personal matter. This is business, nothing personal.

And especially after that guy in Alaska? No dice.

***

The next guests that arrive are a couple. They're a handsome couple, in looks only. They're in their late forties. The woman is the dominant one in the relationship, and the man is passive-aggressive. They aren't a happy couple. It feels to me like she runs a big company, something in the pharmaceutical area. And she, like the others, isn't happy with me.

I can't help but wonder what Leslie is saying to these people, or if other things are happening I'm not aware of. But do I really need to find out any more?

No. I have to stay focused on what I came here for. I don't have the time or energy to deal with that stuff.

That day, the handsome, unhappy couple can't find a trail that leads to an elevated bird observation platform. I ask them to follow me and hike up the trail to the platform, then wish them good luck.

On my way back, I'm looking at the trail ahead of me. On the dirt path about fifty feet ahead is an animal walking on the same path, in the same direction as me. I haven't seen this animal before. It's the size of a medium-sized dog, yet its face reminds me more of a cat. Its fur is sleek and shiny. The animal stops walking and turns around, looking at me. I stop walking. We regard one another for a few moments. Then the animal starts walking again. So do I, while I keep watching the animal.

An inner knowing tells me to be wary of this animal. After walking another twenty feet the animal stops walking again. I stop walking. It turns again and looks back at me. I look back at the animal. After some moments, it turns and resumes walking again. I do too.

The trail turns a corner and then leads farther down into the jungle, where my accommodations and the restaurant are. As I turn the corner I stop and look for the animal. I can't see it. Then I hear loud, staccato barking sounds from high up in the tree I just passed. The animal that was ahead of me.

That evening I eat dinner with the handsome, unhappy couple. The woman sits across from me. She definitely doesn't like me. Her body language and the way she looks at me confirm this. I'm polite to both of them but the meal is decidedly uncomfortable—for me, anyway.

It feels like this is the norm for them.

***

The next morning I'm eating breakfast with the handsome couple. I'm sitting across from the woman again. I sense something and look to my left. The animal I saw yesterday is balanced on a fence rail ten feet away. It looks like a mixture between a dog, a cat, and a wolverine. It's slender, yet it looks powerful, wiry, quick. It has massive, sharp claws on its feet and a small, sleek head. Shiny, short, dark brown fur.

The animal turns to look at us. The three of us are mesmerized. I, however, have slowly grasped my knife. The animal silkily, stealthily, jumps onto a sitting bench, somewhat closer to us. It peers at us, sizing us up. It isn't intimidated by us at all. Nor should it be. Not in these circumstances. I look from the animal to the woman and back to the animal again.

The animal looks me in the eye for some moments, takes a step forward as it moves its head to look at the other woman, while sniffing the air. After a few moments, it jumps into a nearby tree, moving off into the thick jungle canopy.

The handsome, unhappy couple leave for their next destination a few hours later.

I learn this animal is called a Tayra. The Internet says it's a meat-eater. The Internet says it eats small mammals. This isn't true. The locals call it the monkey-killer.

And based on what I saw, I don't think it'd have any issues killing a human if it wanted to.

After this round of guests leave I take a day off and travel to Mindo. I hire a taxi to take me to an Orchid Garden. Taxis aren't a common sight in the rural areas. I also want to visit a Butterfly Garden, but today I'm going to visit the Orchid Garden first. The taxi driver is cute—what I consider normal, healthy. He's open-minded, polite, not fearful and has an authentic, happy disposition. I ask him if he'd like to pick me up later and drive me back to the lodge in the jungle. He agrees to.

The Orchid Garden is run by a woman who runs a hostel within the large orchid garden. She has a piece of land with various huts/cabins interspersed all around and her Orchid Garden, with hummingbird feeders, weaves its way around the property. It's lush and wild, yet also tame in a subtle way.

I spend the day taking pictures of all the different species of orchids. They vary in sizes, colors, and shapes, and I had no idea there were this many. The natural world is amazing on so many levels.

It's like The Light, impossible to fathom.

The taxi driver picks me up after I've spent the day at the Orchid Garden, and we stop at a hut on the side of the road on the way back to my accommodations and drink a beer together. He's doesn't speak any English. Still, we manage to have a few laughs. He's in his late twenties. We have another beer then he drives me back to the lodge.

When we get there, I ask him if he'd like another beer. He nods his head, smiling.

I'm the only one staying at the lodge for the moment.

We hike down the trail, get to the lodge, and drink another beer. As we're sitting drinking side by side on a balcony, I find him trying to give me a hickey on my neck. I stop him from doing that but decide what the hell? He's cute and he's good company. And besides sleeping with the guy in Alaska, which was for the purposes of showing good faith toward Leslie and was decidedly unsatisfactory, I haven't had sex in like... seven years? Maybe more?

Also, I'm making a statement to Leslie, showing him that I'm not stupid, I can recognize a person who doesn't have ulterior motives, and that I know the owner of the business I'm working with is connected to Leslie and has ulterior motives.

Besides, I'm not a nun. I've had to completely forego a personal life in order to try to understand and communicate with Leslie.

Plus, I'm not getting paid to do this. This is my own research project.

My friend doesn't seem confused about his sexuality, he likes women, he seems to like me, he isn't an alcohol or drug addict, he isn't looking at me as a ticket to gain access to Canada, and he's fun to be around. He just doesn't speak English.

I ask him if he has condoms. No, he doesn't. I let him know if he goes and gets some we can have sex. Whoever said you have to learn the language of a foreign country must not have realized that body language, the language of facial expression and eyes, is incredibly effective. Because my new friend seems to understand me just fine. He lets me know he doesn't have any condoms on him but he's going to get some and will be back soon.

When he gets back later he tells me, using drawings and pantomime, that when he got back to his car one of his tires was slashed. He had to change it and put his spare on.

Huh. Leslie?

Most likely. He seems to have a thing for slashing people's tires. Whatever. My job is to help him by warning him, not take orders about my personal life.

And I'll give my new friend his due, what he lacks in style he definitely makes up for in enthusiasm. But I decide if I sleep with him again I'll need to teach him some of the finer points of lovemaking. Enthusiasm is great, but style trumps it.

He shows up unexpectedly a few days later, pleasantly surprising me. We share a beer, some laughs, some pantomimes and have another roll in the hay. I decide I'll be heading back to Quito soon, and from there back to Canada. Which means I probably won't be seeing him again, so there isn't a point to teaching him some of the finer points, for me anyway.

He wants to "friend" on Facebook. I like how he thinks. We're simply enjoying each other's company. He doesn't want anything from me, and I don't want anything from him. I genuinely like him and he feels the same toward me.

No expectations.

***

One day I decide to take a break from the computer. I've been working in the wall-less eating area of the restaurant, occasionally taking pictures of hummingbirds, parrots, and other wildlife. I decide to walk down to the waterfall at the bottom of the trails and take video footage of the waterfall. I take my tripod with me.

Once there I take off my socks and shoes and set up my tripod in the water. As I'm filming the waterfall I see something move quickly out of the corner of my eye. I stand straight and look around. Directly in front of me is a male Purple-Bibbed White-tip hummingbird hovering in the air a foot above and in front of me.

It's looking at me questioningly, with its head cocked to the side. And it occurs to me, I've been taking video and photographs of these creatures as if they are foreign to this world, this planet. Because I've only seen one hummingbird before, in Nova Scotia, and I haven't seen this many hummingbirds, or this many varieties of hummingbirds before. Seeing how they interact with one another is fascinating. They're incredibly territorial.

The way this creature is looking at me, it feels as if I'm the foreign creature. It's curious about me, wondering what I'm doing in ***its*** world. I smile at the hummingbird. The sun is reflecting off its head and throat, the majesty of its colors. We continue appraising one another for a few more moments, then apparently satisfied, it flies off.

Which one of us is foreigner, I wonder?

The next day the owner asks me to travel back to the main location in Quito. I'm catching a local bus. I've made some good headway with the second bird book. It's tedious, time-consuming work and I also need to cross-reference details with another reference book.

During the five-hour bus ride the bus driver has a local radio station playing. A Spanish voice is speaking. It's the news. The Spanish language contains many words that sound like English words. As I listen, I understand that the President is issuing incentives for people to trade in their old cars for new ones. Incentives for people to buy cars.

So. They're trying to westernize South America. Create a want, and then profit from it.

If people want cars, then they'll need gas. If they need gas they can't complain when oil rigs destroy their natural habitat, as well as their traditional way of life.

This isn't very good. The news is mass media. Alongside it they play commercials of things they're trying to brainwash people into thinking they should need, should want. And to a large extent, they're successful, because they're playing on people's fears of not "having" or "wanting" what they should "have" or "want" to be normal. To fit in.

It's somewhat like the drug business. People who aren't ready to or don't know how to heal their own pain, transform it into something positive, seem to pass it along to the innocent, and then those innocent also feel ashamed, guilty, bad, wrong. In turn, they'll want to push those negative feelings aside and become drug addicts, or shopaholics, or alcoholics, workaholics, whatever. Unbalanced. It's all like some kind of terrible wheel of misinformation.

And there are those who bank on this.

***

As I'm riding a public bus to Quito, I take in the atmosphere. Unlike in Canada, the bus driver chooses music to play and it plays on the speakers for all the occupants to hear. The seats are comfortable.

There's a young man standing in the aisle two seats ahead of me. He's looking at his phone. He looks like an average young man. Except I know he's involved in street culture. Something about him doesn't seem right. As if he's watching me. Or has been paid to.

Yes, this would make sense. It also feels right. Leslie would be getting people to tail me.

I observe the young man. His energy seems belligerent, which means he's fearful, which definitely means he's from Leslie's world.

And I wonder, if a bag moved in the holding area above our heads that line the upper sides of the bus, where the passengers can store their bags, backpacks, packages…

I wonder… if one of the bags moved, would this alarm the young man? Because this would alarm someone who is fearful and tailing me. If I'm wrong, then it wouldn't bother them at all.

A few moments later the bus gently turns and my tripod bag, the only bag among many, moves from above me and slides a few feet toward the young man, stopping near the young man's head.

The young man looks up from his phone, stares at me angrily, grabs my tripod bag, which has stopped moving, and slams it down a few times in the carrier above, glaring at me.

I look back at him, expressionless.

Yes, he definitely has something to do with Leslie. That experiment confirmed it.

And I wonder… did I actually make that bag move? Because that was quite a coincidence…

I'm in spirit form only, watching two Ecuadorian women in their mid- to late twenties walking side-by-side down a steep hill. Gray, ominous storm clouds are gathering in the distance. The terrain looks familiar to Quito. Adobe houses and one story businesses flank the street. The two women are the only ones on the street. It's early evening and the eucalyptus smells heavenly.

The pair look healthy and happy. They're lovers. The taller one is wearing a silver-sequined, sleeveless top with dark jeans and boots. The shorter woman is fawning over the taller one. Adoration spills from her eyes. The taller one is laughing and lapping up her partner's adoration, shining her appreciation on her lover as the whites of her teeth gleam. Their skin glows with vitality.

The taller woman has done something, though. She's a drug dealer, but surprisingly isn't a drug addict. But she's done something not kosher in the drug dealing world. I watch as they continue walking down the hill. Suddenly three husky men dressed in dark, baggy jeans and t-shirts run soundlessly out from the shadows beside a building, behind the two women. Too late, the women sense the danger.

As the women begin to run they're both caught. Screaming, grunts; arms and feet are flailing. The shorter woman breaks free. The men want the taller woman. The shorter woman is not of consequence to them. So, they let the shorter woman go. The shorter one doesn't want to leave her lover.

"Michelle!" she screams hysterically at her partner, who's fighting against the arms pinning her arms behind her back and dragging her backwards.

"Run! Run!" her lover screams back at her as she's being dragged away.

I watch the shorter woman running away, terrified and crying, looking back often, and yelling her lover's name. The men drag the taller woman to the door of a nearby, sign-less, building.

In spirit form, I hover closer to the taller woman and follow behind as the men drag her into the building and close the door. They drag her down about twenty stairs to a very long, dimly lit, wide hallway. At the end of the hallway is a closed, steel door. Garbage is strewn on the floor. The air smells musky with old body odor, sweat and fear.

The men push her forward, ahead of them. She knows what lies in the room at the end of the hall. She won't live through this. She leans back and falters. She hears a noise next to her and stops. The men behind her allow her to stop.

Next to her a man is sitting on the floor, his back against the wall. Tufts of hair haphazardly stick out from his mostly balding head. His teeth are rotted. His eyes roll around, showing the whites, in his sunken face. His body is mostly collapsed and shriveled. His naked chest and face are teeming with weeping sores. It's hard to say what age he is. He's shirtless and wearing a very dirty pair of grey khaki shorts. He's a heroin addict. He's also lost his sanity. He has a knife.

He looks at the woman's assailants and in a cackling, sing-song voice says, "I got hungry a while ago," then he looks down at his right calf. A large chunk of flesh is missing from his calf. Dried blood cakes the floor underneath his calf and the knife he's holding. With his lips closed, and a smile growing on his face, he looks back up at the men.

The woman gasps in horror.

The men start laughing and one throws a small packet of paper filled with drugs at the man on the floor. The men push her forward again. I hover closer to her, just above her right shoulder. I know she can feel me. I silently call out to Archangels Michael, Gabriel, Raphael, and Ariel to be with her. To stay with her. To cover their wings over her, protect her soul and give her serenity in her last moments. I stay with her on that long walk down that long hall until I feel the Archangels. They're here.

Most of my dreams I'm in spirit form watching but also my physical self in my dream. In this one I was only in spirit form. It felt like this really happened, which is awful. I wonder, *Could this have really happened? Why would I access energy/information like this?*

Two days later I'm riding a bus through Quito and on a wall, written in very large, red letters is: "I MISS YOU, MICHELLE."

So that dream was showing me something that was really occurring, in real time. I don't know what to think or feel about this.

At this point a lot of my dreams, which I need to access information, are overwhelming me. Somehow, I'm trying to shut down my feelings, my emotions, about the information I'm receiving.

Which is difficult, because in all of them it feels as if I can sense what others are feeling.

I only have four days left in Ecuador...

***

I decide to visit the Poor Man's Galapagos. This will give me more information about the natural state of this place, how healthy it is, if there are any threats, and if there are, what they are.

It will take me about twelve hours by bus to reach this destination. Once there I plan to book a tour to Silver Island. I'll have time to go on a tour for the day, then it's a full day bus ride back to Quito before I have to board my plane back to Canada.

I meet with the owner of the bird touring business and let him know where I'm at with the bird book. Its ninety percent done. He wants me to give him the electronic files. I tell him I can, but that if I do that he's going to have to re-do a lot of the work I've done. Once he opens the main file, he'll need to re-attach all the separate photographs one by one. There are over five hundred of them. I don't think he understands me, although I try to explain this to him three times. It feels like he thinks I'm trying to force him to let me finish the project, which I'm not. But I also don't want to see my work go to waste.

In the end, at his insistence, I give him back the files. He shorts me on the fee we agreed on. Whatever. I let him know I'm going to go sightseeing for the remainder of my trip and ask if I can leave my suitcase at the lodge. He agrees.

Early the next morning, I start my trip. The bus ride is a long, grueling twelve hours, with the bus stopping only four times along the way to allow the passengers to grab something to eat, go to the washroom or stretch their legs. There are few people on the bus. I wish I could fall asleep on buses, but I can't, so I spend my time observing the other passengers, the landscape, the towns we pass through.

I arrive at the small town by the sea at two in the morning. A cab takes me to a hostel near the beach. I sign in and book my tour, which starts in six hours. I'm exhausted.

As I'm unlocking the door to my room I notice a bent, burnt spoon sitting on the low concrete wall opposite the door to my room. The tin roof of the neighboring business sits on the other side of the wall.

I wash up, change my clothes, opting for underwear and a t-shirt as pajamas, and fall asleep immediately.

I'm hovering above myself in spirit form and I'm also my physical self, standing in my private room at the hostel I just checked into. Instead of the wall in front of my bed in my room, separating my room from the next room, there's a large, sunken living room. New-looking rattan furniture with white cushions sits in the living room. Healthy potted plants sit on the floor and hang from the walls.

A thin, unhealthy looking man in his late twenties walks into the living room and up the stairs toward me. His eyes are sunken. He's wearing baggy beige, light cotton pants, no shoes, and a long-sleeved, light blue dress shirt. The shirt swallows his thin frame. He's a heroin dealer and drug addict. I stand and watch him as he reaches the top of the stairs, nods to me, then takes a chair and places it under the handle of the doorknob to my room. He turns and looks back at me. This is thoughtful of him. He's trying to assure me I'll be safe. I don't require this, though. I'm not doing anything wrong. It seems like drug addicts, in my dreams, are fearful and think everyone else is that way too.

I wave my hand in a brushing motion at him and send him, "Remove the chair, please." He nods, removes the chair, and looks back at me. I nod my head at him respectfully, thanking him. He nods back at me and then leaves, walking back down the stairs to the sunken living room.

I wake up to my phone alarm and review this dream. Okay, another dream about someone I don't know. There's no doubt in my mind that the man in my dream owns this hostel, and he either lives close by or in the hostel. But I don't have time to think about that anymore right now. It really isn't relevant to what I'm here for anyway.

I wash, brush my teeth, dress and find a restaurant to eat breakfast. After that I go back to the hostel and wait for the tour guide. There are about twelve people going on the tour today. We're riding on a boat out to Silver Island. The day is sunny and beautiful. Fishermen have already laid out their day's catch on the beach.

Once we reach the island only two of us want to hike around the small island. The tour guides warn of muddy, slippery trails and advise against it. Two of us insist. A guide takes us on a hike around the island. The island is full of Blue Footed Booby birds, the rarer Red Footed Booby, and multiple other species of birds, along with different species of cacti, trees, and flowers. I take a lot of pictures and struggle to keep up with the guide. We spot a Peregrine Falcon.

After the tour and boat ride back, I visit with a few of the locals on the beach and learn that an oil refinery will be built nearby soon. It's a big project.

Naturalists are concerned about the impact this will have on the fishing and tourism industry, including the tour I'm on, as well as the effect it'll have on their natural environment.

And I know, if big business weren't encouraging people to buy vehicles, they wouldn't need to build this oil refinery.

Most the oil won't stay in their own country anyway. Their land and waters will become polluted and the profits will go to people who don't live where they've polluted. On top of that, there seems to be a high percentage of people who work on oil rigs or at oil refineries who have drug or alcohol addictions, or if they don't initially, they eventually do. This also negatively impacts the local people.

Eventually they're going to run out of spaces that aren't polluted, though. I wonder if they've thought of that? Or if they realize the compounding implications each one of these incidents have on the overall balance of the natural world…

I don't think they do.

I catch my bus and take the long ride back to Quito. Once there I call the owner of the bird tour business. I need to collect my suitcase and want him to know I'm heading to the hacienda to do this. I also want to thank him for the opportunity to intern for him. As soon as the call connects and he realizes it's me that's calling, he's angry.

He's saying the electronic file I gave him doesn't work. The book isn't there. I try to explain to him again that the book is there, but that all the photographs will need to be re-attached to the main file. I'm not sure why he doesn't understand this. I offer to finish the project again. He declines.

I retrieve my suitcase and fly back to Canada.

Once I arrive I'm stopped in customs and asked to move to the side.

A customs officer is standing at a desk with my suitcase on top of the desk. He's opening it, but I notice someone has already looked through my suitcase. He's acting as if no one has opened my suitcase yet.

He searches through my suitcase while asking me questions about my trip: where I went, why I went there, how long I was there, where I visited when I was there. Lots of questions. I answer the best way I can. I haven't been stopped by a customs officer before. This situation seems odd. I haven't done anything illegal, haven't been around anyone who is doing anything illegal as far as I know, and it was a "pleasure trip", as far as anyone else is concerned. Also, I'm exhausted and this is annoying.

I've been to Thailand, the Dominican Republic/Haiti, Mexico, Korea, and some states in the U.S., and I've never been detained like this.

Leslie?

Yes, most likely.

Eventually, I catch a cab to my home, settle in and think about my trip. I'm overwhelmed by the amount of information I've gathered, both in terms of my intuition, consciousness, and my dreams, as well as the information I gathered about the current state of the land containing the lungs of our earth.

I'm in spirit form watching the physical me. Physical me is standing in a white room, but there are no walls, ceiling, or floor. There's a window in front of me. It's round-looking, like those little round windows on the lower decks of a ship, or like a window in a spaceship. I'm walking forward to look through the window, the portal.

I get a feeling as I'm walking toward the window, the portal, that the place I'm going to be looking at is a time/space that rests alongside what we call "reality." I can climb through this portal and "be" in this dimension if I want. But for right now, I just want to look through the portal.

Wherever it is, it's dusk, and the sun is slowly setting in the sky. Brilliant reds, golds, purples, and oranges are flowing into one another, painting a warm, glowing horizon.

A healthy forest brimming with ferns, shrubs, multiple varieties of trees in various stages of growth and plant life are busy singing life into the air. Birds are insistently calling out to each other.

To the left a body of water gently meets a sandy shore, littered with small, gray stones. Each stone is uniquely shaped and different from the other. Every small, gray stone has a white circle around it. A large silver fish suddenly bursts from the water ecstatically, sending diamonds out as it lands in the calm, clear turquoise.

My distance from this piece of land is about twenty feet.

Then a being walks out of the forest toward the water. The being is shaped like a human: head, eyes, ears, nose, mouth, arms, hands, torso, legs, feet. Its skin is a tawny, golden brown. The being somehow glows with vitality. Life. There is something else very different about this being. A feeling comes to me to regard it as I do the Archangels, with reverence and respect. I sense the being knows I'm watching. I sense it feels I've earned the right to observe it.

The being's ears are small and lay flat against its head. It doesn't have hair on its head, as such. The texture of its hair looks mossy, like dark brown fur... dense, thick, and very short, ending un-neatly at the nape of its neck.

Three-inch circles of this same fur cover the being's body. The width of the circles is one inch. Inside the center of the circles is the being's skin. The being's chest is flat. The being is neither male nor female; it has no genitals, but somehow seems to be an elegant combination of both male and female. The being stands about five foot eight.

I watch as the being walks toward the water. Its movements are graceful, contemplative, yet animal-like. It's neither slender, nor stocky, but somewhere in between.

Power emanates from its pores.

Somehow, with my mind, the portal zooms in closer on the being as it begins walking slowly into the shallow water, until the water is to its knees. Then the being begins lying down on its side in the water, in a semi-fetal position.

The being is completely submerged in the water. No bubbles rise to the surface. The being can simply exist in the water. I watch as the being closes its eyes. It's going to sleep in the water. Sleeping in the water. Yet it looks humanlike, and walked out of a forest moments ago.

So, the being can live in both an air and a water environment. Interesting.

But why? Why does it sleep in the water?

This felt real. This place or dimension I was looking at was real, somehow. I don't know how. It must be another dimension that lives in a similar time/space. Or one that lives in our time/space but on a different level, a level we can't perceive. Yes. That feels right. The being I observed is as real as I am.

The being has something very important to do with the natural world I live in. It just feels that way. I don't know what, though. I haven't ever dreamed the same dream twice. Or returned to the same place I've dreamed about.

I think about wanting to re-visit this place, though, to learn more about this being, learn more from this being. I'm not sure how to get back there, though.

This also makes me think about the time/space continuum. It isn't as lateral as I've been taught. While we use a calendar and a clock to operate in day-to-day life, there's also another layer, or layers, of time/space that exist, ones that don't operate laterally. My dreams have given me plenty of evidence to this effect.

I've been looking for work since I arrived back in Calgary. It's been about a month and I haven't found anything yet. It feels as if Leslie is hounding me still. I don't know what he wants from me. The sneaking around and doing things underhanded is getting on my nerves.

I've continued practicing meditation and continue to eat as healthy as I know how to. I'm struggling with giving up coffee, though. I love the taste of it. I keep switching to decaf and then stopping altogether, which means a few days of withdrawal symptoms. Headaches.

When I drink coffee, decaf or not, because my system is so clean, my system reacts to the chemicals in the coffee. Red splotches appear on my face beside my nose after I drink it. So, I know it isn't good for me and I know it's negatively affecting my intuition. I'm having a difficult time removing it from my diet, though. Much harder than I had removing meat from my diet.

I'm in spirit form hovering above myself, and I'm also myself in physical form. I'm standing near a vacant lot in a city. Weeds and garbage litter the unused, wasted space. It's later in the afternoon; storm clouds are gathering in the distance. The sun is being filtered through long, wide, wispy clouds.

Kyler is standing in front of me, his hands open, palms facing up and stretching toward me. He's asking me something. He pulls at my hand, then kneels on the ground, mind to mind asking me to look down. Then, grabbing a nearby twig, he starts drawing something in the dirt. Directions. He's giving me directions.

He's offering me a place to hide out. With him. And with whoever the people are he hangs out with. I respectfully watch him until he's done. The directions are intricate. It's a well-hidden place. He's offering food, shelter, safety, and protection. But he's a heroin addict, and he hasn't shown any signs of stopping. So, he's involved with lower energy stuff, drug dealing, stealing—that kind of thing. I have no intention of living there and want nothing to do with that world.

Each to his own and everything. It's not my thing.

He's done drawing and is looking up at me expectantly, waiting for an answer. Although I'm not interested, I appreciate his gesture. I don't need protection.

"I'm really not very good with directions," I tell him with my mind.

I don't want to hurt his feelings. He's doing the best he can. I bite the inside of one cheek nervously.

A stunned look begins dawning across his face as he looks back at me. I raise my shoulders slightly and look away. Out of the corner of my eye I watch as his head drops, and sighing heavily, he looks from side to side.

It feels to me as if Kyler has been doing a lot of things since this journey began, to protect me, or what he believes is protecting me. I think whatever he's been doing has also been causing a lot of problems. I wish he'd stop whatever it is he's doing. I don't want to try to find out what he's doing because I don't want to know anything more about his world. I have enough to deal with trying to figure out how to warn/help Leslie.

I've figured out, though, that Kyler doesn't understand he has to begin by believing in himself, loving himself and wanting to live a life that's healthy for himself. He has to want to heal, to give himself a chance, and know he can un-brainwash himself, re-train his brain, re-parent himself.

He has to be willing to give up his old lifestyle and everything and everyone in it, though. I'm not sure he will. And in that case, I can't do anything for him. I consciously decide I'm not going to share any dreams with him again. As much as I appreciate what he's done for me, I can't repay him.

At least, I haven't figured out how to yet. And I'm not sure I ever will.

I need to let him go.

***

I'm hovering above myself watching myself standing with my hands clutching the handle of an empty shopping cart. I'm at the top of a twenty-foot-long, concrete walkway that gently descends. Six feet high, almost white, smooth concrete walls are on either side of me.

Ahead of me the path ends, a wall closing it off. I can tell to the left is an opening. To what, I don't know.

What I do feel, and know, is that few make it here. The empty shopping cart signifies no attachments to people, places, or things, to the ego. But even the cart holds significance. Even it must go.

I begin pushing the cart down the walkway until I reach the end. Then I turn left and step off into the slate-colored blue water. The frigid temperature takes my breath away. Gasping, my hands release the shopping cart handle as my head submerges, and then my reflexes kick in and I'm using my arms vigorously, swimming back to the surface.

The water is choppy, churning, smacking against itself and sending drops of water raining out in all directions. I see the cart bobbing and turning in the waves about six feet from me.

Ahead of me stands a thousand-foot rocky cliff, its sharp edges jutting into the air daringly, insolently. The sky is a whirling mass, a rainbow of grays. Wildness permeates the air and every pore of the water and stone cliffs.

I'm treading water, with a lot of effort. Every so often an errant wave slaps me in the face.

I look up at the top of the cliffs and realize, understand. This is where they live. The Archangels. They ruminate, meditate, and gather here. They perch on top of the cliffs. This place. So, full of life, so wild, so full of passion.

This dream felt authentic. It also feels I've passed many series of tests to be able to go there. Obviously, I have more to go, but it's a positive sign.

***

I'm toying with the idea of starting my own business. I'm not sure doing what, though. I think about what I have fun doing. I have fun being creative. Using my creativity when I made the wedding video for that couple—it was gratifying to see how much they, especially the woman, appreciated the result. It brought them happiness and would for years to come. They'll be sharing it with their loved ones. I consider how I could create a business based around video.

Some days later I'm sitting on the couch, drinking a tea, and looking out the window. And I'm thinking about all the travelling

I've been doing and how my intuition has been correct. I think about how many times Leslie has been disrespectful toward me during the course of this journey.

And then I start thinking about the wildlife I saw on my drive to and from Alaska. The hummingbirds in Ecuador, the orphaned baby woolly monkey, the oil rig in the cloud forest, the firefly in the jungle, the daughter of the seed geneticist, the way the people in Ecuador were being encouraged to buy more gas-powered vehicles, the flying squirrel and the whales in Nova Scotia, the spies in Nova Scotia, the being I dreamed of, the beautiful, wild one, the being-with-the-brown-circles-on-its-skin ... and as I'm thinking, reviewing all of this, I feel an anger growing in me.

A frustration and an anger at all the nonsense Leslie has brought me. How he's chosen to be ignorant, act like he and those he does business with know everything, control everything.

And I'm getting angrier and angrier.

After some moments, it feels also like I'm touching base with feelings of pent-up frustration inside me too.

Then I decide.

They don't control everything. They just think they do. They wouldn't be here if it weren't for The Light. If it weren't for the air we breathe, the water we're provided with, the land and the plant and animal life The Light created, the sun... we wouldn't be here.

I'm angry at their arrogance, at their lack of taking responsibility and honoring these things, so generations to come will have the benefit of a natural world that we, all of us, are supposed to be protecting.

How they're so **certain** of their actions and their beliefs, when nothing is certain. And how their certainty negates the opportunity to learn more, accept, adapt and change.

How I've been seeing all this nasty stuff, this stuff that has to do with Leslie's world, that I wouldn't have to see or know if I wasn't try to help/ warn him, so he could help others, the ones he seems to feel he's protecting, but really, he isn't; he's using them, feeding off of them.

Then, for ten seconds, I imagine and fully concentrate on water flowing. A lot of water.

And it's as if, for those ten seconds, I'm suspended in a different time and space.

Then I come out of it, finish my tea, and ask The Light to provide me with the next step. Because The Light hasn't told me it's time to stop trying to communicate with Leslie. I dearly want to, though. I just can't see a win-win situation in this anywhere. I've been trying.

And I watch as over the next six days, the city I live in experiences a flood.

A big flood...

It shuts down the downtown core for a week.

I live in a city of a million people.

Holy.

Crap...

I'm stunned.

Because... I think I may have done that.

It feels like... I did that.

And a multitude of feelings flows through me, sometimes a combination of some of these and sometimes each one by itself: shocked, horrified, excited, apologetic, ashamed, exhilarated, bewildered, amazed.

At times, I'm in denial and at other times I'm not.

The shock of it eventually wears off...

After about two years.

But initially I realize, I did make my tripod case move toward that young man on the bus in Ecuador. So, energy works like this too!

Huh.

And I wonder, can I flip vehicles? Can I flip semi-trailers... can I create tornadoes?

The feeling is very strange... It has an addictive flavor to it. And I realize this is what it must feel like to people who get a taste of power. It's addicting.

A trap.

And I stop myself from thinking thoughts like this, although in certain life-threatening circumstances I can see where having this ability would be a plus...

But what I'm most excited about is the discovery that all human beings have this capability. If I can do this, then that means all human beings have this capability. We are so much more than we think we are!

But I decide never to concentrate on something like that again, to only use my mind like that in situations where my well-being depends on it. Even then, maybe not. I'm okay with where I'm going after this place.

Obviously, I'm going to have to really watch what I think about and concentrate on.

This seems to be a recurring theme I'm having a difficult time understanding.

What I think is important.

That the thoughts I focus on I give energy to. And energy is powerful.

Thoughts contain their own energy, and emotions are tied to thoughts...

Wow!

I had no idea...

No idea how much power thoughts contain...

It seems those who've been harassing me didn't know either. And there's nothing I can do about it after the fact.

As far as I know, there isn't anywhere to train or learn how to use energy. Or if there are, I don't know about them and they aren't to be found on the Internet.

I try looking.

Nothing.

It isn't like the X-Men or Harry Potter—there's no school you can go to in reality.

So, I'll just have to endeavor to keep learning.

I also decide it's time I stop trying to learn more in order to communicate with Leslie.

Obviously, I find it too frustrating.

For over ten years now I've been trying to communicate with him about the importance of the environment.

And I'm making no progress.

What I'm receiving for my efforts is being attacked personally, in real life, online, and in my dreams.

This is what they do, I suppose.

But I decide until I receive a message from The Light on what I'm supposed to do next about Leslie, I'm not going to warn/help him anymore.

The thing is, it feels to me that while I accepted the challenge of believing in my intuition, others have accepted the challenge of believing in their own intuition too. It feels as if there's been a shift in the consciousness of many, many others over these past ten or so years, as if many others are waking up, deciding to wake up.

Making a choice.

Maybe this is evolution? Maybe this is energy. Maybe it ***does*** matter if one person tries, if one person begins, if one person starts experimenting with energy and thought, if one person pushes boundaries.

I'm not sure...

But I do know it isn't easy, and lots of people don't or won't like it, people who aren't open to change, to seeing things differently, seeing themselves differently; but it is possible.

And incredibly worthwhile.

Because it feels like Leslie and the world he belongs to are part of the old world, a world that relies on violence to obtain power. But the new world has no use for these things and understands them as being a detriment to the survival of our species.

When I began this journey, I thought The Light was asking me to have compassion for Leslie, and try to help him understand, so he could help himself and others survive. But that might not be the reason why The Light chose Leslie and me.

They say if you want to look at how healthy a society is, look at one of its offenders, one who has been hurt. Then look at how that society has treated and continues to treat them. Because people will naturally point fingers, instead of looking at themselves, instead of looking at how the "offender" reflects their own shadow side, the side they keep hidden, the wounds they won't heal, the wounds that infect and fester over time.

I thought The Light chose Leslie because he's a leader. But true leaders educate, inspire, and encourage. They motivate by example. Leslie is ruled by his fears, which he was taught, and he hasn't been able to break free from them.

And I know, the future depends on those who ***will*** be able to do this, break free from attachments/fears/illusions. Because the adaptable will be the survivors. Not the strongest, and not the smartest. The most adaptable.

From what I know so far, Leslie isn't adaptable. He's stuck in his beliefs, making it impossible for him to learn, grow, change—not unlike a lot of us, including me. I've been stuck in my beliefs, one of them being that it's important that Leslie understands what I'm trying to tell him.

But then, as long as we're living and breathing, we can become adaptable.

We all have the gift of free will.

And I'm struck, again, by the unbelievable way The Light weaves its way in my life. The love and the beauty, the wisdom, and the patience. I remind myself, I need to be kinder to myself.

Because it feels like I'm frustrated with myself because I couldn't convince Leslie.

Angry with myself.

Disappointed with myself.

I know I'm hard on myself.

I always have been.

It was part of my upbringing. Nothing was ever good enough. I wasn't good enough...

***

One of my earliest memories was when I was four years old. I was sitting at the kitchen table with my family eating dinner. One of the side dishes was peas and carrots—you know, the kind that come frozen together in a bag? Well, they smelled weird to me. Smelled like chemicals. The smell caused my stomach to contract. And I knew, if I ate them I'd throw up. I also knew if I didn't eat them my parents would be angry. So, I silently sat at the table, with my parents and my siblings, as tears streamed down my face, while pushing the small cubed pieces of carrot and peas around my plate with my fork.

"Eat your vegetables!" my mom admonished me.

I looked imploringly from my dad to my mom, as my siblings stopped eating and looked at me.

"They'll make me throw up," I said.

"Don't be ridiculous and stop being difficult! There are children in the world starving; you're just being a spoiled brat. Eat your vegetables now!"

But I couldn't. And I sat while everyone else finished their dinner. Then my mom said, "Fine, you want to be stubborn? You can sit there all night until you eat those peas and carrots!"

So, I sat. Alone.

While the sun warmed my back consolingly, shining through the kitchen window. But even the sun couldn't stay, and as it made its gradual departure, casting long shadows on the kitchen table, I knew I'd have to eat the peas and carrots.

Finally, I picked up my fork and began eating the peas and carrots. My mom came into the kitchen and watched me. I finished eating them, then laid my fork down on the table.

"There, that wasn't so bad, was it?"

And two minutes later I threw up on myself, the kitchen table, and the floor.

"Oh, for God's sake!" she exclaimed.

And silently I cried, feeling ashamed and guilty for knowing this is what would happen and being incapable of stopping it.

So, this mentality I have, some of it is just a natural progression of my experiences growing up, what was expected of me, what beliefs I chose to agree with and adopt. And I need to look at how I can make changes to this. I am good enough, more than good enough. My worth isn't determined by anyone else's choices.

I can't control anyone else. It's okay if I couldn't convince Leslie. I can only be with myself, become more myself. Become more forgiving and accepting of myself.

Unconditionally love myself despite, and because of, my flaws. The Light does. And by doing this I can be more compassionate, loving and forgiving of others.

This last thought strikes a nerve in my heart and tears of gratitude flow down my face. The Light is so beautiful and gives me so many blessings it takes my breath away.

I wonder if I'm supposed to be more forgiving of Leslie, to ask for The Light's forgiveness on Leslie's behalf. If by forgiving him I'll actually be showing myself more love.

Yes, this feels right.

It also feels like Leslie feels as if he'll die if I win.

If he says, "You're right, I know you're right," that, to him, means he loses and I win.

It's as if he thinks this is a competition somehow. And Leslie can't lose.

He feels that if he loses, he dies. I don't know why he feels this way, but that's the way he feels.

Because that was never my intention—to make him feel that threatened, like his life is at stake.

It isn't even that I expected him to do anything about it, other than believing me, believing my intention was sincere and beginning to open up to the possibilities of looking at alternatives. Solutions.

But I'm reaching the understanding that Leslie's beliefs negate the opportunity to reach compromises. To Leslie, everything is a fight-or-die situation. There is no middle ground, no discussions, no compromises. Only drama. High stakes, fear and drama.

It must be an awful way to live life. A very high stress life for him. Full of fear.

***

I'm standing in a kitchen in a house. It appears to be a house I think is mine. My kitchen. A 5x3 foot window is behind me, above an empty, clean double sink. The cupboards are an ivory color and the counters are a pale yellow. Sunlight is flooding in through the window, casting a warm glow on the silver toaster and plug-in kettle. A scarred oak table with plain wooden chairs sits in the corner of the kitchen. I'm alone in the kitchen. Something is baking in the oven. I sniff the air. Cinnamon and apples. Apple pie. I'm making homemade apple pie.

Two men enter my kitchen. They're wearing suits. One of them is a political leader, well-known in North America. The second man is not well-known, but he helps the political leader. They're looking at me questioningly.

And I'm annoyed suddenly. Because they have a problem. And they want me to help them. Do I care to? No. I don't. I don't care what their problem is. I want them out of my kitchen. Out of my cozy, homey, peaceful, apple pie-smelling home. I'm almost hostile in my body language. They lower their eyes and sit at the kitchen table. Then they look at me, eyes pleading. I squint my eyes and purse my lips. Why? Why should I help them?

And then a woman with a child walk into my kitchen. The woman sits down on a chair at the kitchen table and the child sits on her lap. The child is about eight years old, a girl. No one has spoken and I know no one will. We don't have to. I don't pay attention to the mother and I watch as the child appraises me, not belligerently but resignedly. I look from the child to the two men, understanding.

The child is powerful. I can feel the power emanating from her. And she's decided. She's going to obliterate a lot of people, create a lot of chaos, because she doesn't feel there's any point to it all. No point to life. She's overwhelmed by all the ignorance and violence in the world.

I can sympathize.

And that's why the men have brought her. They don't know how to stop her, and they can't stop her. So, they want me to try.

But I don't care about them or their motives, because it makes my heart hurt that one so young can feel this way. And that's why I'll try. Because her life is important. And doing what she's planning to do will mean she doesn't value her life.

I look at the men and mother and send them, "Don't mess up my kitchen and when I get back don't be here." Because if they are, they'll wish they weren't. The men look in my eyes and then look down at the table.

I look at the child, smile and send her, "Want to come for a walk with me?"

Her eyes lower and then look at me, a very small smile on her lips. Then she stands and slowly walks to me. I hold out my hand and wait for her to put her hand in mine. After a few moments, and I'm not sure she will, she does.

Then we walk out the back door and into a forest. Trees are everywhere. Twigs crunch beneath our shoes. We meander through the forest for some time. At one point, I stop, let go of her hand, and mentally send her an image of a St. Bernard dog. She smiles back at me.

Then with my mind I explain to her that a St. Bernard rescues people who are trapped under a lot of snow, snow so deep no one can see that they're trapped under it, like when there's an avalanche. But the St. Bernard knows they're there. Because the St. Bernard can smell them and sense them. And the St. Bernard does this because that's its gift, its gift of love. Its gift of life.

She looks back at me while I'm explaining, sometimes cocking her head. After I finish explaining I smile at her, waiting for her to understand. She looks down at the ground, then up at the sky, contemplating what I've said. Then the corners of her mouth rise, rise, rise and her eyes are twinkling.

She reaches her hand out to mine and slowly intertwines her fingers in mine. She understands.

We begin walking in silence again and after a while we come upon a turning curve of an old dirt road. In the distance, we can hear children laughing and shouting at one another and soon we see them leaping and pushing one another as they're running toward us. I look down at the little girl. This is what she needs. To play. To not focus so much on the serious side of life, to be a child.

As the children get closer they see the little girl with me and they're shouting out invitations to her to start running with them, playing with them, as they turn the corner of the dirt road in front of us. The little girl looks up at me, asking if it's okay. "Go play," I send her. "Have fun!"

"Come play with us," she sends me back excitedly, imploringly, tugging on my hand.

"No little one, this is for you. I want you to go with them,"

She understands and lets go of my hand, and I watch her as she joins them running, smiling, and shouting into the wind, watching their backs until I can't see her anymore.

I'm not sure what to think of it.

***

Next I find out my dad has fourth stage cancer. I go visit him. He lives outside the city, on an acreage. He has two old horses and a dog. He's single and has been for a very, very long time. He never re-married after he and my mom divorced.

When I arrive, I can see he's lost weight. He's moving slower. He tells me he's experiencing a lot of pain. He's been told he has tumors throughout his body. In particular, he has one growing next to one of his lungs and another in his throat, making it hard for him to breathe.

My dad experienced some kind of trauma as a child. He never told me this, but I sense it. Because of that, and his reticence to heal from it, he's never watched his diet, and because of that he has stage one diabetes. He wasn't born with diabetes; he developed diabetes because he ate too much meat, starch and sugars and not enough vegetables and fruit. And he doesn't exercise regularly or drink water.

He's not that old, though. He's in his mid-sixties. But he's lived like this all his life. This body we're given is a gift, but it needs proper care.

The doctors have given him, at most, a year to live. That's with chemotherapy and radiation. He won't consider other options, like changing his diet and exercising. Or other alternatives, like homeopathy. He won't consider combining "modern medicine" with other alternatives.

I can see he's visibly shaken by the news. He's frightened. He doesn't want to die. He's an atheist so he doesn't have spirituality to lean on. So, I visit him a lot over the next few months. I tell him about what happened to me when I drowned, hoping it gives him peace to know that there's a lot of beauty on the other side. That there will be for him. This is what I feel. It doesn't seem like he believes me, though.

I'm in spirit form hovering above myself, watching physical me standing in a thriving, healthy forest. Rainbows of greens erupt under and all around me. The air hums with life, with energy. The sky is a dreamy dark blue. Sunlight dances across my face as the wind whispers private messages to the trees. Songbirds joyfully string stories together in their forbidden language.

Closing my eyes, I let my pores drink in the sun, the wind, the sounds, the earth. The true essence of nature, a magnificent paradox—so simple yet comprised of intricately connected, complicated, beautiful patterns, beautiful matrixes.

I sense something and opening my eyes, I begin turning my head to the left. Standing beside me is a healthy, white Clydesdale. My head reaches almost to the bottom of its belly. The contours of the beast's muscular form surprise, delight, and humble me. It's standing still, waiting. Tilting my head back, I look up at the horse's head. The horse shakes its massive head and its silky mane dances gracefully, mesmerizingly, back and forth across its back.

Then the horse is gazing down at me. My breath catches. The liquid, dark brown eyes gleam and glitter with ancient wisdom. Wisdom and a dash of humor. I reach my hand up cautiously and hesitate. I'm waiting for a reaction from the horse, to see if I'm allowed to touch it.

The horse blinks, then lowers its head until I can feel its breath against my palm. Slowly and gently I touch the tip of its nose. The moment hangs, suspended in time. Then a mischievous glint flashes into its eyes and it snorts loudly—abruptly lifting its head in the air.

Startled, I gasp, fall backwards and, losing my balance, fall on the ground, on my ass. I look up as the horse swings its head back and forth, neighing.

Laughing.

"Hey!" I yell at it, a grin spreading across my face. I stand up and next we're running together, side by side, through the forest. An endless forest.

I look up the significance of the color white, horse, and forest. Then I feel into the dream. It was telling me something. The next step. What I need to do next.

White horse.

I'm to go to Whitehorse, located in the Yukon Territory in Canada.

I feel into this.

Yes.

This is what I'm supposed to do next.

***

I talk with my dad to find out what he needs, what he wants. He wants to keep living in his home. His greatest fear is going to a Hospice. I don't know why. He wants to live out the rest of his time in his home. He's made arrangements for someone to watch over him, somewhat. This concerns me. He isn't well and he needs someone cooking healthy meals for him, taking him for daily walks so he gets fresh air, making sure a nurse checks him out every other day. But I know my dad. He's stubborn and doesn't want this. I just have to accept what he wants.

I let my dad know I'm leaving but I'll be in touch, and if he needs me I'll be there for him.

Which is odd. For my whole life, it's seemed to me I've behaved more like a parent to my dad. He and my mom divorced when I was about four years old. My mom took me with her. My siblings went to live with my dad. She left my dad for another man, the man who brought a lot of violence into my world for the next seven years. My dad knew this was happening at the time but felt helpless to do anything about it. He did try, in his own way, to help, though.

He taught me downhill skiing starting when I was two years old. On small, red, plastic skis. On most weekends in the winter he would have us out on the ski hill. When he and my mom split up he'd pick us up every other weekend and take us skiing in the winter. As I got older, he spent less time with me on the hill, preferring to ski on his own or with his friends. But I loved skiing.

When I was eight years old I was scouted by someone representing the Nancy Green Ski Team. They wanted me to join their club. But neither my mom nor dad felt able to commit to the schedule. It meant very early drop-offs at the hill on the weekends.

After my mom and step-father split up when I was about ten years old, visits with my father became less and less often. I only skied after that when I made arrangements to.

He didn't attend any of my gymnastic competitions or piano concerts. Aside from the ski trips when I was young, I never went on a holiday with my dad. Conversations with him were stunted, kept to a polite, stranger-type level.

What I was realizing as I grew older was that it felt like my dad was afraid of emotions, of people expressing deep-felt emotions to him or around him. It felt as if he needed me to respect this, even at the cost of expressing myself, which, at times, I resented[7]. He repressed so much of his own feelings that he ended up getting colon cancer later in life.

It took me a while to just accept who he was and not expect too much from him. I didn't see him much in my teenage years, or my early 20s. After that it was clear to me that while I knew my dad loved me, he wasn't capable of the type of relationship I'd hoped for.

That the relationship we had was all he was capable of. And I finally accepted that.

So, I'd visit with him, usually every few months. Or I'd send a letter, or call. He was always happy to hear from me. We'd have long conversations, with him telling me about the various wildlife he was seeing on his acreage, how his dogs were, what book he was reading, how his life was going. I understood that he couldn't deal with any more than that. It would've been a lot better for him if he could've stretched. Tried.

At times, I found it frustrating, though, mostly because he put the onus on me to extend energy and time toward him. It was always up to me to call him and go out to his acreage to spend time with him, as if this was my duty. If I wanted to have a relationship with him, it was my responsibility to do way over 50% of the work.

In my 30s and 40s I would visit him, but only as often as I could without feeling resentful. Our relationship blossomed in these years, because I accepted my dad's limitations and adjusted my expectations. I understood that I could enjoy his company, if I didn't overextend myself with him.

Now that he's sick, it feels like he's pulling me into his fear. His fear of death, of what he could've done better throughout his life, of many things. But I know he's reeling from the news. It's odd, we all know we could die any minute... get hit by a car, our plane could go down, any number of things, but when a person is given a timeline for how long they're going to live, they're forced to face their mortality and all it encompasses. Not that the timeline we're given is something we have to believe, though; it's just that some people do. I know my dad does, which is too bad.

I suggest to my dad to consider talking with someone, a worker in the hospice field, who would be an incredible help during this difficult time in his life. But he won't consider this. There's little else I can do for him, other than keep in contact with him.

***

I'm hovering above myself in spirit form looking down at myself. I'm walking out of a large, one story, community center type of building. It's an overcast day. It feels like I am at a community garage sale or something. As I'm walking out the front doors I see Leslie standing on the far-right side of the front doors, on the grass, near the front door.

His arms are crossed in front of his chest and he's looking at me with a stern look on his face. He's wearing a light blue sundress, with small dark blue and yellow flowers on it. White threads hang loosely from the shoulders, where it looks as if the sleeves have been ripped off the dress. The dress reaches his knees. It hangs baggily on him in a lot of places, and is way too tight in other places. He's wearing a pair of really worn, brown leather work boots.

I walk by Leslie and continue walking toward my car, which is apparently parked about a hundred yards away, in a parking lot. As I reach the parking lot I turn right into it. On the right side of the lot a tin roof hangs, covering the cars that are parked against the fence. I walk to my car and as I'm getting into it I see Leslie running, jumping, leaping in the air while hooting and hollering. He's heading toward the opposite side of the lot, where I see a hangar-type building. One of the doors to the hangar is open and a black car sits waiting for him.

Then I see four other men dressed like Leslie running behind him, scattered. They're all hooting and hollering while they're jumping, leaping, and running toward the same car. His friends. Then a huge fist comes down from the sky; it's the size of a house, and it slams down on one of the clown guys, crushing him. No hooting and hollering from him anymore. There's no blood or anything. He just disappears.

Undaunted, Leslie and the other clowns jump into the car, which looks like an old-style jalopy, the kind you see clowns at an old-time circus riding in. Leslie starts the car and starts driving out of the parking lot, while his three clown friends are jumping around in their seats, arms flailing around, hooting, and hollering as the car drives away.

I open my eyes when I wake from this dream. Then I close my eyes and shake my head. What was that? I breathe deeply for a few moments and slowly get my bearings. I concentrate. I've had a few other dreams where Leslie is either wearing a wig and/or makeup and/or a dress. Anytime my dream combines Leslie with these things it's not a good sign for me in my dream. It means he's angry. Not necessarily with me, although he directs his anger toward me, just that that's his state of being. I usually zap out of dreams like this right away.

Somehow it feels to me like it has something with him being angry with the feminine part of himself, and/or females in general. Again, it feels like he's angry with his mom for not protecting him from whatever trauma he experienced when he was young, that what he experienced caused him to be confused and angry about his sexuality.

I get that. I can't fully understand it because I didn't experience this, but I do understand trauma and what a confusing effect it can have on a person, how the effects can last into adulthood, and even into old age unless healing takes place.

It doesn't mean you can't find healing, happiness, and peace, though. It just means you have to work at it. Chances are high that something happened to his mom too, in order for her to be incapable of protecting him. So, a lot more compassion, love, patience, and tolerance is needed here.

This is why the LGBT community is **so** important.

Everyone needs a supportive, loving environment where they feel safe to be who they are, who they feel they are, who they're most comfortable being. We all make up what's considered to be "society," and we're all different in our own ways. *And society is **all the richer for it.***

...And I wonder about the huge fist that came down.

Was that The Light, letting me know I'm being protected in my dreams?

I'm not sure.

I really want to stop having dreams with Leslie in them now.

I can't do anything about his situation.

I can't help him.

Even if I could, he wouldn't accept help from me, because I'm female. This is what it feels like; the fact that I'm a female is the main reason why he behaves the way he does toward me. I don't get it, because personally it doesn't matter to me if a person is male or female, but there it is.

I already made a conscious decision I didn't want to have dreams of Leslie anymore. Why did I have this dream then?

I don't know.

***

Before I leave for Whitehorse I send a message mind-to-mind to Kyler, not knowing if he'll receive it or not. I'm telling him I don't know how to repay him, that I'm thankful for everything he's done for me. That I have to work on my own life now. On what I need to do next. I know it has nothing to do with Kyler or the world he lives in. I thank him again.

The thing is, I feel indebted to him.

If it hadn't been for him I would've thought I was going crazy, losing it. Because of him I was able to move forward into this journey, with some semblance, however small, of understanding of what was going on. He gave me proof my intuition was right. I just don't know how to repay him without getting involved in his world. So far, when I do, I suffer negative consequences.

I've already been suffering the consequences when I try communicating with Leslie.

I catch a plane to Whitehorse. I have no idea for how long, or why I'm supposed to go there. People I've come across since I started this journey often ask me what I'm doing, where I'm going and why. I tell them the truth. I don't know.

They give me odd looks, as if I'm hiding something or lying. I'm not. I just don't go into detail about my dreams, what I've been learning about intuition, energy, or consciousness, or how I live my life. I don't know if anyone would believe me anyway. It's a lot to digest. I still haven't digested all of it. But if one of my dreams tells me to do something then that's my intuition, and that's The Light speaking to me—guiding me.

After I arrive in Whitehorse I book a bed in a hostel. I spend some time getting used to where things are—the grocery store, the walking trails. I meet some of the people who come and go from the hostel.

The air smells unbelievable. The Yukon River is an aqua color I've never seen before. It reminds me of the dream I had with the being-with-the-circles-on-its-skin. The body of water it walked into, and then went to sleep in, was the same color as the Yukon River.

I see a red fox sometimes, first thing in the morning, running down the street.

I visit a local business and offer to create a promotional video for them. They accept. I begin taking footage in the storefront business. I end up shooting over sixteen hours of video, because every time the store owner notices me pointing my camera at them, they freeze. This look comes into their eyes and they stiffen. So, I have to try to get footage when they aren't aware of it.

It takes me hours and hours to edit the video footage to create a two-minute video. I end up interviewing the business owner and cutting the audio of their voice into the video, instead of using the video of them I have. They just don't look relaxed in the video. I use background music that suits the business. I'm hoping the owner likes it and wants to use it. I'd like to begin creating a video portfolio.

While I was shooting the video footage some of the customers and workers for the business owner suggested to the business owner they create a Facebook page. But they look at me when they're talking to the business owner. I'm not sure what that means but I take note of it.

The business owner loves the video when I present it. When I ask where they're going to put it they tell me they don't know. They aren't into computers. I suggest on their Facebook page. I learn the business owner doesn't have one, and they don't want to spend much time on computers. They don't understand or like computers and they'd rather be doing what they love.

Based on what the owner's employees and customers have been saying, I encourage the owner to use a Facebook page and offer to create one for them and teach them, for a fee.

They agree and I begin creating a business page for them on Facebook and teaching them how to use it.

***

In the meantime, I've offered to volunteer for a local nature conservation society. I spend some time getting to know some of the people who work for it. I talk with a man who works for the conservation organization, who tells me he's involved in the mining area of conservation.

I learn that any corporation, owned by anyone in the world, can mine in Canada.

Every mining corporation is required to have a sum of money set aside, legally, to clean up after the mining project shuts down. What typically happens, though, is the corporation will file for bankruptcy after they've mined and made their money. So, no cleanup ends up occurring.

This, apparently, is legal. The poisonous aftereffects on the land, water and animals are devastating. For many years.

***

A woman from Europe books into the hostel and is staying in the same room as me. Something doesn't feel right about her. I can't put my finger on it but it doesn't feel right. It feels as if she has something to do with Leslie.

She asks to join me on a walk. Warily, I agree. During our walk, she begins talking about an "environmental terrorist." She's talking about a man and a tree. I don't know. What I do feel is that's what she's calling me. What Leslie is calling me.

Which is funny. Apparently stalking, assaulting, bullying, and harassing someone for years isn't considered "terrorism" in their books. But I make some water flow and I'm an environmental terrorist.

Well, whatever. I didn't know I could do that and there's nothing I can do about that now, other than **not** do something like that again.

What it feels like is they're angry because I showed them nature isn't something they can control. Which I find astounding. Some people, in their arrogance and ignorance, have come to the point where they think they can understand and control the unfathomable and uncontrollable. No one controls The Light. The Light created The Wild.

The European woman is in it. It has something to do with feces. I can't remember it very well; it was short and I zapped out quickly. Whatever it was, it was distasteful. And she meant it to be.

When I wake up the next morning the European woman in the same room as me excitedly asks me if I remember my dream. I tell her I don't, because I don't remember it the way I do other dreams, and it feels as if she invaded my dream, which means I don't remember it as vividly, and now I'm able to block these types of interferences better.

What she did do was let me know who she was and what she was about.

And I spend no time around her after that.

Many months later I hear her voice on the computer. She now reads tarot cards on YouTube under a false name, without showing her face.

Where does Leslie find these people?

***

I end up spending a few months in Whitehorse. I call my dad every week to see how he's doing. He's gradually getting worse.

After I finish the project for the business owner I fly back to Calgary and begin the process of starting my own business. I've decided to train business owners to create their own videos, to help them overcome their fear of using video for their business.

The only problem with this is I'm terrified to get in front of the camera. How am I supposed to teach other business owners to do it when I haven't done it myself? And it takes me a few months to advance on this fear, look it in the face, deal with it and overcome it. I set up a rigorous schedule where I make myself go on camera at least four times a week. And gradually, over time, I become more comfortable being on camera.

One day when I'm taking a break from the computer, during a walk on a sunny afternoon, I feel a mental tugging. What is this?

Kyler.

Then a download occurs. It's as if a bunch of information just dropped into my consciousness and I know things. I don't know how I know what I now know. This is somewhat confusing, disorienting and unbalancing when it happens.

What do I know?

That Kyler has been recruiting; whatever he does he recruits people to work for him, and that one of these recruits is a spy. That if he changes one small detail in some kind of a large meet-up that's soon to happen, he'll know who this person is and know not to let this person into his organization.

I think about this for a minute.

What would be the implications if I send this information to Kyler? Would harm come to the person who was a spy? I feel into that. No. I determine this is the way I can repay Kyler. If I send him this information, then we're even. I've repaid him. I'm no longer indebted to him.

I send Kyler the information. It feels like he received it.

And I don't owe him anymore.

A few days later I feel Kyler tugging again. I feel into it more.

He wants more information.

The information I sent was accurate.

He traded that information for drugs. For his drug habit.

Instantly, I'm angered. I gave him the information a few days ago as a sign of thanks, for his help.

Then I stop walking and think.

He's a drug addict. He hasn't stopped this whole time. At times he's been cleaner, yes, but he hasn't made the choice, he hasn't had the courage to hope. Then I feel frustration mixed with guilt and shame that he could believe in me so much, yet believe in himself so little, and I can't do anything about it.

I have to let him go.

There's nothing more I can do.

I make a conscious effort to cut ties with him, send him good wishes, and goodbye.

***

The following months I continue conquering my fear of being in front of the camera by practicing. A lot. And I gain some clients. I work with them diligently. I've continued to stay with the changes I made to my diet and practice yoga/meditation daily. I'm spending time with my dad every few weeks. The radiation and chemotherapy are taking a toll on him, affecting his appetite. He's losing more weight.

***

One day I'm helping a family member arrange to have a piano removed from their home. I hire two men to move the piano. One of the men acts

as if he's interested in me. I haven't dated anyone for about eleven years now. I decide, maybe, maybe I could try dating again? That would be normal. We text one another for a few weeks. He communicates as if he's a single person.

Then one day, I'm working at the computer and I receive another download.

About the piano mover.

He's currently living with a woman he's been with for a number of years. They have three children. He doesn't care about his relationship with this woman. Stopped caring years ago. She kept trying for some time, even after he stopped, but then finally gave up. He doesn't have much interest in their children. She's currently seeing another man, who loves her children, loves her and she loves him. She's going to leave the piano mover. Piano mover knows she's seeing someone and is going to leave him. He doesn't care. He doesn't care because he doesn't love himself, so he isn't capable of loving someone else. Somehow, he's connected to Leslie.

This information both feels accurate and is accurate. I feel no need to look for proof. I stop texting with him.

I review this internally. This is twice in a row, in quick succession, I've received these downloads.

What is this and how can I know so much, without knowing how? I try searching for information on this but I don't even know what this is called. All I know is it has something to do with energy and consciousness. I find it confusing. Completely illogical.

I'm thankful for it, though.

***

I've been meeting a lot of people online, using video. One woman in particular seems to have sought me out. I don't know why. She teaches a healing modality. But something seems off about her. I can't put my finger on it, but something's off. She's asked me to help her with a few video projects and I agree to. I'm trying to get as much practice as I can, so I can provide good services for my customers. Once the second project with her is coming to a close, I have this dream.

I'm in spirit form hovering above myself standing in a house. The house is large. Something feels wrong with the house. I walk into rooms. Most of the rooms in this house are bedrooms. Children's bedrooms. There are bedrooms connected to bedrooms. So many of them. All are furnished homey-like—you know, knitted afghans, knick-knacks. Some of the rooms have baby cribs in them. Sometimes the cribs are small;

sometimes they are larger with the bars on the sides. I continue walking through these rooms until I see a set of stairs leading down.

I walk down the stairs and see the teacher woman. She's smiling and standing off to the side. I walk into a room off the basement and see it's like a shower area in a gym or something. There's a large shower area, bathroom stalls and sinks lining one wall. Off the shower area are smaller rooms, private shower areas. I know. The teacher woman's husband assaults children. This is where he does it. They're wealthy people. Financially.

This is why she teaches a healing modality. She's trying to offset what her husband does.

I don't want to know information like this.

A few weeks later I answer a video call from the teacher woman. She tells me she took a few days off and travelled with a friend somewhere in the U.S. When she and her friend were sitting at a table outside at a cafe/ bar two men joined them. She tells me the men seemed friendly, yet also threatening.

They gave her a business card. It had something to do with them working for a GMO corporation. She felt they sat with her and gave her the card because she has a connection to me. I don't speak much during our conversation, because it feels to me like she's telling me I should be scared. That she is. But I'm not.

I already died; I know what's waiting for me. I'm good with that. Whoever these people are, and whatever their reasons are for trying to warn or scare me, their reasons have nothing to do with me. Their reasons are about their own fears.

Also, because the dream I had about her is still too fresh... and disconcerting, all I know is I don't want to have communication with her anymore.

I know I'm not to be judgmental. I try not to be. But I also know these same children who are being assaulted? A lot of them are going to grow up to be drug addicts, or some kind of addict. They'll have to fight to bring balance, peace, and happiness into their lives because of the shame and guilt that's been passed onto them that isn't theirs that was forced on them because the person who passed it to them didn't have the courage or the strength to overcome their own fears, their own pain.

I decide to definitely not communicate with her anymore.

I feel into this. Am I being judgmental?

No. I'm being discerning.

I don't want to have access to that kind of energy.

I don't know how to stop it or control it, though, so the best I can do is stay away from people who have anything to do with this kind of thing.

Afterwards I consider the general facts I have so far.

What do assaulting children, wealthy people, GMO corporations, oil corporations, the military, and organized crime have to do with me? The only link I can see to any of this is Leslie.

I wonder again, why did The Light give me this job? I'm only one person. It feels to me as if Leslie has brought in a whole bunch of people I don't know, who are just as fearful as he is, who are threatened by me.

I'm the messenger.

I didn't create the message.

The message is there to help.

But it's starting to feel to me like it's not just about the lowering energy in the environment, it's about people learning to heal and let go of their fears and learn to love themselves unconditionally. If they can do this, they'll naturally care about the environment, nature, because they'll feel it, understand it more, be more connected to it.

But how can this be accomplished?

***

I've been working most days, and into the evenings, as well as a lot of weekends.

I decide to take a break. Go for a drive. For about a week. I've been west, north, and east in Canada and I decide to drive around the U.S. I haven't done this before. It'll be interesting to see the different landscapes.

So, I set out. When I get to the border there seems to be a problem. I don't have a destination and wanting to drive through the U.S. sightseeing, without a destination, appears to be cause for concern. I don't have a record. After thoroughly searching my car they determine I don't have any bombs.

I'm held up at the border for twenty-five minutes, giving me time to wonder if I've done something wrong, or if this happens to everyone. At which point they allow me a pass to be in the U.S. for ten days. If I'm not back by then I'll be arrested.

I continue on. I've brought my camera to take pictures. The first day I drive a long time, into the night, and end up stopping at a roadside turn-off, populated by about eight other cars and a few big hauling trucks, to sleep for a while. I plan to stay in motels the rest of the trip but I wasn't looking at the signs on the road when I was driving so I don't know how far away from a motel I am.

I stop to go to the bathroom in a roadside facility, wash my face and armpits and change into more comfortable clothes. I'm going to catch some sleep here, then buy a map and plan to stay in a motel the next night. After I get back in my car it feels like someone is looking at me.

I turn around in my seat and see a man in his late fifties, with short gray hair, in a khaki green military uniform, lots of bars on his chest, standing ten feet behind and off to the side of my car. Just standing there. Looking back at me.

That's odd.

I turn around and look at my map, thinking about the route I'll take when I wake up.

Then, climbing into the back seat, I cover myself with a blanket and shut my eyes.

About two hours later I hear noise… something wakes me.

It's pitch black outside. I can't see a thing. I grab my flashlight and hold it. No need to turn it on yet.

People are talking, close to my car, behind it.

"Who does she think she is?" I hear a voice snarl.

Leslie.

"Yeah, it's time she got taught a lesson," another male voice says, laced with malice.

"She's not doing anything, leave her alone," says yet another male voice, softer, younger, kinder.

It's like Leslie has a good angel and a bad angel on each of his shoulders. I check to make sure my flashlight is close to me.

What ***is*** he doing here anyway? What does he ***want***? What ***is*** this guy's problem?

Taking a deep breath, I close my eyes, figuring if something happens then it happens. I'll deal with it if and when it does. I go back to sleep.

"If you are irritated by every rub, how will your mirror be polished?"

— Rumi

The next morning, I brush my teeth using a bottle of water and my toothbrush and continue driving. I notice as I'm driving that at different times loud motorcycles seem to be following me. I don't think I'm being paranoid.

I stop at a motel in the early evening and get a room. After I bring my knapsack into the room and close the door I hear a loud motorcycle drive up to the parking space in front of the door to the room next to mine. The engine to the machine stops and then the door to the room next to mine opens and closes. It sounds like one person. A man. Then five minutes later I hear their door open and close again. Someone has joined them in the room. Then I hear grunting.

I know Leslie is having sex with whoever the guy was that first went into the room.

What is the deal with this guy anyway? Who cares? Why does he feel it necessary to let me know when he's having sex and who he's having sex with?

Does he have nothing better to do than go out of his way to let me know this information? How can he be so confused as to think that me trying to warn him means I care about his personal life or the choices he makes? I don't. His personal life is his own business. I only wanted to know as much as I needed to try to communicate what The Light wanted me to communicate to him.

Why does he find this so hard to understand? This is a very confused individual.

I wonder.

Is there something I'm not understanding about this situation? What am I not understanding?

I don't know.

The Light hasn't given me a sign yet to stop. I'm trying not to jump into any dreams with him. As far as I know I'm not subconsciously trying to dig for any more information. I just don't know what to do next.

It feels like I'm between a rock and a hard spot.

The rest of my road trip goes like this. Loud motorcycles following me.

I do end up enjoying the drive, though. I just keep my windows rolled up, turn up the volume on my music and sing. I also stop and take pictures of scenery I haven't seen before and appreciate the different, varied landscapes. I drive through about seven states.

As I'm waiting in line at the border crossing from the U.S. back into Canada I notice the car in front of me. It's stopped beside the customs window.

It's a black, shiny, new racecar. The top is down. I don't know what kind of car it is; I don't pay attention to that kind of thing. But it looks expensive.

Leslie is driving. He has no passengers.

Again, I wonder. What is the point to this following me around stuff? What is he trying to accomplish by it? Is it just his narcissism? It probably is. He feels the need to make everything about him. Which it isn't. There's what, seven billion people on the planet? He's just one of them.

But I still wonder... what am I missing here?

***

After I arrive back in Calgary I'm asked to spend a week with my dad. He can't be on his own at this point and no one is available to stay with him. I let my dad know I'll need to work during the days but that I can look after the horses, bring in his firewood and make and share meals with him. He seems happy about it.

I spend the week with him, enjoying our time together. He seems to be enjoying our time together too.

He frequently pops in on me during the day to say hi. I work with great people online and have been meeting some amazing individuals. I'm having a lot of fun with it. Dad's dogs are constantly trying to play with me, interrupting me.

I'm hovering above myself, looking down at myself sleeping. I'm sleeping in the spare room at Dad's house. I watch myself in spirit form as my physical self wakes up from sleeping to noises... shouting. Someone, a male voice...

"Move! Come on, move!" he's shouting agitatedly.

I turn my head and look toward the open bedroom door. I hear more shouting.

"Let's go, I said!"

This isn't Dad's voice.

As I'm getting out of bed I notice something odd. I sense a lot of energy above and around me and can hear voices loudly murmuring—much like you'd hear at a performance when people are waiting and looking forward to it before it begins. It feels as if rows of tiered seats surround the house, from above, in a circle, looking down into the house, as if there isn't a roof. But when I look up there is. I register this in my dream.

Amongst the murmuring from above, I start walking toward the shouting, which sounds like it's coming from the kitchen. Entering the kitchen, I see Dad in his current attire that passes for pajamas: baggy gray sweatpants and a large, baggy beige cotton t-shirt. I see the familiar bulge under one side of Dad's t-shirt, his colostomy bag. Dad's brows are furrowed and worry emits from his squinting eyes. His arms are extended out in front of him, palms facing outward, close together, as if he's protecting his chest. He looks scared. He's facing me but it's as if he doesn't see me. I'm standing behind someone. The someone who's standing in front of him.

This someone is a younger man, who has his back to me. I walk toward him and stop when I'm beside him. It seems as if he can't see me. He's wearing dark, baggy jeans, some popular brand name, white but dirty athletic socks and a red and black checked flannel long-sleeved shirt, open, its tails waving in the air as I watch his arm darting forward, toward my dad. The younger man has straight, mouse-brown, fine hair, cut close to his head.

I continue walking toward Dad to see what the younger man is doing. It's as if Dad can't see me. The young man is holding a knife, the blade three inches long. His face is contorted. Disgust, anger, and arrogance roll like waves across it. The air tastes like sulphur. He's jabbing the knife he's holding at my dad, herding him from the kitchen into the living room. It's as if the two of them are in their own world.

Suddenly a circular, five-inch-thick, wooden pole is in my hands, about five and a half feet long. The ends are sawed off flat.

"Stop! Leave him alone!" I shout at the younger man, while using the pole I'm holding to hit him firmly on his left shoulder. I'm not trying to hurt him, but I am trying to get his attention.

He pays no attention to me. His eyes stay glued on Dad as he keeps stabbing at him and shouting at him. All the while I'm using the pole to hit the young man on his shoulders and sometimes on his head. But foot by foot he's effectively herding Dad out of the kitchen, through the living room, down the hallway and into my dad's bedroom. The murmuring above is escalating, getting louder.

He keeps stabbing at my dad, herding him to the far side of the bedroom, to an open space. I stand in the doorway watching. He's pushing Dad to the floor. There are small tears in Dad's t-shirt where the knife has cut through the fabric.

Dad is now lying flat on his back, tears streaming from the sides of his eyes, over his temples and dropping onto the floor. The man is raising his knife above his head with both hands, while he's standing, straddled, with both feet on either side of my dad's body.

The young man is going to kill my dad.

I look at one end of the pole I'm holding. It's now transformed into a sharp-tipped point. A spear. I lower my stance and, stepping back, I pull my spear-wielding arm back. With a primal yell as I begin stepping forward, pulling energy from my lower belly up through my torso and into my arm, I release the spear and wait. I aim for the young man's head.

The escalating murmuring above is cut off. Silenced.

Seconds seem to be suspended. The silence above turns into a collective gasp as the spear flies straight and connects with the young man's third eye, and his head and body burst into nothingness, as if he were never there. From above I hear nothing and yet in that nothing there is a heavy understanding. I look at Dad. He's okay. He's shaken but he'll be okay.

What was that about? My dad's fear of death? I feel into it. Yes. The young man represents my dad's judgment of himself, how he doesn't forgive himself, love himself enough to forgive himself, to give himself peace. That feels authentic. And I wonder. Did I share that dream with Dad? What was with that murmuring stuff going on above me? That was new.

I fall back asleep and wake to the sounds of Dad puttering around in the kitchen in the morning, making his morning coffee.

I get up and as I'm changing my clothes my dad sends me a thought with his mind. "Have you been alone all this time?" he asks incredulously.

"Of course I have," I reply with my mind, exasperated.

Who does he think I'm with anyway? He knows I've been on my own.

It doesn't occur to me until later to be surprised that Dad sent me a thought, that he was communicating with me using his thoughts and that I communicated back with him. It seems we did share that dream then. His question confirmed that.

***

The last day I spend with him he seems peaceful, content, happy and relieved. We laugh a lot. We spend time sitting together outside, enjoying the birds, the sky, the sun, the wind.

I tell Dad again about what it was like when I drowned. How beautiful it was over there. How amazing it was. He listens intently, nodding his head, looking me in the eyes, smiling. He doesn't say anything. But I know he believes me.

I travel back to Calgary and continue working.

***

I'm hovering above myself in spirit form and I am myself.

I'm wearing a skin-tight, black leather, one-piece outfit, and chunky three- inch heeled black leather boots.

The boots cover my calves.

I've landed as if I've dropped from the sky.

I'm in a crouched position, one foot in front of the other, my right hand stretching out across the ground below me.

My head is looking down at the ground.

Raising my head slowly, I look around, noticing less than a foot away, on my left, is a handsome young man, maybe sixteen, wearing a bathing suit, lying in a lounge chair. He's mostly hairless. Thinner build. Shaggy, dirty blond hair. Blue eyes.

I've startled him and he's moving from a semi-laid back position to an upright one, while turning to look at me at the same time.

His mouth is shaped like an "O" and his eyebrows are raised. Ignoring him, I stand up and look around.

The room is long, about a hundred and fifty feet.

There are lounge chairs spaced two feet apart from one another and four rows deep. There look to be about eighty lounge chairs. They're filled with beautiful young women between the ages of about fourteen to seventeen, all wearing bikinis. All have long hair. They're sunbathing. I look back down at the young man. And I realize they are all courtesans. These people belong to Leslie. He uses them and he gives them out to his associates to use. It's a business thing.

What the hell was with the outfit I was wearing? And why were my legs three inches longer in this dream? Shaking off these thoughts as distinctly unimportant, I re-center and review the dream again.

Ok.

Why did I dream of anything related to Leslie again? I decided not to.

Crap.

What information was I looking for? Am I trying to figure out if I can help him? I already determined I can't.

Maybe I'm trying to determine the extent of Leslie's fears?

So... ok, courtesans. Not a big surprise. Leslie has a sex addiction. Pretty much falls in line with power/money and drugs. Actually, with the whole organized crime thing.

So, his fears, stemming from his childhood traumatic experiences, have manifested as illusions/attachments to power/money, drugs, and sex.

That's quite a lot of ego attachments. A lot of fear. A lot of illusions.

And I ask The Light again, what am I supposed to do next? If it's useless trying to warn/help him about the lowering of energy in the environment, what am I supposed to do?

Why am I still having dreams that have something to do with him? Because Leslie is going to know or find out I was there and, as usual, he isn't going to be happy about it. Crap.

I'm in spirit form, hovering above myself looking at myself, while at the same time I am myself, standing in the aisle of a shopping mall. It's about five o'clock in the afternoon and the traffic is light; there're only a few people milling in and out of the stores, mostly window shopping.

I'm walking now, passing the storefronts. I'm looking for a specific store. After about fifty yards, I stop in front of a store. It's a spa-type store. They offer facials, hairstyles, massages, and holistic products related to these services.

I walk into the store and begin scanning the shelves and feel into the ambience. It's relaxing... calming. It's decorated with fresh, clean lines and colors. The products are holistic, no harmful chemicals. I taste sandalwood in the air.

Then I feel an energy. It's a younger energy. Not a child, but a young man. A young man works here. He's very quiet. Very smart.

Then he walks out of a room and behind the cash register and looks at me. He's about five feet eight inches tall, slender build, with dark brown hair styled in a way that highlights his cheekbones and liquid brown eyes.

With our eyes, we recognize one another. Not as if we know one another, but we recognize each other's energy. He walks out from behind the counter and approaches me and facing one another, we sit across from each other cross-legged. For a time, we simply look at each other, communicating with each other soundlessly.

He has much to offer whomever owns the establishment, but he hasn't been speaking up, sharing his ideas with the owner. The owner may be his father or someone related to him, I'm not sure. It doesn't matter. But he cares about this person. Wants them to do well. To succeed.

After a time, I uncross my legs and stand. He follows suit.

I leave the store and begin walking down the aisle of the mall again. Except now someone's following me. An older gentleman. This is the owner of the store.

I understand the younger man has already spoken to him and the older man was impressed and thankful. He loves the younger man's ideas and is going to begin implementing them. The older man is following me because he's curious about what I did.

This felt authentic. I don't know these people, though. I haven't met them in real life. Maybe I will one day. It doesn't really matter. I don't know how I did what I did, though; I just did it automatically, reflexively.

I'm hovering above myself in spirit form, looking down at myself walking down a residential street. The area looks well-maintained. Bees buzz amid the well-tended front gardens. It's summertime and golden rays caress my skin. Fluffy, marshmallow-like clouds occasionally dot the sky.

I'm nearing a curve on the street when I see a man sitting on a concrete bench in the front yard of a house nearby. As I'm approaching the front of the house he's sitting in front of, the man is walking down the yard toward me. I continue walking until we meet and stop, facing one another.

"Someone really rich was sitting on that bench a little while ago and a huge diamond fell off their ring. They looked and looked for it but couldn't find it. I looked all over for it too, because the person who finds it can keep it. If you look for it maybe you'll find it," he says to me.

"Okay, thank you," I reply to him.

He continues on his way, walking past me. I look at the bench and start walking up the lawn.

But instead of going to the bench, I'm walking around the side of the house into the unfenced backyard.

There are people milling around the backyard. The backyard is incredibly big and smells of fresh-cut grass.

The people milling about are from another era. They're wealthy Americans from the 1910s or 1920s era. Their hair, clothing, parasols, lace handkerchiefs, the way they hold themselves, look at and talk with one another is fascinating.

They don't seem to see me, which is good. I would stand out in my blue Sketcher sandals, light blue cotton shorts and dark blue, short-sleeved cotton t-shirt.

I watch them for a while then walk to the edge of the lawn where no one seems to be standing. The edge gives way to water. I look up and there's a lake spread in front of me. The water is a clear, calm, light turquoise.

Looking back down into the water in front of me, I see five white roses waving in the water just below the surface. The roses are massive, each flower head the size of a lawn chair. Underneath them I glimpse their stems connecting to the bottom of the lake. The white of the roses is dancing elegantly in the turquoise.

To my right I spot a raft and pole sitting haphazardly on a bank. The raft is made of light wood and has been tied together with a coarse, woody twine. I pull the raft to the edge of the water and set it in. Leaning down with one hand holding it, I press down firmly with my other hand on the surface of the raft. It doesn't take on any water. I grab the long pole and cautiously step onto the raft, keeping low to the surface. The raft is holding me, not sinking. Smiling, I stand up a bit more, spread my legs and use one end of the pole to push away from the bank. The thin, light pole is about eight feet long.

After pushing away from the side of the bank, I turn my head and torso to face forward and see five large stones sitting in the water ahead of me. Each is shaped differently than the other. The large stones stand about ten feet above the water and their surface is smooth. Their color is a range of warm browns combined with deep burnt oranges and light reds.

It feels like there's an ancient knowledge and energy within and around them.

The five stones sit in a semi-circle about twenty feet apart from each other.

Reaching the closest stone, I use a piece of twine to secure the raft to the stone and begin to hug it, splaying my hands and feet, groping for footholds and handholds.

The stone feels warm against my body. I lay a cheek against it and close my eyes for a moment. Its energy is rejuvenating and calming at the same time.

Fossils lay engraved in the stone's surface, here a shellfish, there a centipede. I trace their patterns with my fingertips. The stone feels older than time, before the concept of time.

Climbing down from the stone I reach the raft then, closing my eyes and bowing my head, I thank the stone for its wisdom and peace. I repeat this process three more times, using the raft to make my way to each stone, then exploring it. Each stone is subtly different in shape and energy.

As I use my pole and raft to navigate to the last stone, I look up at it, taking in its shape.

I notice a dog. The dog is sitting on a flat portion of the rock looking down at me. The top middle of the rock looks like a chaise lounge chair-shape, with a back, seat, and a portion of stone to stretch your legs out on. At the tip of it is a hollowed-out heart shape to rest your feet in. The dog is sitting in the seat area.

We look at each other. His jowls hang loosely from his jaw and his eyelids droop sleepily. Skin sags underneath his eyes. His long, flat ears hang floppy-like beside his face. He's about ninety pounds, a larger dog. His light beige coat sinks and sags with age. His whiskers and the hair around the base of his whiskers are white.

But his eyes.

They're my dad's eyes.

He's been waiting for me. I fasten the raft to the stone and climb up, reaching the old dog.

"Hey boy, how are you?"

The dog smiles up at me and gratefully accepts scratching behind his ear, his eyes closing as his head lowers a little.

I look at the hollowed-out heart in the stone and realize the dog is gone.

I sit in the seat, still warm from the dog, and stretch my legs out in front of me, resting my feet in the center of the heart.

That was Dad. He gave me that.

He's also warning me. He's going to die soon. He wanted to give me this gift before he left. This brings tears of joy to my eyes, because he understands. He isn't afraid any more.

***

A week later my dad passes.

My family is seated around my recently-deceased dad's kitchen table. The doorbell rings. Someone answers the door and then brings in the first bouquet of flowers. A bouquet of white roses.

> *"Don't grieve. Anything you lose comes round in another form."*
>
> *— Rumi*

***

A week later I'm in a grocery store, accompanying a friend while they grocery shop. My friend has to go to the bathroom. I don't, but I go there anyway to wash my hands. After I wash my hands and dry them I look down into the waste bin. There's a bouquet of mini carnations, all white, sitting in the bin. They're fresh. Nothing's wrong with them. I pick them out of the bin. Aside from wildflowers, carnations are my next favorite flower. Carnations smell wonderful and last a long time.

White flowers. These are from Dad. He's letting me know he's watching over me in spirit. I thank him.

***

My dad's celebration of life takes place on a Saturday, in a town hall near his home. My dad's favorite song was "Seven Spanish Angels." I sing it, accompanied by other family members and a pianist, at the celebration. As I'm standing outside taking a break from the people, a fleet of loud motorcycles drives by.

Leslie.

Great.

I still haven't figured out what I'm supposed to do next about that situation.

I'm still missing something. I need to figure out something but I haven't figured it out yet.

I'm feeling frustrated. I just can't understand what *it* ***is*** I'm missing!

***

In the weeks that follow, the song I sang for my Dad at his celebration of life, "Seven Spanish Angels," keeps popping into my mind. It feels like the song is tugging at me.

Which is different.

I haven't had this experience before.

It feels like the song is trying to tell me something.

A few months go by and this feeling is getting stronger and stronger, until it feels like I have to do something. And I don't know why I'm doing it, but it feels like I have to. Sometimes twice a day, every other day, for about a month, I'm pulled to concentrating on calling the "angels" from the south to the north. Or at least farther north than they are. I think I'm calling to people who live in South America.

This confuses me, because this hasn't happened before.

Ten months later the Zika virus hits. Then I understand why I felt strongly about this. Somehow, I knew it was going to happen. I accessed this energy/ information somehow. I don't know if anyone heard me and it doesn't matter. I did what I could. That's good enough for me.

And I wonder, how did I pick up on this? Know when something like this was going to happen before it happens?

I don't know.

***

One day I'm walking through the grocery store. I just need a few items, and I notice I seem to be being "shadowed" by a younger couple as I walk through the aisles.

They look like they're in their mid-twenties. After my items are in my basket I head to the checkout counter. As I'm waiting for the teller to finish scanning my items, I notice the young man is standing beside me and his friend or girlfriend is standing six feet behind him—the ones who it seemed were shadowing me.

He's wearing a pair of nouveau yoga pants, made of cotton, and a cotton shirt. He looks new-agey as does his girlfriend.

As I'm standing waiting for the teller, I hear him speak to me mind-to-mind.

"I can do this," he says strongly to me with his mind.

In seconds, I pick up on what his intention is.

His energy is saying he feels he's ready to use his intuitive gifts, he feels strong, he's confident, he wants to test himself. He's a bit arrogant, though, which means he doesn't understand.

Without thinking about it I send back to him, "Put that away before you get yourself hurt." I don't yell this at him mind-to-mind, but I do send it strongly.

The young man turns his head and stares at me, his eyes widening as he looks at me.

I ignore him, pay the teller and leave.

As I'm walking home I think about this.

Sending thoughts, mind-to-mind, is a lower energy form. It isn't difficult. Although we're taught it isn't possible, it is. But just because someone realizes they can do it doesn't mean their intuition is fully formed, or that they know how and when to use it. Sending thoughts, in the intuition realm, is the first stepping stone of many.

Knowing you can do this doesn't mean you understand how important it is to use it with integrity. So far, I've learned intuition is something we're all born with, but those who've experienced an unhealthy or unbalanced home life, as children, tend to have an enhanced sense of intuition. So, they're able to access energy, but they also have a low vibration until they begin unconditionally loving themselves. A low vibration combined with some intuitiveness isn't a good combination.

But all a person needs to do is make concentrated efforts to raise their vibration, by healing themselves, so they can use their intuition with integrity and bring benefits to themselves, as well as others.

I think about how I've been doing integrity-wise.

I'm not sure. Especially in my dreams, where it seems like sometimes my subconscious is leading me. For the most part I seem to be either defending myself or looking for clues, though. I'm not sure—is looking for clues considered bad? I decide this is something that needs to be determined case by case, depending on the person and their circumstances.

But thinking about the boundary thing again, I realize, in my case, I've been stepping over Leslie's boundaries. Regardless of my reasons, I've been overstepping. There must be a way, though, a way to reach him, to show him, to help him understand.

The Light would tell me I was done if there weren't, right?

Sigh.

I don't know.

What I do understand so far is, if you use your intuition with integrity it will lead you to higher levels of understanding, higher levels of truth—both in the physical and spiritual realms. Sure, you can use it to benefit yourself monetarily in "real" life. But if you do, you stagnate your growth. Stop yourself. While it requires courage, effort, and the ability to say no to things and people who can't support your growth, your own journey will be all the richer for it.

It allows you to keep growing.

It seems to be like computers in a way. Someone at a higher level can go to lower levels, but someone at a lower level can't go to higher levels. You have to earn your way to higher levels. The only way you can do that is by healing and exercising, growing - integrity. It's also the only way you can experience true freedom, peace, and joy.

Which I'm still striving for.

I'm not sure that was the message the young man received from me. I hope so.

I actually didn't like that, him communicating with me mind-to-mind. I didn't know him.

It felt invasive. Not polite. Sort of like a stranger jumping in front of you, unexpectedly, and demanding something from you.

But it also helps me understand. There are people out there who've developed their intuition and want to learn more. Understand more. They want to understand it better, but aren't sure how to go about this. That's all he was doing. Reaching out.

I'm satisfied with my response, though, because the more you value yourself and your intuitive gifts, the more responsibility you have, but also the more opportunity you have to keep growing, keep learning. Provided you use them wisely.

Which isn't easy.

***

Its dusk and I'm walking in a residential neighborhood. The air smells as if something is going to happen. There's a suspension and a charge to it, like how everything gets very calm just before a storm. I look around me. No one is on the street or the sidewalks. I keep walking until the sun goes down and the blood red sky dims and goes a murky gray. There's a hill beside me. I stop walking and then I hear it.

A drum beat. It's a low, slow, persistent beat. Then other beats join in. It's as if people are joining in the beat using whatever is around them. Trash can lids, hub caps, crow bars on fenders. It's getting louder and faster.

I climb up on the hill and look around below. There are young men with bandanas around their foreheads banging on things, in time with one another. Their skin is darker, South American looking. They're starting to yell while they beat. Some of them seem really angry.

And I watch as a few very expensive cars and some SUVs slowly drive out of the neighborhood in single file.

And I know these young men are claiming this area as their territory, they're a gang, and they're driving out someone who's been operating here. A great amount of violence isn't going to happen because they've left, whoever it is they wanted to leave.

I wake from this dream. *Sigh.* Okay, this has something to do with calling the angels from the south north. A by-product of it. So, by sending out the intention and energy, anyone, no matter who they are, heard it and have moved up north, I'm not sure where and I don't care, but it proves to me it was heard.

***

I'm hovering above myself in spirit form, watching myself.

I'm a passenger in a beat-up, small-sized, manual transmission car that Kyler is driving.

We're driving down a dirt road in the country. I would zap out of this dream but something about it feels important to Kyler. He knows and accepts that I said goodbye so this must be important to him. So, I don't. I stay. Stunted green grass grows between the two dirt tracks we're driving on. Fields of wild grass, weeds and wildflowers flank the car.

Kyler presses the clutch in, gears up and releases the clutch. He's intent on arriving somewhere.

We drive in silence, both of us looking ahead.

Sometime later we pull into a makeshift dirt parking lot. A small ridge sits beside the car to the left. Wordlessly we get out of the car.

I see a wooden shack-like store a few hundred meters away and start walking toward it. The shack sits on three-foot stilts. A small, wooden hand-painted sign hangs from a nail above the door. Five steep wood steps lead up to the wooden door.

I climb the steps and open the door. A somewhat dirty-paned window on the opposite wall greets me. Dust motes swirl in the air in front of me. I look down at the makeshift shelves and see white plastic buckets sitting on them. No colorful labels scream for attention. A simple address label sits on top and in uneven handwriting says, "Unpasteurized honey. $10."

I pick one up in each hand, the plastic handles digging into my palms, and look for a counter. I see one. A bald old man with age spots on his scalp looks back at me, smiling. His smile grows, revealing he's mostly toothless. His sunshine eyes dance with humor. I smile back and walk toward the counter, lifting the buckets up onto the counter, and reach into my pocket to find two ten dollar bills. I give him the bills.

He takes the money, places it in a tin box and closes the lid. We nod at each other and I pick up my honey and leave the shack/store. I stand at the top of the steps and look for the car.

It's gone. I set the buckets of honey down and stand still for a moment.

Something's wrong. Something's really wrong.

I walk down the steps and across the lot to the ridge, climb it and look in all directions. I don't see Kyler or the car. Next, I'm holding a ruby red umbrella over my head, looking across the fields. In the distance, I see storm clouds gathering quickly. And then I hear the low, ominous rumble of thunder and see a flash of lightning.

It feels like Kyler's gone. Like he's not alive anymore. And he knew he was going to die. He was angry. Angry and frustrated with himself and others. That he couldn't believe in himself. Angry with the ones who claimed to love him, who he felt caused him to live the life he lived. He felt trapped by them. Trapped by their insanity. He dreamed this last dream with me.

To say goodbye.

Honey.

Sweet.

The next day I hear through an acquaintance that Kyler was found dead in his apartment. They say he overdosed.

But I know. He didn't overdose.

He'd being doing heroin for long, long time. He knew how it worked.

He made a choice, because he felt it was his only way out. I know it wasn't, but he didn't feel that way.

I feel numb...

I was expecting my dad's passing, and that was difficult. Still is difficult, even though I know he's okay, not in pain, and in a realm where he's happy.

But I wasn't expecting this. Everything feels muted...

hollow...

empty.

> *"Out beyond ideas of wrongdoing and right-doing there is a field. I'll meet you there. When the soul lies down in that grass the world is too full to talk about."*
>
> *— Rumi*

The next day there's something trapped in the fireplace.

A bird. A sparrow.

I open the doors to the fireplace and the sparrow flies out and toward the window in the back door.

It hits the window but keeps flying. It flies down the hallway, into a bedroom, and lands on a windowsill next to a closed window, where it sits, stunned from hitting the window in the back door.

I get a plate and a colander and gently move the bird onto the plate.

As if it knows, it gingerly steps onto the plate. I place the colander on top of the plate—a temporary makeshift bird cage.

I take the sparrow outside to the back deck and remove the colander. The bird sits on the plate.

We stare at one another for moments that seem to stretch, bend, waver.

As I'm looking at the sparrow I get a strong feeling.

This is somehow Kyler, or Kyler's spirit.

He's telling me he has wings now. He can fly.

His spirit is free.

And he's watching over me. He appreciated what I tried to do for him. That I believed in him. That I was thankful for what he did for me.

Salty tears escape from my eyes… rolling down my cheeks… creating rivers.

I know he's close by in spirit, and I also know I'll meet him again one day.

One day.

***

I'm hovering above myself in spirit form, watching myself. I'm walking purposefully through a living room in an unfamiliar house. A woman is following behind me. I open a closed bedroom door, walk in and to the far corner of the room. The woman following me enters the room but stays close to the door. I look back at her and meet her eyes, then turn and look at the child in the corner.

It's a little girl, about three years old. She's wearing a pink Dora t-shirt and a cotton, short, light green ruffled skirt. No socks or shoes. Her hair is dark brown and slightly wavy.

Round face, and big brown eyes.

Her back is in the corner and she's whimpering and writhing against the wall, pulling at her shirt and skirt frenetically. Large tears roll down her cheeks. It's as if she's trying to crawl out of her own skin.

I reach down and pick her up, placing my hands under her armpits. She allows me to. Her whimpering subsides somewhat, not much. Pulling her chest against me and using my forearms as a seat for her, I start walking toward her mother.

Her mom takes a step toward us, concern and love showing on her face. The little girl turns her head suddenly to look at her mom. She stops crying and whimpering and the sides of her mouth stretch; her upper lip curls under. The skin across her cheekbones and forehead pulls back, her eyes squint and her body stiffens.

"Be right back!" she snarl-screams at her mom.

"Be right back!" she screams again, accusingly.

The little girl's teeth are pointed and sharp. Hatred spills out of her pores.

I stop walking and look at her mom. Horror crosses her face and she takes a step back. I turn around and walk back to the far side of the room where I picked the child up and turn again so the child is facing the wall, not her mom. Using one hand I cup the back of the child's head, then I close my eyes and concentrate on pulling the dark energy out of the child into me. The child relaxes.

After some time, I realize there's too much of it. I can't take all of it. I concentrate on calling the Archangels Michael, Gabriel, Raphael, and Ariel. Soon I hear the beating of powerful wings and sense their talons and feet landing.

Keeping my eyes closed, I lift the child by her armpits, keep her positioned facing the wall and turn myself around, exchanging my arms under the child. I hold the child up high in front of Archangel Michael.

"Please help her, Archangel Michael... pull it out of her," I plead with my mind.

Archangel Michael looks down at the child, then extends his arms out, taking the child and pulling her close to him. He closes his eyes and looks up, his neck extending. I can sense him pulling the dark energy from her. After a while he holds the child out toward me.

"Thank you," I send him.

She still has more, though. Although what we've done has helped, she needs more taken out of her. I give her to each of the Archangels, one by one, thanking each. Afterwards I hear their wings beating and then they're gone. I sense this has helped the child. She's now only crying softly against my shoulder, her body relaxed.

Slowly I turn around and walk back toward her mother. This time the little girl cries out when she sees her mom.

"Mommy! Mommy!" She extends her arms out to her mom. Relieved tears flow down her mom's cheeks. I pass the child to her mother.

"Don't leave her alone again," I say quietly to her.

The mother nods at me silently, as she's hugging and kissing her child.

I walk out of the room into the living room. Two young girls are sitting on the floor, quietly coloring. They look about seven and nine years old. Stopping, I look down at them. They look up at me and their silent question hangs heavily in the air.

"Is she okay?"

I smile at them. These are her sisters.

"You give your sister lots of love and hugs now, okay?" I say to them.

Relief waves through their tense bodies and relaxing, they smile back at me tentatively. I start walking again and leave the living room.

It felt authentic. But I don't know these people. I don't recognize any of them. But wherever it was, that little girl won't grow up thinking there's something wrong with her. She won't feel guilty or ashamed. Her family is loving and accepting.

Two days later I'm driving and as I'm slowly turning a corner I see two little girls. They look familiar. One of them recognizes me and raises her hand, waving at me. I smile back.

Then the smile freezes on my face. I realize. These are/were the sisters to the little girl from my dream. These are actual real people I haven't met yet. Again.

I wonder, how does energy work? Somehow the mother knew something happened and in a different state of consciousness called to me to help her.

I need to explore this more.

Because so far, my job has been to try to communicate with Leslie. It doesn't feel like I'm supposed to do that anymore; I'm supposed to do something else concerning Leslie.

I just don't know what yet.

But I do want to learn more about healing using consciousness. This I find fascinating. Using consciousness and energy to heal.

I think and feel into that more.

It can be used to heal.

***

My business helping business owners create video for their business is going okay.

Not awesome, but okay.

It doesn't feel like this is what I'm supposed to keep doing, though. It's an important part of my journey but it isn't the destination or at least, what I'm supposed to keep doing. But I'm not sure what that is yet.

I've recently met a psychic through video livestreaming. She's very open and positive about her abilities. I find this incredibly shocking and refreshing.

So far, most the people I've met who are "psychic" have been criminals and spies. And they hide what they can do. I've met very few people who are open and don't have ulterior motives, who have a more advanced understanding of energy and consciousness.

She tells me I have "mad psychic skills."

I've been so trained to "act normal" and not talk about my dreams or how information comes to me that her comment shocks me.

Which is awesome. It shocks me out of feeling like there's something wrong with me, with what I can do. Because I've been feeling, all these years, like I'm doing something wrong or something, by experimenting, by trying to protect myself, and by gathering information.

This "psychic" word kind of unnerves me, though. It brings a picture to my head of someone wearing a big purple turban sitting in front of a crystal ball, talking with a heavy European accent. I can't identify with this word, or identify myself with this word. I think everyone can access energy, and energy is information. Why it has to have a label like "psychic" escapes me. But anyway, she isn't like that.

She's... normal.

So, I endeavor to be more accepting myself, love myself, by finding out more about this psychic stuff. I learn more about the things I've been experiencing. But to me, these things aren't psychic; they're just different ways energy works. Energy is information. Energy is intuition. It's been helping me. Continues to help me.

***

Then one day, I understand.

It hits me like a lightning bolt!

I'm still having dreams that have something to do with Leslie because I'm trying to learn if I can help him in any way. Because he's in pain and I'm trying to alleviate his pain. But The Light didn't ask me to do that. The Light asked me to have compassion for him! Yes, try to communicate the lowering of energy in nature also, but I've done that. By trying to do that I've learned why he can't understand the importance of it!

So, what I haven't done is have **compassion** for him, because I haven't simply accepted him, accepted that his reality, his understanding of "pain," isn't the same as mine. He doesn't feel he's in pain. So, this was about me! Because I can sometimes actually feel Leslie's pain, feel it like it's my own, so I've been trying to figure out how to help him because I don't want to feel his pain; I want his pain to stop.

I've been doing what I've been trained to do since childhood, make other people's lives easier, fix problems. Fix him. The fact that I haven't been able to has been making me feel guilty, like I'm doing something wrong.

But he doesn't want help from me.

He's probably insulted and doesn't feel he needs any help. He's okay with his pain. Might even be addicted to his own pain. How crazy is that? But still, it's his pain; he's entitled to it, right? You can't take fear or pain away from someone. They have to want that for themselves.

He doesn't understand what he's missing though. How can he? You can't miss what you've never had, right? He has to want to use his own free will to remove his own fears.

I did learn it's possible to help people, though, if they're willing, able, and ready to take steps in that direction. But you can't do it for them. The most you can do is have compassion for them, and if they want to take positive steps forward, and they're open, willing, and able, offer a helping hand.

That doesn't mean you have to be involved in their world, though.

I realize that the problem isn't only environment-related, per se. It's people.

Not being able to face their own fears to unconditionally love themselves. Like Leslie feels he can't.

I also realize I haven't been that grateful for what he was trying to tell me. Teach me.

Well.

I haven't been grateful at all toward him.

I try to figure out a way I can thank him, a goodbye gift.

I'm hovering above myself in spirit form, watching myself sitting on a couch.

I'm wearing a baggy cotton t-shirt and shorts, my pajamas. Leslie is standing off to the side of me. His attention is elsewhere.

I pull a letter-size brown envelope out of the cushions next to me, in the couch, and hold it out toward him. The movement causes him to look over at me. He takes the envelope.

He opens it and reads the paper inside. Then his face begins changing color, growing extremely red, his eyes bulging. He looks up from the paper toward the wall. The tendons in his neck are standing out.

"Someone's going to have a very long yesterday..." he says in a low voice, between clenched teeth. He looks as if he's getting more and more upset. I'm looking at him.

I wait a few moments.

"Are you ok?" I ask. "You look really upset."

Leslie, alarmingly, instantly snaps out of it, his lips forming a smile. But it never reaches his empty eyes. He puts the paper back in the envelope, leans down and kisses me on the cheek.

"Sure, I am!" he says enthusiastically.

Okay, I paid him back. I gave him information that had something to do with someone in his organization stealing from him. I don't know how I did that, and I don't know who or what it was, and I don't want to know. It was the least I could do, though.

Because if it weren't for him I wouldn't have learned everything I have about energy, consciousness, intention, and healing.

That probably hasn't been his goal, but it was because of him I learned all of this. Because I felt I had to, to survive and at the same time do what The Light was asking me to do.

And again, I smile, because The Light uses everyone.

Then it occurs to me. The reason Leslie doesn't know who is stealing from him is because of his fears. He has intuitive abilities, but only the lower ones, like sending or receiving thoughts, because his fears prevent him from accessing other, more important information.

I know he doesn't have good dreams like I do, doesn't have moments of downloads of accurate information. He doesn't have beautiful moments in nature, or with other people, because he hasn't taken steps toward unconditionally loving himself, facing his fears, releasing his attachments. If he did, then he wouldn't be in a place where he'd be worried about others stealing from him. His world is a world of not enough, whereas the world really is about ***more than*** enough for everyone. The natural world teaches that.

Chapter 9

Reward

Later on that day, a feeling comes over me. The Light is telling me I'm done. I've learned what I needed to. I've done the hard work. There's no need to try to understand or learn more from Leslie or about his world. And no need to try understanding or communicating with him anymore.

That was what The Light was waiting for me to understand.

Now my task is to understand the truths of what I've learned.

> *"There are only two mistakes one can make along the road to truth. Not going all the way and not starting."*
>
> — *Buddha*

And the most profound one is...

Gratitude toward and for Leslie.

Because Leslie taught me a lot. As I think about this, the more I realize just how much I learned because of Leslie, whoever this individual is or was. I learned:

- Every living organism is energy and we're all connected.
- The constructs of time and space are very different than what I've been taught and lean toward the teachings of indigenous peoples around the world.
- There is much, much more to this life - much more to the unseen.
- How powerful my thoughts are and to re-train my brain to think positively.
- To create balance in my life.
- To have faith in my intuition.
- Practicing meditation is a way to connect to my higher self, the self who knows what I came to this place to learn, do, and understand.
- To be aware of the food and drinks I consume, and how they affect my mind and body.
- To be aware of the products I have in my environment and use and how these affect my state of being.
- I can heal, un-brainwash and re-parent myself.
- The value of patience.
- To set emotional boundaries with others.
- Not to overstep others' boundaries.
- That if someone isn't ready to heal, they won't and there's nothing you can do about it. The best you can do is focus on your own growth and well-being.
- That unconditionally accepting and forgiving myself are integral to my quality of life.
- To appreciate every moment of every day, and that each moment is incredibly precious.

- To believe in myself, regardless of what others say or do.
- That people who are full of anger are really in pain, pain they haven't figured out how to heal from yet.
- That people who feel powerless feel the need to try to exert their power over others.
- The difference between pity and compassion: pity is ego-based and compassion is on a higher plane that brings peace, harmony, freedom, and flow into my life.
- It's okay if people are in pain; their journey will include it, just as mine has.
- That emotional pain is transitory and choosing to mentally relive painful experiences is unproductive.
- That we're all doing the best we can with what we have.
- I can ***create*** a life that supports me in a loving way.
- The value of surrounding myself with positive people who are like-minded.
- The main person I need to appreciate, seek approval from and seek to understand is myself.
- What the illusions in this life are and what tools I can develop and use to overcome them.
- That my thoughts are energy, and I can either attach or detach myself from thoughts if I want to.
- That my values and my ethics are just that: mine.
- That in order to be adaptive I need to accept that what I believe to be true about myself and the world around me isn't certain - it's always changing, and so must I if I want to embrace acceptance, change and positivity.

- The more compassionate I am toward myself, the more compassionate I can be toward others.
- That investing in myself is the most gratifying gift I can give to myself, and therefore others.
- That it doesn't matter what the crowd is doing, if it doesn't serve me or work for me, then I'm free to walk away.
- Every moment of every day I'm being given opportunities to identify and transform my fears.
- Every moment of every day I can see myself in new ways, to change, to make new choices that serve, help, grow, strengthen, and uplift me.
- To focus on what brings me happiness.
- To have gratitude for everything and everyone.
- How incredibly amazing we human beings are.
- That unconditional love is the most important gift I can give myself.

Does Leslie know he did me a great service? Did he mean to give me these gifts?

Probably not. But it doesn't really matter. Because in the end, it wasn't about him. It was about **my** journey.

But without him, I wouldn't have understood or learned these things. So I'm grateful to him and wish him courage, peace, and unconditional love.

> *"Those who don't want to change, let them sleep."*
>
> *— Rumi*

And as the relief washes over me, more waves of gratitude and peace set in.

No longer do I have to rise so high above, meeting this army of opposition which is essentially the mass subconscious. Leslie was only a representative of it, to understand why our planet is facing the challenges it is, why humanity faces extinction, and what we can do to avoid it.

No longer do I have to be open and try to access as much information as possible, so I can communicate with Leslie while at the same time defend myself against him and people like him.

I understand now. I can come back down now...

Down to earth.

And resume a life of one person, one simple, solitary person who understands the impact I have and can have.

I can resume the life of one more extraordinarily ordinary person.

Just like everyone else.

I can start to begin enjoying my life again.

Rediscovering myself, who I am, what I believe in, how I want to live my life, who I want in my life. Understanding how energy works. How my energy works.

Looking forward to enjoying meeting new like-minded friends, spending time in nature, using my gifts to help others, being creative and incorporating more balance and peace into my life.

Knowing that we all have the potential to be so much more. To know that unbelievable happiness awaits us.

As long as we're open to change. To adapting.

To transformation.

To *unmasking*.

And, I realize, even though I'm more tuned into the environment, that this is the energy I perceive the strongest, it's impossible to address one thing, improving the way we treat the environment that nourishes us and supports our ability to survive as a species, without addressing all the other aspects of humanity.

Like how pain, unconditional love, fear and all its faces, healing, compassion, forgiveness and self-acceptance interconnect with our social, political, economic, societal, psychological, emotional and spiritual sides.

Everything and everyone is connected.

So to try to address one aspect, our environment/nature, or politics, without addressing the other aspects, won't work.

First, we need to have the courage to take responsibility for healing ourselves, unmasking ourselves, because we contain energy, and our planet is merely a reflection of our collective energy. When we do this we'll automatically be affecting the overall energy of the planet, healing the planet.

If we use our free will to access our personal power, we'll have the courage to love ourselves unconditionally, which includes having the courage to detach ourselves from the ideas that we've been indoctrinated with that limit our freedoms and can un-brainwash ourselves, re-program/re-parent ourselves, and begin living the life we were meant to live, full of happiness and positivity; we can access our higher intelligence and higher forms of our intuition.

And we'll be able to value ourselves in a way that doesn't detract from our ability to admire and encourage others.

This will have a positive impact on our environment and our ability to support an abundant, thriving planet and therefore ourselves in the years to come, all the while knowing there's a presence, whatever name you want to call it—God, The Light, Source, Spirit, whatever—that loves us unconditionally and wants the very best for us and knows we came here to learn what's important and what isn't important for our own individual growth. Each one of us is striving to learn something different. Each one of us has different reasons for "being" here.

One of those reasons is to learn how incredibly unique and valuable we are, every single one of us.

How strong we are.

How we can overcome any obstacle placed in front of us, can heal anything we want to in our lives.

How we asked for this chance - this life, this challenge, this opportunity.

In realizing this I'm able to fully comprehend the extent of what I've experienced and learned. It's been fifteen years on this particular journey, which felt like a crash course, but really, I realize I've been in training my whole life.

And it's been incredibly rewarding.

Of course, it looks as if I've been digging around into big problems.

And I have.

Because it's impossible to come up with solutions unless you're willing to honestly look at problems.

Typically, people who bring problems to light are seen as the ones who created them, which isn't true. They're simply bringing the problem to light, noticing it, identifying it, studying it, and looking for solutions. And I've gained a lot of understanding about my own opportunities for growth, what my own perceptions are and how they've impacted me and the choices I've made.

And I'm still learning.

You see, I don't see the point of pretending a problem isn't there, which makes some people feel uncomfortable, people who want to pretend the elephant isn't in the room. But those who want to pretend the elephant isn't in the room are the same people who want to point a finger at someone and "blame" them. The same people who don't want to "look within."

But blame isn't the answer. Courage is.

Just like a child who is being hit at home will usually hit other children at school. The child isn't the problem. The parent who doesn't know how to heal, accept and unconditionally love themselves is simply teaching this to the child. The parent was taught this by their parents. They aren't the problem either. Nor are they bad.

Problems aren't bad and people aren't bad. People just react to problems.

And problems are just opportunities. Opportunities to look at what's really going on, look at it from different perspectives and come up with creative solutions.

The fact that it wasn't appreciated by some that I was doing some digging around meant the process was painful for them. Shedding light on what is dark can seem painful. It's been painful for me at times too, but that's okay; releasing ego attachments is disorienting and can seem like it's painful.

Really, you don't get to live this life without pain and pain isn't the end of the world. Physical, emotional, and spiritual pain are simply part of the journey. But how I allow myself to perceive it, my perception of reality, is what matters the most. Because I can allow it to negatively affect my emotions for the remainder of my life, in the form of unhealed pain, which I'll then need to create a mask for, or I can choose to accept it and heal it. Because unhealed pain will come back again and again, until I recognize the lesson and honor and respect it as the gift it is from The Light. Pain is simply one of the tools in the Universe's toolbox that helps to guide me in the right direction—toward wholeness, completeness, Oneness, happiness.

> *"Yesterday I was clever, so I wanted to change the world. Today I am wise so I am changing myself."*
>
> — *Rumi*

Releasing ego attachments which don't serve me will allow me to embrace things that are unequivocally priceless, that do serve me, like self-acceptance, giving myself unconditional love, freedom, peace, happiness and living authentically.

So while I learned the causes of our current condition, as a species—socially, economically, mentally, politically, psychologically, and spiritually—I also, in the process, learned humility. Because throughout my journey I encountered incredible amounts of disrespect and ignorance. I understand these things now as the other person expressing their own fears, and at times, also a reflection of my own fears.

***

I'm sitting on the C-train heading northbound from downtown Calgary in the afternoon on a weekday. The train is almost empty. I'm not listening to music or reading; I'm practicing deep breathing and being in the moment. Appreciating the calmness.

A man gets on the train and sits opposite me, facing me. He's about sixty years old. He's wearing khaki brown pants, sturdy black shoes and a light brown, thin ski jacket. No hat or gloves. It's winter here and about minus eighteen degrees Celsius. I look him in the eyes and we study one another for a moment.

And he sends me a package of information, mind-to-mind.

He works for a spy agency, the CIA, and knows about me, knows what I can do. He's offering me a position. I'll be well paid.

I look back at him and can't help it. "Seriously?" I ask with my mind, but not in a way that means I'm excited or interested, in a way that's well… offended.

Because really, does he think that I've gone through all of this, that I explored all of this, just to start spying on other people for money? Yah. No.

This has been an incredibly important journey, my soul journey, and if I do this, it means I don't get to continue growing, my soul doesn't get to continue growing. It means all the hard work I've accomplished will be wiped out and will mean nothing. And that's not going to happen. He seems to understand my point of view. He blinks and looks down. I understand he's merely extending an offer, an offer he's been paid to extend to me.

I look out the window and don't look at him again.

And I think about how grateful I am to have had the opportunity to learn all I've learned. Because one of the main things I've learned on this journey so far is humility. Because in my zealousness, my headstrong attempts, I missed what Leslie had been trying to communicate to me, personally.

I had expected Leslie to ignore the messenger, me, and instead receive the message. But I didn't realize he would reciprocate and ask me to do the same.

How ironic!

And I have to laugh at this, because I can be stubborn. But while some may see stubbornness as a fault, for me my stubbornness is a strength.

I never give up.

I don't give up on myself. Because I'm here for a reason. To learn. To be open to learning.

My job now was to ignore the messenger, Leslie, and receive the messages he was delivering to me. To release my attachment to what I perceived he is/was, to release my attachment to what I was ordered to do. Everything has a place and a time. And I completed my task.

> Now my challenge is to release any personal attachments I have to who he is/was, what his opinions are/were - release any importance I placed on it. Because it isn't important.

It isn't and wasn't about him.

It's about what I choose to learn. It's about my free will. About what I take away from it and choose to incorporate into my being. About what I choose to release. About what I take forward with me that strengthens me.

Sure, it was a bit confusing—spy, organized crime, military and big business stuff—but in the end, it wasn't about any of that. Those were just illusions.

It was about the human condition.

It was about unconditional love and healing.

And for me personally, it was about the need to accept myself and give myself unconditional love. That I have the ability to use my energy, my power, to do this. Because energy, and how I choose to use it, is all that matters.

***

So now it's time for me to focus on myself.

Although I know I'll need more time to process everything, I'm now able to understand what all of it was for.

Now it's time for me to take a good look at how I'm living my life, how I've judged myself in the past, how I view myself now, how I've valued myself, how I value myself now, how I've been caring for myself.

Because in order to go on this journey, I needed to metaphorically sacrifice myself in order to begin to look at life differently—to understand how my spirituality is a major component of my being, a component that plays an incredibly powerful, positive part in my life, that it's always been there for me, and that it connects me to myself as well as to what I consider "reality". My spirituality has helped me gain new understandings about the different facets of our current condition.

And I understand there's no way I could've learned how the parts of me, the spiritual, emotional, physical, and mental parts of me, are all connected, intertwined. Not separated, as I was taught to believe. I was taught to believe in borders, walls, and only to believe what is right in front of my eyes. To believe in illusions. To believe illusions have power. And they don't. They are a puff of smoke on the wind.

So my worst enemy has also been my best friend.

Huh.

A paradox.

So, just as The Light needed me to deliver messages to Leslie, The Light also used Leslie to deliver messages to me.

The Light uses everyone, whether they know it or not.

Just the way it works.

The Light is the craftiest thing going.

Never, ever think you can one-up The Light, my friend. The Light is a hundred steps ahead of you.

Okay, now, my main goal is to accept what I've experienced and heal any wounds I have, by unconditionally loving and accepting myself. Because I've taken some hits for sure.

> *"The wound is the place where the Light enters you."*
>
> *— Rumi*

I'm all in one piece, though. And as I already know, you don't get to live this life without experiencing pain; it's part of the package. It's about how I choose to acknowledge this energy, move through it, ingest it, transform it, and create something beautiful.

This is another journey in itself. But I already know this feels good. This feels awesome. This feels amazing, to live my life with happiness and peace from a place of wisdom and experience, knowledge and humor, because pain, like childbirth, can be forgotten. Memories can evaporate into nothingness. I can choose what's dead weight, what doesn't serve me, and what to take with me going forward.

Because there's no doubt in my mind I've been indoctrinated by my parents, television, magazines, school, my community, society, government—all of it—into believing not only what constituted their beliefs about reality, but about who I am, and what I value and what makes me happy. And how I've been reluctant to discard their viewpoints, because to me it seemed if I did that I was discarding their value as a human being.

But that was a mistake. As a human being I'm entitled to discard viewpoints that are made in ignorance, from a standpoint of no experience, while still honoring the human being expressing their viewpoint.

I understand and acknowledge now that I don't need to explain "who" I am or justify "why" I do anything. If I do, it is a courtesy, a gift I'm comfortable sharing in the hopes it eases someone else's journey.

***

So, like a phoenix, I begin burning away all that hasn't served, doesn't and won't serve me in the future. I transform the illusion of duality, the illusion that anyone is truly separate from anyone else, because consciousness isn't dual—only the components of our personalities are.

This is one of the cycles of life, of a life within a life. Because I've been given this life, this opportunity, to destroy, create, learn, understand, heal, incorporate, and transform aspects of myself, my energy, my consciousness and my subconscious. To use my free will.

> *"Chaos is merely order waiting to be deciphered."*
>
> *— José Saramago*

I've been given the gift to now choose the path of unmasking.

And I often re-visit the place I went to when I drowned and died, to accept and receive all the unconditional love I need. Because drowning was a gift. If I hadn't received that gift, I wouldn't have had the courage or conviction to carry out what The Light asked of me. And I go back to re-discover myself as a child, who I was, before

I began believing in the negative nonsense passed on to me—before the indoctrination began. Because this is my true self, the self I've been longing for. The self I've been fighting for. The one who came here to learn, laugh, do and be, knowing that would be more than enough.

Chapter 10

The Road Back

And the way back from this journey is a process, just as life is a process.

I dream one last time of Leslie, who visits me briefly, wearing a different face. He's had a facelift and I tell him so in my dream. Because it's easy to distinguish a person's essence. And I have a few dreams of others who were trying to take from me, who were lost, confused and in pain. They were unsuccessful. Now I'm dreaming in ways that show me things but aren't infringing on others' boundaries. I'm healing. Which is part of this journey.

Healing by taking steps in what we consider "reality" by taking a good look at what's going on with me, focusing on me, and only me now. What I want, what I want to do now, how I want to live, who I want to be in contact with.

I have a lot of choices to make.

I start with the basics.

I haven't been to the dentist in many years. Turns out I need three fillings replaced.

Instead of going to the doctor, I visit an Iridologist who prescribes food as medicine. The Iridologist prescribes a strict list of foods I can't eat: meat, wheat, refined grains and dairy. I've been mostly doing this except for refined grains. This is one thing I haven't cut out of my regular diet yet. I've noticed for years though, that when I eat a piece of wheat bread a crevice forms on the end of my middle finger of my right hand. When I eat no wheat, this crevice doesn't form. So my body has been trying to warn me all along. I'm also prescribed bone broth and one tablespoon of apple cider vinegar (with Mother) daily.

And walking. Daily. Grounding. I follow this advice.

As time moves on I feel better and better.

The walking also seems to be helping diminish where I go in my dreams and how often, which I'm incredibly grateful for. Because now it's time to focus on myself, my peace of mind, my creativity, my unconditional love of myself and life, fun, nature, and good friends who are like-minded.

My love of life begins returning, the flames of my curiosity burning brighter.

I feel a growing sense of renewal.

Revival.

Playfulness.

My sense of humor is returning, filling my heart and soul.

***

People have approached me while I was on this journey, wanting to know more. I don't know what people thought they knew about me, but I wasn't able to provide them with any information, because I wasn't done. I've been called names like "badass", "oracle", and some others than don't deserve mentioning. But the fact is, I hadn't completed the journey. And I hadn't had time to process everything.

What I've done, whatever this has been, has been incredibly difficult, seemingly impossible at times and exhausting. And until I was done I didn't feel I had the right to share anything with anyone. I also didn't have a context for what I was experiencing along the way. Plus, I didn't know if I'd survive, either physically, emotionally, mentally or spiritually.

And I hadn't heard from The Light that I was to share any of what I'd learned. There's no way I would've made it through this journey without The Light.

And as the months go by, and I slowly put together the pieces of my experiences, The Light quietly tells me, orders me, I need to write a book about my experiences. I need to share what I've learned.

A book?! I ask.

Yes, The Light softly replies.

But on many levels, I'm not sure I can do this. Good grief, haven't I done enough already? But then no, that isn't how it works.

I've been given so many gifts; of course The Light wants me to share. But I'm not sure about this. One of the things that was instilled in me since childhood was to hide who I was, that I wasn't okay, that something was really wrong or off with me. Shame.[8] Again, I'm astounded by The Light.

And I realize why The Light is asking/ordering this.

Another re-parenting/un-brainwashing myself exercise. I'm very grateful. Because everything The Light asks me to do brings me closer to my higher self. Closer to The Light.

Closer to who I'm comfortable being. Me.

The Light is saying that I'm okay, just as I am.

I don't have to try to be stronger, smarter, or more than anyone. I'm okay just as I am.

And this is why I love The Light so much.

> *"Your task is not to seek for love, but merely to seek and find all the barriers within yourself that you have built against it."*
>
> *— Rumi*

At one point, during a meditation, I cry forlornly, because I don't know how I'm going to do this. How can I do justice to and for The Light?

How can I express how amazingly beautiful The Light is?

How I can share what I've learned in a way someone would understand?

> *"What? Are you still pretending you are separate from the Beloved?"*
>
> *— Rumi*

And to be honest, I'm also uncomfortable doing this. Because I know what I've experienced and experimented with isn't the norm.

But also, sharing my story means I'm sharing my dreams, some of them beautiful - and the beautiful ones I want to keep for myself. So it'll be painful to share, because it won't be "just mine" anymore. But I know that pain is a necessary ingredient for growth, just as healing is necessary for growth. So I have to let that attachment go.

If I'm being completely honest with myself, I'm afraid I'll be seen as too different too. So there's a fear of not fitting in. Even though I love spending time in my own company, need it in fact, I've been programmed to believe that I won't be accepted if I'm not like everyone else.

I'm also afraid the mistakes I've made will be unforgiveable. Perhaps to some they are. I don't know. But I do know how illusions work, and fear is the basis of all illusions.

The more power I give it, the more power it has.

Fear will not stop me, because at the very least, others can benefit from my experiences and my mistakes.

Just because I've been knocked down for making them and, at times, accepted the assertion that making them was a bad thing, doesn't mean I have to accept that assertion now, because I wouldn't have learned unless I tried, experimented, and made mistakes.

After all, even though I was raised and taught to be an automaton, to "fit in," I'm not supposed to. And even though I don't admit it often, I'm more interested in learning than fitting in. I mean, I like fitting in and all, but it doesn't drive me, not like my curiosity does.

Which is why The Light chose me, I suppose. I was open to learning why everything is the way it is and understanding what needs to change.

But who will believe me? Because what I've encountered, experienced, gone through—is not your typical run-of-the-mill stuff. Sure, my upbringing was; a lot of people experience an unbalanced childhood. So there's that. But maybe, just maybe, someone will identify with some of the intuitive experiences I've had.

Or maybe someone else was told they were "too sensitive" when they were young. Or maybe someone else has felt weird, uncomfortable, or unaccepting of themselves at some point in their lives, and maybe, just maybe, writing about what I've experienced will help them understand they aren't alone. They never have been alone. Separateness is an illusion.

And that being different is just fine. More than fine.

***

And I move on to other areas of my life that I want to heal or transform. So I look at my relationships.

I look at what relationships, family or otherwise, have historically taken more from me than they've given. Nothing is ever a hundred percent even, but I can see where I have relationships that are more than unbalanced, relationships I've participated in that aren't healthy for me, where I've continued with a pattern because it's all I've known, a pattern where others have taken more than they've given and where I've allowed this because I didn't understand or learn healthy boundaries, healthy emotional boundaries.

I now know it isn't my job to "fix" everything and everyone. That I take away from their journey, the blessings of their own, unique journey, if I try to do this. That this is a choice I have, not something I have to automatically do, like I was raised to believe. This is a belief threaded throughout many societies, a societal belief held in many parts of the world, about what a "female" is supposed to do.

What I've learned goes far beyond gender biases. I see myself as a human being, an equal to every other human being.

This viewpoint is shocking and threatening to some. But that isn't my concern.

Chapter 11

Resurrection

And I decide my only responsibility is to do what's best for me, regardless of the norms of society or anyone else. Not in a selfish, mean way, but in a

way that's accepting of others, accepting of their journey and understanding their journey doesn't have to include me if it doesn't serve my growth in a healthy, balanced, loving way.

It's my responsibility to honor, respect and accept others' journeys and their free will.

It's also time to devote to doing what's best for me, allowing myself to focus on what matters to me, what I'm passionate about.

A new road. A new journey.

This causes me to look at the root of what I feel about myself. Because I've always been told that my creativity and intuitions were "silly." Were wrong. Weren't to be entertained.

But they've led me to this place.

My intuition, The Light, led me to write this book, which I was reluctant to do because I haven't written a book before. Just like when I started experimenting with replacing using pot by using yoga/meditation. Just like when I began investing in and growing my understanding of how the unseen works with what we consider "reality." Just like when I was afraid to put myself in front of a video camera. Just like when I first started my journey and didn't know how to use my intuition.

A person can only learn by doing, by trying, by being open to the possibilities, by admitting their mistakes, by asking for help when they need to and by holding themselves accountable.

And it's at this point I stop writing this book.

Why?

Because during a morning meditation the feeling was sent to me that I wasn't done with the journey.

The Light was telling me to wait.

To have patience.

I needed to learn something more.

Learn the reason why The Light was asking me to write this book. It has been a part of my healing (and I have no doubt I have more to heal), a part of my accepting myself, my journey, and seeing all the possibilities ahead of me.

And three months go by and some very beautiful things happen.

The work of Elaine Aron comes into my world. She is a scientist who wrote a book called *The Highly Sensitive Person* (HSP) and I learn this is what I am. A person who has a highly developed nervous system, which is a trait you're born with, is a person who picks up on a lot of things non-HSPs don't pick up on (like energy and information). What's more, I'm an HSP with HSS (a High Sensory Seeker) tendencies. HSS means you're incredibly curious, which made me the perfect person to make all these discoveries.

Wow.

Just.

Wow.

It doesn't mean you're weak, if you're an HSP. In North America "sensitive" is viewed as a weakness. Approximately 10-20% of the population have this trait in both the human and animal worlds. It's by design. This trait is naturally built into nature as a survival mechanism for the species. I learn HSPs pick up what others don't notice, because their nervous system is highly developed and tuned into their environment.

I realize this is why I pick up on energies and information, why my dreams speak to me, why caffeine and other environmental factors affect me more so than others, why I feel the negative effects humanity is having on nature, why I can feel the effects of GMO foods in my body, chemicals in my environment, and why I'm concerned about the effects these things will have on our species surviving in the future.

This is why 80-90% of the population doesn't understand how and why HSPs are the way they are.

In fact, most HSPs don't even know they're an HSP, which is why so many HSPs suffer, feeling isolated and misunderstood. And some HSPs, especially in North America, force out and negate their trait, a vital part of their being, because they don't know what is different about them, and they don't know how to use their trait in a way that benefits them and others. Which is why a great many HSPs develop depression.

But wouldn't you feel depressed if you were one in ten people who received information all the time and fully felt the effects of everything, and you didn't have the tools or understanding to know how to use your trait to enhance your life?

Plus, a lot of HSPs had a similar upbringing to mine, which is why we struggle. But we don't need to. It isn't necessary.

I want you to know, though, my experiences aren't typical for an HSP; they're simply my experiences of how my trait has showed up, developed and how I've chosen to accept and incorporate my trait in a healthy way. Every HSP is unique. There's an HSP continuum; some people are a little HSP, some a bit more and some are a lot.

Regardless, we're all unique, every single one of us, whether you have the HSP trait or not.

Chapter 12

Return With the Elixir

Whether you have the HSP trait or not, if you are someone who was raised in an unhealthy, unbalanced family, or you just plain know you aren't living your life in a way that feels true to you, feels good to you, brings you happiness, where you're using the gifts you were born with and embracing life playfully—please know, you're to step into The Light now. Be courageous. Be grateful for and learn how to use your gifts to benefit both yourself and others. You have free will and the ability to un-brainwash and re-parent yourself, heal and move positively forward into the future.

This book is for you, to help you on your own unique journey, because we aren't supposed to "be like everyone else;" we aren't supposed to be cookie-cutter images of one another. We're supposed to be the amazing, unique, one-of-a-kind, awesome individuals we were born to be—we came here to fulfill our own unique journey of learning and growth!

And in this writing I realized I've learned another lesson from The Light.

The power of vulnerability.

I've learned another reason The Light asked me to write this for you.

Because it takes immense courage to be vulnerable. And The Light knows I have courage, but wanted me to see yet another benefit of having courage, and I realize that in sharing this journey with you I've been given the gift of recognizing a long-lost facet of my soul, one I haven't felt free to accept, embrace and grow. But I am now, because I understand. I understand that by recognizing my own vulnerability I'm moving closer and closer to my soul, and vulnerability isn't a weakness, but a strength and a tool I can use to further connect with my own soul, as well as with others.

Oh, how the gifts keep coming...

And my gratitude deepens, for life, for myself, for All.

***

So, I finish writing this book while at the same time creating an HSP Meetup Group in my city, the first in my province.

But I don't lead it. I'm part of it. A member of the group. I'm part of the whole, learning with others as I go. Because anyone who tells you they have ***all*** the answers is lying. There are those who have experience and knowledge, but lack wisdom, compassion and unconditional love for themselves and therefore others. So I know it's important for me now to choose who I listen to wisely, choose what information I'll hold close to my soul on the rest of my life journey.

Because we're all part of the problems and we're all part of the solutions.

It's by working together, side by side, with each other in a way that allows everyone to just "be" who they are, learn from and support one another on our journeys—that we begin to get closer to and strengthen this current energetic evolutionary shift that'll allow us to step into a higher state of being, a state of being connected to everything and everyone on a higher plane, a higher plane that includes loving ourselves unconditionally and therefore, ensuring the survival of our species.

And I'm amazed. Amazed at my persistence. Amazed at my courage. Amazed at the hope and faith I've kept all along.

At times, especially after my dad and Kyler's passing, I've had to just stop for a while. Stop and try to process what's happened. Grieve. Regroup. Try to look after myself the best way I knew how.

Without talking to anyone, because I didn't think anyone else would understand.

Because at times, its felt like my soul imploded and particles of my soul were floating haphazardly around until slowly, as like attracts like, they began moving closer together until, over time, they merged. One painful merge after another, until they collected into bigger pieces, pieces of my soul that, as part of an age-old process, gathered themselves, fortified themselves, while the energy of love was weaving my soul together, until finally a whole soul was formed. A soul woven of scar tissue.

A soul much stronger than it was before.

How can I thank The Light? What can I do? Other than publishing this book?

One of the things I decide to do is give back. Give back because I've been given so much.

So I search for a not-for-profit I resonate with.

Who'll get it.

And I find... The Doorway.

Remember the prophetic dream I had with the huge staircase I was climbing, with the lions and lionesses? Where the small man showed up at the end with a ring of keys when I was standing in front of three doors?

Can a person get a stronger serendipitous sign?

I learn this not-for-profit works with young individuals familiar with street culture, who're taking steps to improve their lives.

They're showing tremendous courage: the courage to try to think differently, to learn, imagine, hope, dream, and take small, decisive steps towards their dreams. Their future. A future where they'll feel good about themselves and their choices.

To un-brainwash themselves.

To re-parent themselves.

There are no psychiatrists or psychologists at this not-for-profit. No one is trying to diagnose anyone, tell anyone there's something wrong with them, put them in a box or label them. They're simply accepted. Everyone's history is in the past. They're supported in a positive way that rewards them for trying to reach their goals. Because it's in the trying that you win.

We have today, we have now, and in our now we can choose to use our free will.

It's elegantly simple.

So ten percent of the proceeds of this book are going to support this not-for-profit.

You did that.

Just by buying this book.

You supported someone who has the courage to begin making

changes that will positively benefit them and bring them happiness. Maybe that person is you.

Either way, thank you. **Thank you for being wonderful.**

We're all connected. Everything and everyone.

And this journey ends here.

And a new journey begins. Another journey within this amazing journey called "life."

A continuation of transformation.

A journey for me that includes embracing the knowledge that I have this HSP trait and, knowing this, I can explore why I am the way I am, what it means for me and make new discoveries and decisions about and for myself.

Because I now know I've locked away a secret, beautiful, sensitive side of myself, an amazing creature. I've locked this part of me away for a very long time ago.

Because I had to.

That creature wouldn't have been able to survive.

But that creature... has been alone.

Neglected.

For a very, very long time.

That creature is a part of me. The part of me that isn't afraid to be open, loving, and kind. Isn't afraid of anything. Doesn't and won't acknowledge or understand what fear is.

But that creature needs a lot of loving, tender care.

That part of me needs to learn more about how to live as a healthy Highly Sensitive Person and to learn more about the Highly Sensitive Person Trait (otherwise known as Sensory Processing Sensitivity).

Not to mention I need to balance my serotonin levels and learn about Cognitive Behavioural Therapy.

But just as important to me is to explore how others with the Trait work with their trait so I can learn from their perspectives and experiences.

So first I begin meeting other Highly Sensitives and working together to create a blog for Highly Sensitives where we share our perspectives, you can visit it here: www.Blog.HSP.World and I begin by using my creativity with others in ways that'll benefit other highly sensitives: www.HSP.World.

Life is my muse and I am my own muse. We HSPs are quite interesting.

We're the thinkers, the dreamers, the healers, the inventors, the seers, and the movers and shakers of the Slipstream.

So stay tuned…

Because I'm very much looking forward to this new future, to this new journey that begins as each day begins, with new life.

Epilogue

I've always been curious and wanted to know about that being-with-the- brown-circles-on-its-skin that I dreamed of—why, when it walked out of the forest and into the water, why did it go to sleep in the water?

I've wanted to know that ever since I had that dream. Why was it sleeping in the water?

I know there's an important reason behind it and I want to know...

So one day, I try lucid dreaming, which is basically, for me, just being awake but really relaxed and using my imagination.

I haven't tried to re-access a dream before doing this. Actually, I haven't tried to re-access any of the dreams I've had.

So...

Another experiment!

So I begin a meditation and when I'm relaxed I start imagining that portal I was looking through...

What the forest looked like. The sky, sun, the white circles on stones, the sand, the water, the birds. How the air felt, tasted, smelled.

I'm looking through the portal again.

Then I climb through the portal and am in that world. That world that sits beside ours, with ours, just in another dimension.

I'm swimming in the water with dolphins. I can swim as fast as they can and sometimes I ride them; other times I jump through the air with them. I play with them for a while and then walk out of the water onto the beach, a beach full of light brown sand.

Lying on the beach and letting the sun kiss the water off of my skin. Feeling the sand behind my calves and on my back. Listening to the waves caress the shore. Feeling the wind's cooling touch. Hearing the leaves move with and against each other in the trees.

Then I'm running on the sand, alongside the water, and there's a horse on the beach ahead of me. Chestnut brown and curious.

It shyly walks toward me a few paces, stopping ten feet away.

I slowly walk toward the horse, holding out my hand.

When I reach it, the horse nuzzles my hand and lets me stroke it.

I send a question to the horse. "Will you let me ride on your back?"

The horse bends a knee, letting me climb onto its back.

Then we're running, galloping through the sand, faster and faster.

I throw my arms above my head, laughing and shouting.

The horse stops at the far end of the beach.

This is close to where I saw the being the first and last time.

The being-with-the-brown-circles-on-its-skin.

I slide off the horse's back and thank the horse by putting my forehead against its forehead and sending it love.

Next, I'm standing on the beach looking into the shallow water.

I can see the being-with-the-brown-circles-on-its-skin lying on its side in the clear, light turquoise-colored water.

It's in a semi-fetal position.

I can feel the power, the majesty, the peace and the beauty emanating from it.

I walk into the water slowly until I'm beside the being.

Its eyes are still closed.

Quietly, slowly and gently I lie down in the water beside the being, facing it, copying its posture.

I patiently wait. Watching.

After a time, the being slowly opens its eyes and looks back at me.

"Hello," I say to it/him/her/? with my mind as I smile.

The being slowly blinks and begins smiling back at me.

"Why do you sleep in the water?" I ask with my mind.

After some moments the being sends, "Look," in a gentle voice, and looks towards its left arm.

I follow its/his/her/? gaze and look down at its arm, and watch as tiny dark turquoise-colored particles begin floating to the surface of the water, glowing as they gracefully dance upward.

These particles are coming from within the being's skin, traveling from within the being, rising to the surface of its skin, and then leaving through its pores.

Then the being is sending me information, and I understand that these particles are nutrients. Nutrients from the forest that the being absorbs, makes more potent, and then releases back into the water, that will then feed back to the forest.

A cycle of nature.

This being plays an integral part to the health of this planet.

And I'm amazed.

Then images of myself flash through my mind, at different ages.

Images of me picking up rocks with white circles on them.

And now I know these rocks are rocks that have touched this being's skin.

Smiling, I gently send, "Thank you."

The being smiles and quietly sends back, "You're welcome."

The most important, amazing journey you'll ever have ***is your own life journey!*** No one is more interesting, complex, innovative and creative than you are. And your everyday life is your art canvas.

Use these lines to write down positive aspects about yourself. These can be things other people have told you, or just what you know inside you to be true. Be kind to yourself, and come up with **at least** 20 things.

1	
2	
3	
4	
5	
6	
7	
8	
9	
10	
11	

12	
13	
14	
15	
16	
17	
18	
19	
20	

I also invite you to write down how your journey has gone so far—what masks do you wear? What illusions do you put your energy into that don't serve you? How would your life look if you *Unmasked*?

CPSIA information can be obtained
at www.ICGtesting.com
Printed in the USA
BVHW041941120519
548071BV00014B/207/P

9 780995 916753